HUMAN CLONING

Since Dolly the sheep was born, controversy has swirled around the technology of cloning. We recoil at the prospect of human copies, manufactured men and women, nefarious impersonators, and resurrections of the dead. Such reactions have serious legal consequences: lawmakers have banned stem cell research along with the cloning of babies. However, what if our minds have been playing tricks on us? What if everything we thought we knew about human cloning is rooted in intuition rather than fact?

Human Cloning: Four Fallacies and Their Legal Consequences is a rollicking ride through science, psychology, and the law. Drawing on sources ranging from science fiction films to the Congressional Record, this book unmasks the role that psychological essentialism has played in bringing about cloning bans. It explains how hidden intuitions have caused conservatives and liberals to act contrary to their own most cherished ideals and values.

Kerry Lynn Macintosh is a member of the law and technology faculty at Santa Clara University School of Law. She received her BA from Pomona College and her JD from Stanford Law School, where she was elected to the Order of the Coif. Professor Macintosh is the author of *Illegal Beings: Human Clones and the Law* (2005). She has published articles in the field of law and technology in the *Journal of Law, Technology & Policy*; *Harvard Journal of Law & Technology*; *Boston University Journal of Science & Technology Law*; *Berkeley Technology Law Journal*; and other journals. Professor Macintosh is a member of the American Law Institute, a law reform organization.

CAMBRIDGE BIOETHICS AND LAW

This series of books was founded by Cambridge University Press with Alexander McCall Smith as its first editor in 2003. It focuses on the law's complex and troubled relationship with medicine across both the developed and the developing worlds. In the past twenty years, we have seen in many countries increasing resort to the courts by dissatisfied patients and a growing use of the courts to attempt to resolve intractable ethical dilemmas. At the same time, legislatures across the world have struggled to address the questions posed by both the successes and the failures of modern medicine, and international organizations such as the WHO and UNESCO now regularly address issues of medical law.

It follows that we would expect ethical and policy questions to be integral to the analysis of the legal issues discussed in this series. The series responds to the high profile of medical law in universities, in legal and medical practice, as well as in public and political affairs. We seek to reflect the evidence that many major health-related policy debates in the United Kingdom, Europe, and the international community over the past two decades have involved a strong medical law dimension. With that in mind, we seek to address how legal analysis might have a trans-jurisdictional and international relevance. Organ retention, embryonic stem cell research, physician-assisted suicide, and the allocation of resources to fund health care are but a few examples among many. The emphasis of this series is thus on matters of public concern and/or practical significance. We look for books that could make a difference to the development of medical law and enhance the role of medico-legal debate in policy circles. That is not to say that we lack interest in the important theoretical dimensions of the subject, but we aim to ensure that theoretical debate is grounded in the realities of how the law does and should interact with medicine and health care.

> *Series Editors*
>
> Professor Margaret Brazier, *University of Manchester*
> Professor Graeme Laurie, *University of Edinburgh*
> Professor Richard Ashcroft, *Queen Mary, University of London*
> Professor Eric M. Meslin, *Indiana University*

See series list after Index

Human Cloning

FOUR FALLACIES AND THEIR LEGAL CONSEQUENCES

Kerry Lynn Macintosh

Santa Clara University School of Law

CAMBRIDGE
UNIVERSITY PRESS

32 Avenue of the Americas, New York NY 10013-2473, USA

Cambridge University Press is part of the University of Cambridge.

It furthers the University's mission by disseminating knowledge in the pursuit of education, learning and research at the highest international levels of excellence.

www.cambridge.org
Information on this title: www.cambridge.org/9781107669598

© Kerry Lynn Macintosh 2013

This publication is in copyright. Subject to statutory exception and to the provisions of relevant collective licensing agreements, no reproduction of any part may take place without the written permission of Cambridge University Press.

First published 2013
First paperback edition 2014

A catalogue record for this publication is available from the British Library

Library of Congress Cataloguing in Publication data
Macintosh, Kerry Lynn.
  Human cloning : four fallacies and their legal consequences / Kerry Lynn Macintosh.
    p. cm. – (Cambridge bioethics and law ; 21)
  Includes bibliographical references and index.
  ISBN 978-1-107-03185-2 (hardback : alk. paper)
  1. Human cloning – United States.   2. Human cloning – Moral and ethical aspects – United States.   3. Human cloning – Law and legislation – United States.   I. Title.
  QH442.2.M253   2013
  176'.22–dc23   2012023251

ISBN 978-1-107-03185-2 Hardback
ISBN 978-1-107-66959-8 Paperback

Cambridge University Press has no responsibility for the persistence or accuracy of URLs for external or third-party internet websites referred to in this publication, and does not guarantee that any content on such websites is, or will remain, accurate or appropriate.

To MaryAnn Balyeat Macintosh

Contents

List of Tables	page xi
Acknowledgments	xiii
Introduction	xv

PART I THE SCIENCE OF CLONING 1

1	**Animals Born Through Cloning Are Ordinary Members of Their Species**	7
2	**Animals Born Through Cloning Are Unique Individuals and Have Their Own Lifespans**	27
3	**Humans Born Through Cloning Will Be Unique Individuals and Have Their Own Lifespans**	43
	Summary of Part I	61

PART II THE COGNITIVE PSYCHOLOGY OF CLONING 63

4	**Identity and Essentialism**	69
5	**Artifacts and Essentialism**	103
6	**Impostors and Essentialism**	125
7	**Resurrection and Essentialism**	147
	Summary of Part II	165

PART III THE LAW OF CLONING 171

8 **Essentialism and the Law of Reproductive Cloning** 175
9 **Essentialism and the Law of Research Cloning** 199

Conclusion 221
Notes 233
Index 303

Tables

1 Cloning Is Used to Create Copies	*page* 79
2 Cloning Is Associated with Manufacture	110
3 Cloning Is Used to Create Impostors	132
4 Cloning Is Used to Resurrect a Person	149
5 Cloning Is Used for Spare Body Parts	152

Acknowledgments

This book has been an exhilarating but challenging project. I could never have completed it without the aid of many people.

My colleague, Gary Spitko, offered me helpful advice. So did the two academics who read the book manuscript for Cambridge University Press. H. Clark Barrett, who is an expert in psychological essentialism, was kind enough to discuss this project with me at an early stage and provided me with useful suggestions.

I am also indebted to my many talented research assistants. Richard Seifert, Michael Pittman, Michelle Woodhouse, Jason Mendelson, Shannon Pedersen, D. Ashley Richardson, and Kevin Isaacson are now graduates of Santa Clara University School of Law. Their dedicated research brought me the biological, psychological, and legal sources that I needed to write this book. In addition, these assistants read my drafts and offered helpful comments on how to improve them.

I also thank my editor at Cambridge University Press, John Berger, my project manager Bhavani Ganesh, my copy editor Sheila Elmosleh of PETT Fox, Inc., and the staff at Cambridge University Press and Newgen Knowledge Works for their efforts in bringing this project to fruition.

Last but not least, I thank my husband and children for their patience and support during the creative process.

Introduction

MAMMALIAN CLONING IS A RELATIVELY NEW SCIENCE, one that burst onto the scene at the end of the twentieth century. In 1996, scientists took a cell from the frozen tissue of a long-dead sheep and used it to clone a lamb named Dolly. When this achievement was announced in 1997, the public immediately realized that the technology might be applied to human beings.

Safety was an immediate concern for many observers. Initial experiments with animals had low success rates, leading to legitimate concerns that cloning might cause physical harm to mothers and children. However, safety was far from the only objection that the prospect of human cloning inspired. People from all walks of life, from scientists to journalists to political leaders, framed the technology as a means of manufacturing copies of living or deceased persons. Responding to public hysteria, federal regulators in the United States prohibited the cloning of babies, and many state legislatures followed suit.

Sixteen years have passed since Dolly was born. During that span of time, researchers all over the world have continued to experiment with the cloning of animals. Birth rates have climbed and healthy animals are common. Meanwhile, other scientists have succeeded in cloning human embryos. Their goal is to create cloned stem cells for research and therapy. However, the same research that could create new drugs or replacement organs may render human cloning not only possible but reasonably safe. The day may come when cloning is no more hazardous for mothers and children than in vitro fertilization. Therefore, before the first cloned baby is born into a hostile world, it is important to reexamine objections to cloning that are not based on safety concerns.

This book proceeds in three parts. Part I updates the science of cloning. It explains that researchers have experimented with new methods of animal cloning and improved birth rates. Contrary to public expectations, animals born through cloning are individuals rather than copies. They are ordinary members of their species, not designer products or resurrections of the dead. Extrapolating from this data, Part I explains why humans born through cloning[1] will also be unique human beings with their own lifespans.

Part II contrasts these scientific realities with the psychology of cloning. Drawing upon popular culture, the media, and government reports, it documents the existence of popular fallacies that construe animals and humans born through cloning as copies, artifacts, impostors, and resurrections. Part II traces these fallacies back to psychological essentialism – a cognitive heuristic that some scholars believe evolved tens of thousands of years ago.

Finally, Part III focuses on the law of human cloning. It shows how false intuitions have masqueraded as reasoned public discourse and spawned regulatory actions, bills, and laws that ban not only the cloning of babies but also stem cell research. These bans violate the American commitment to reproductive freedom, scientific freedom, and egalitarianism. Part III advocates a fresh approach toward the regulation of human cloning, one in which education and counseling play a leading role.

---

[1] Scientific articles, popular culture, the media, and government reports often describe animals and humans born through cloning as "clones." However, as Chapter 4 explains, the word "clone" has become a synonym for copy in our culture. Also, when used as a common noun, clone reinforces essentialist intuitions that are scientifically inaccurate. Therefore, in this book, I seldom use clone as a noun (except when I am describing or citing a research source that itself employs the term). Instead, I have used the word as a verb ("to clone"), gerund ("human born through cloning"), or adjective ("cloned human").

PART I THE SCIENCE OF CLONING

THE YEAR WAS 1997. THE NEWS WAS AMAZING: a team of Scottish scientists that included Ian Wilmut and Keith Campbell had cloned a lamb from an adult sheep. Although Dolly had been born on July 5, 1996, the team had delayed the announcement to protect their ability to publish their work,[1] which they did nearly eight months later in the science journal *Nature*.[2]

Dolly promptly became a media sensation. The outpouring of scientific research, academic analysis, and public discussion makes it likely that the reader already possesses some information (or misinformation) about this first and most famous mammal cloned from an adult cell. Also, the experiment that produced her serves as a basis for discussing later developments in cloning science. For these reasons, Part I will begin the discussion with a review of how Dolly was made and what we know about her.

A. The Story of Dolly

Dolly's story begins with cells harvested from the mammary glands of a long-since deceased ewe of the Finn Dorset breed.[3] The cells were retrieved from storage and placed in culture. Each cell in the culture contained in its nucleus the nuclear deoxyribonucleic acid (DNA) of the donor ewe, arrayed in structures known as chromosomes. Embedded within those chromosomes were the donor's genes. Genes are discrete DNA segments that specify the sequence of amino acid chains[4] that form the building blocks of proteins. Proteins are major structural molecules that form single cells; groups of cells assemble to create larger tissues; and collections of different tissues form the body of an organism.[5]

Thus, all the information necessary to make a sheep was present in each individual cell in the culture. However, most of the genes in those cells had been switched off during the process of differentiation, through which embryonic cells diverge in function and take on specialized roles in the body.[6] Only genes necessary to the function of mammary gland cells were still active in the cultured cells. Wilmut and his team had to find some means of reprogramming the gene expression of these donor cells so that the nuclear DNA could support the development of a new organism.[7]

To accomplish this feat, the scientists relied upon the magic of the egg, which contains factors that promote the replication of DNA.[8] The scientists retrieved eggs from Scottish Blackface ewes (a different breed than the Finn Dorset cell donor) and removed the chromosomes, leaving the eggs without any DNA of their own (a process often referred to as *enucleation*).[9] Meanwhile, the scientists readied the mammary gland cells for reprogramming. They deprived the cells of the nourishment needed to grow and proliferate, starving them into a quiescent state.[10]

The next challenge was to transfer DNA from the mammary gland cells into the empty, waiting eggs. This transfer was accomplished in two steps: first, one scientist passed a donor cell into an egg via pipette; second, another used electrical pulses to fuse the donor cell to the egg and simultaneously activate that egg so that it could begin the reprogramming process and initiate development of a cloned lamb.[11]

Wilmut and his team obtained 277 fused couplets from this process. Twenty-nine of those developed into embryos and were transferred into thirteen surrogate ewes. One Scottish Blackface ewe became pregnant and delivered Dolly, a healthy lamb. In terms of lambs born per embryos transferred, the experiment had a birthrate of 3.4 percent.[12]

Dolly did not share the breed of her egg donor or surrogate mother. In appearance, she was a Finn Dorset sheep like her cell donor.[13] DNA analysis further confirmed she was cloned from the cell donor.[14]

This accomplishment was striking for a number of reasons. Ordinarily, mammals conceive new life through the combination of *germ cells*, that is, sperm and eggs. Dolly had been conceived using a non-germ, or *somatic cell* (which explains why cloning is sometimes called somatic cell nuclear transfer). Her method of conception was asexual, rather than sexual. Another happy surprise was the success in reversing the differentiated state of the adult donor cell. Although Wilmut and Campbell had already cloned sheep from embryo-derived cell lines,[15] biologists had long believed that the cloning of a mammal from an adult cell was impossible.[16]

Granted, the experiment was inefficient, and that raised eyebrows. Moreover, many politicians and reporters misunderstood the 276 fused couplets that either never became embryos or failed to produce a pregnancy, viewing them as deformed or dead lambs.[17] This, however, is incorrect. There was only one pregnancy derived from adult cells, and that resulted in the birth of a healthy lamb (Dolly).[18] Moreover, Dolly stayed healthy as she matured. Defying those who questioned her fertility, she gave birth to six healthy lambs conceived the old-fashioned way.[19]

Still, skeptics questioned whether she could possibly be normal, and the media eagerly reported every indication that she might not be. For example, after she turned one year old, the Wilmut team measured her telomeres (repetitive DNA sequences that protect the ends of chromosomes against degradation)[20] and found them to be shorter than normal for a sheep of her age.[21] Noting that the difference could have been due to natural variations among sheep, the team pointed out that it was not certain that telomere length reflected physiological age. In fact, at age one she was healthy and typical for a sheep of her breed.[22] However, the team also stated that Dolly's telomere length was consistent with the age of her DNA donor (who had been six years old when the mammary gland cells were harvested) and the length of time the cells had been cultured prior to her cloning.[23] This captured the attention of the media, which reported that Dolly had been born prematurely old.[24]

When Dolly developed arthritis in her left hind leg at age five, critics again raised the specter of premature aging, discounting the explanation that Wilmut gave: she was a celebrity and stood on her hind legs to beg for treats and attention from visitors.[25] When she was euthanized at age six after contracting a contagious lung disease that was spreading among the sheep in her barn, reporters wrote premature aging into their obituaries.[26]

The idea that a lamb had been born six years old blurred the distinction between Dolly and her DNA donor. It reinforced the popular misconception that cloning was a means of resurrecting the dead. Even people who realized that resurrection was impossible had a tendency to conceptualize Dolly as a copy of the DNA donor. It was easy to forget that she had been born as a lamb because the reports of her birth (and accompanying photos) came much later, after she was nearly eight months old. The absence of the sheep that had donated the DNA made it impossible to draw comparisons that would have revealed her unique characteristics and individuality.[27]

B. Updating the Science of Cloning

Dolly was born sixteen years ago. Since then, cloning has proven to be a popular field, attracting interest from scientists all over the world. These scientists have conducted countless experiments in many species, including our own. Accordingly, the goal of Part I is simple: to bring the science of cloning up to date for the reader.

Chapter 1 discusses methods that have been used to clone animals, and the efficiency rates that scientists have obtained. It also examines the health status and function of cloned animals.

Chapter 2 shifts the focus to the individuality of animals born through cloning. Applying basic biological principles and experimental results, the chapter explains why these animals often do not look or act the same as the animals that donated the DNA for the cloning procedure. It also discusses scientific evidence showing that animals born through cloning are not born old. Rather, they start life as infants and enjoy healthy lifespans.

Chapter 3 carries the discussion into the human realm. It explains that human embryos have been cloned for research purposes but no babies have been born thus far. The rest of the chapter uses biological principles and animal experiments to predict the characteristics of humans born through cloning.

1 Animals Born Through Cloning Are Ordinary Members of Their Species

THE CREATION OF DOLLY THE SHEEP RAN CONTRARY TO biological dogma. Some scientists questioned at first whether Ian Wilmut and Keith Campbell had truly cloned her from the somatic cell of an adult animal.[1] Fifteen years later, scientists now realize that Dolly was the vanguard of her kind.

A. Which Species Have Been Cloned?

Working with differentiated cells taken from young and mature animals, scientists have cloned a menagerie: livestock such as cattle, sheep, goats, and pigs[2]; experimental animals such as mice, rats, and rabbits[3]; and pets such as dogs, cats, and horses.[4]

Cloned species are not limited to familiar domesticated animals. Scientists have also turned the technology to more exotic uses. Although no dinosaurs have been cloned (apologies to *Jurassic Park* fans), some labs have cloned other species that are threatened or extinct. For example, South Korean researchers have cloned the gray wolf,[5] which is still considered endangered in some parts of the United States.[6] An American team has cloned a gaur, a type of wild ox that is on the brink of extinction.[7] Some Japanese researchers are even attempting to clone the extinct wooly mammoth.[8]

There is one notable gap in the menagerie: not a single primate has been cloned from a live animal.[9] However, that momentous event may

7

be drawing closer. In 2007, Oregon researchers took DNA from an adult rhesus monkey, cloned dozens of embryos, and used the embryos to create two stem cell lines.[10] This accomplishment hints that cloned baby monkeys may not be far behind.

1. Which Species Are Most Commonly Cloned?

Scientists and researchers clone animals from certain species far more than others. Approximately 75 percent of cloning labs work on livestock. Cattle lead the herd, serving as research subjects in nearly half of all cloning labs.[11] Pigs are also popular, functioning as research subjects in approximately 15 percent of cloning labs.[12] The main reasons for this interest are commercial. The food industry wants to replicate individual animals with desirable genetic traits – not so that they can be eaten, but so that they can sire offspring.[13]

The biomedical industry is another player. It is interested in *transgenic cloning* – that is, cloning animals from cells that have first been altered in the lab by adding or inactivating genes. One of the first transgenic cloned animals was a sheep named Polly. Ian Wilmut cloned her from DNA to which he added a human gene. Her milk was modified to contain human factor IX, a clotting protein used to treat hemophilia.[14] Similarly, transgenic cloned cows may one day produce milk laced with proteins that can be used in medical therapy.[15] Other scientists have engineered cloned pigs. Their goal is to create hearts and other transplantable organs that the human immune system will not reject.[16]

Moving beyond livestock, one finds that cloning is more than a commercial activity; it is also a valuable research tool. Scientists can use cloning experiments to investigate fundamentals of cell biology, genetics, and epigenetics.[17] Mice are useful research animals because they reproduce rapidly and prolifically and have relatively short life spans.[18] Thus, it is not surprising that mice are research subjects in nearly one-fifth of labs; only cattle are cloned in more labs.[19]

B. How Efficient Is Animal Cloning?

The original Dolly experiment was not very efficient. Only one of the twenty-nine embryos transferred to surrogate mother sheep resulted in the birth of a lamb. In other words, the birthrate was only 3.4 percent.[20]

In 2010, Dr. Keith Campbell made headlines by revealing that he had cloned again from the same stock of frozen mammary gland tissue that had produced Dolly. Improvements in cloning technology resulted in four healthy sheep born in 2007. This time, one out of every five embryos transferred to surrogate mother sheep resulted in the birth of a lamb.[21] In other words, the birthrate was an impressive 20 percent. That increased rate is a big leap forward from the original Dolly experiment.

Further details on these sheep were not available at the time this book went to press. However, in the past fifteen years, scientists have conducted hundreds of experiments involving various species. These scientists have utilized different cloning methods. Their success in generating animals has also varied.

This book presents data on the two animal species that are most commonly cloned: cattle and mice.[22] Although cloning experiments can be rather technical, it is worth examining the data for what it can reveal on the methods and efficiency of cloning.

1. Cattle

Researchers working with cattle most commonly clone from *fibroblasts* – that is, a type of progenitor cell that is not yet terminally differentiated and can develop into bone, cartilage, fat, or muscle.[23] Early pregnancy rates can be high: as many as 65 percent of embryos transferred lead to a pregnancy. This rate is comparable to early pregnancy rates achieved through bovine in vitro fertilization (IVF). After seven weeks of gestation, however, few IVF fetuses miscarry while most cloned fetuses do.[24] Judging by reports in the literature, approximately 9–20 percent of cloned embryos transferred to the womb produce live-born calves delivered at term after nine months gestation.[25] This birthrate falls short of the nearly 40 percent birthrate achieved in bovine IVF.[26] Why is cattle cloning less efficient than IVF?

a) Genetic Abnormalities

Genetics offers one possible explanation. A cloned embryo will not develop properly if there are errors in its genetic code. For example, suppose the nuclear DNA in the donor cell mutates while the cell is still in the body of the donor. Or, suppose the nuclear DNA is fine when the donor cell is harvested from the donor but mutates in a Petri dish while it awaits transfer to an egg.

However, experiments have not yet shown that mutations are a major obstacle to cattle cloning. Indeed, the evidence we have cuts the other way. Cattle have been successfully cloned from cells taken from an older donor and cultured for several months; the birthrate was comparable to rates obtained in experiments utilizing cells harvested from younger animals and cultured for shorter periods of time.[27]

b) Reprogramming

Other biological barriers to cloning involve not genetic but rather *epigenetic factors* – that is, heritable changes that go beyond alterations in DNA sequence.[28] For example, epigenetic modifications switch genes on and off, leading to the differentiation of cells.[29] Such modifications make it a challenge to clone from the nuclear DNA of an adult cell. The egg must remove the modifications so that all the genes are once again available for expression.[30] In other words, the egg must reprogram the nuclear DNA of the cell.

Some scientists believe that animal cloning is inefficient because of inadequate reprogramming. To test this hypothesis, one group of researchers studied the gene expression profiles of cloned bovine embryos. To their surprise, the profiles for cloned embryos were quite similar to those of embryos created through artificial insemination. Less than 1 percent of the more than 5,000 genes studied were differentially expressed.[31]

ANIMALS BORN THROUGH CLONING ARE ORDINARY

This experiment showed that reprogramming can be successful and fairly comprehensive. However, some of the genes that were abnormally expressed in the cloned embryos control embryonic development or the function of the placenta (the organ within the uterus that delivers nutrition and removes waste from a growing fetus).[32] Consistently, some scientists claim that aberrant placental function accounts for the high rate at which cloned fetuses miscarry – a tempting theory examined later in this chapter.

c) Technical Elements

In an effort to improve birthrates, cattle researchers have also experimented with the technical elements of cloning. For example, certain types of donor cells may be easier to reprogram than others. To test this possibility, scientists have cloned from fibroblasts taken from various organs and blood leukocytes. Unfortunately, a dearth of comparative studies makes it hard to know if one donor cell type is more efficient at generating cattle than another.[33]

The process of enucleating an egg and combining it with a donor cell might compromise development by damaging the egg or the donor nuclear DNA.[34] To test this hypothesis, researchers have compared two methods of enucleating the eggs used in cattle cloning: aspirating nuclei with glass needles versus cutting the eggs in half to get the nuclei out and then reassembling them. Either way, cloning efficiencies remained similar.[35] Researchers have also tried different methods of reconstructing eggs into embryos. They have fused entire donor cells to eggs and microinjected just the nuclei of donor cells into eggs. Again, such variations did not have a noticeable impact on birthrates.[36]

Other technical elements include the chemical agents used to activate reconstructed eggs and the *culture media* (a mixture of biological and chemical substances) in which embryos are grown. Experiments with mice have shown that the right blend of chemical activators can aid reprogramming.[37] Similarly, culture media are important because they can affect gene expression and alter the developmental trajectory of embryos.[38] Unfortunately, when it comes to cloning cattle, chemical activators and culture media have had little apparent impact on birthrates.[39]

In sum, although researchers have not yet ferreted out the biological reasons for inefficient cloning, it would be a mistake to assume that they never can or will. Cloning cattle is more than a curiosity; it is a commercial enterprise. Companies have a profit motive and will continue their research into methods of achieving higher birthrates at lower cost.

2. Mice

Birthrates for mice cloned from adult animals have been low, generally ranging from 1–3 percent of transferred embryos (although higher rates are possible, as discussed later).[40] Most cloned embryos fail before implantation or immediately thereafter.[41] Mice that survive to birth are likely to have overlarge and abnormal placentae, suggesting abnormal nurture during gestation.[42]

The genetic[43] or epigenetic sources of these inefficiencies are not entirely clear. However, unlike those who work with cattle, researchers who work with mice have discovered some means of improving birthrates significantly. A complete review of this research is beyond the scope of this chapter, but several experiments are worth mentioning here.

a) Cell Type and Genotype

Some scientists have reviewed the literature and concluded that donor cell type does not matter to success when cloning mice.[44] However, others believe that certain donor cell types and genotypes do facilitate reprogramming.[45]

In 2003, a Japanese research team cloned mice and achieved a birthrate of 3–5 percent.[46] The DNA donors were newborn males, and the donor cells used in the cloning were immature Sertoli cells, which aid in testicle formation and sperm production.[47] The team was not sure why cell type mattered, but noted that smaller donor cells tended to support development better than larger donor cells (at least in mice).[48]

The Japanese researchers further discovered that genotype also can affect reprogramming. When they used immature Sertoli cells from a genetic mouse strain known as 129, birthrates jumped to around 10 percent.[49] The reason for this success was unclear, but the 129 strain excels at producing embryonic stem cell lines and could be more epigenetically malleable than other genetic lines.[50] In 2009, these researchers cloned from immature Sertoli cells derived from the offspring of a 129 strain father, and reported an impressive 13.8 percent birthrate.[51]

Other scientists who clone mice have also experimented with donor cell type. In 2007, a New York research team theorized that adult stem cells had an intermediate state of differentiation and might be easier to reprogram; accordingly, it cloned mice from multipotent keratinocyte stem cells harvested from hair follicles. The birthrate for males was a higher-than-average 5.4 percent, but for females it was only 1.6 percent.[52] The team speculated that the males were easier to clone because females had to undergo X chromosome inactivation.[53]

b) X Chromosome Inactivation

A brief explanation may help clarify that last point. Males carry one X and one Y chromosome; females carry two X chromosomes. How does nature avoid giving females a double dose of the proteins associated with the genes on the X chromosomes? Early in the life of a female embryo, chemical marks randomly inactivate one of the two X chromosomes in each cell.[54] Once these marks are established, they are maintained during cell division in later stages of development. Thus, if an adult female animal is to be cloned successfully, the epigenetic mark that silenced one of the X chromosomes in the donor cell must first be erased so that random inactivation of the X chromosome can occur anew in the cloned embryo.[55] Although some researchers have found X chromosome inactivation occurs as it should in cloned mice, others have found aberrant inactivation.[56]

The Japanese researchers who conducted the 2003 experiment discussed in the preceding section have also investigated the role of the X chromosome in cloning. In 2010, the researchers discovered that numerous genes on the X chromosome were down-regulated in cloned mouse embryos.[57] The culprit was *Xist*, a ribonucleic acid (RNA) that is supposed to inactivate one of two X chromosomes in females. Xist was expressed when it should not have been: from the single X chromosome in the male embryos and the active X chromosome in the female embryos.[58]

The researchers cloned mouse embryos from donor cells that had been engineered to render the active X chromosome Xist-deficient. Elimination of Xist not only decreased the numbers of down-regulated genes on the X chromosome, but also the numbers of down-regulated genes on other chromosomes. This outcome may reflect a network of genes that controls embryonic development.[59]

The Japanese researchers also implanted the Xist-deficient cloned embryos in surrogate mice. For females derived from cumulus cells, the average birthrate per embryos transferred was 12.7 percent; for males derived from Sertoli cells, the birthrate was 14.4 percent. These birthrates represented an eight- to ninefold increase over birthrates achieved for wild-type cloned mice.[60]

In 2011, the Japanese researchers followed up with another experiment. This time, they cloned mouse embryos from Sertoli cells and injected a short interfering RNA into the embryos, thereby temporarily disabling Xist (a technique known as RNAi-mediated gene knockdown).[61] Unlike the method used in the 2010 experiment, this knockdown method did not require a permanent genetic alteration. The results were impressive: a 12 percent birthrate compared to 1 percent for controls. Moreover, the knockdown technique normalized the gene expression profiles of the newborn mouse pups.[62] The researchers speculated that other mammalian species could be cloned successfully using this method.[63]

In short, controlling the negative effects of Xist on gene expression could lead to dramatic improvements in birthrates of cloned animals.

c) Chemical Treatments

Scientists have also experimented with chemical agents. By adding the chemical trichostatin A (TSA) to the activation and culture media, one research group increased the birthrate for cloned mice to 6–7 percent.[64] Although the precise reason for this success is unclear, the TSA may have relaxed the degree of association between DNA and its associated structural and regulatory proteins, making the genetic code easier to read. The TSA may also have facilitated erasure of the chemical marks that inactivated most of the genes when the donor cell was in its original somatic form, thereby making reprogramming more efficient.[65]

The mice in this experiment grew up to be normal and healthy,[66] but chemical treatments have a mixed record of success in other species. For example, when scientists treated cloned rabbit embryos with TSA, all of the bunnies died shortly after birth.[67] Yet, when cattle researchers pretreated donor cells and embryos with TSA and another chemical, they not only achieved higher birthrates, but also produced calves that were more likely to survive beyond the critical neonatal period.[68] Another group of scientists cloned healthy inbred miniature pigs from fetal fibroblast cells with the aid of a chemical that is less toxic than TSA but has a similar effect.[69]

Perhaps the true value of chemical treatments lies in their combination with other birth-boosting strategies. In 2011, Japanese researchers reported that they had combined their Xist knockdown technique (discussed in the preceding section) with TSA treatment and achieved birthrates for cloned mice as high as 20 percent. This big increase in birthrate suggests that scientists may be on the verge of a cloning breakthrough.[70]

C. Are Animals Born through Cloning Ordinary Members of Their Species?

In the fifteen years since scientists announced the birth of Dolly, many other animals have been born through cloning. The critical question is this: are they as healthy and functional as animals conceived and born the old-fashioned way?

Because these animals are cloned in a lab, they remind many people of the novel *Frankenstein*.[71] In that story, a scientist tries to create a man from body parts. What he gets instead is a "creature" that is physically grotesque, psychologically warped, and so morally flawed that it sees murder as the only effective tool with which to achieve its goals.[72] In keeping with this horrific tale, some argue that animals (or, potentially, humans) born through cloning are necessarily the flawed products of a technological process and can never be functional members of their species – a point of view that I label the *artifact fallacy*.

In examining the artifact fallacy, this chapter proceeds in two steps. First, it reviews experiments that have raised questions about the health and normalcy of cloned animals. Second, it shares the contrary evidence: cloned animals that are healthy at birth not only remain so but exhibit development and behavior that fall within the appropriate range for their species.

1. Large Offspring Syndrome

Large offspring syndrome (LOS) affects a substantial proportion of cloned cattle and sheep.[73] Rates for cattle can range as high as 40 percent.[74] The syndrome encompasses a wide variety of abnormalities such as oversized body and organs, cardiovascular and kidney defects, respiratory problems, oversized umbilical cord with patent blood vessels, vulnerability to infection, inability to regulate body temperature, and slowness to stand.[75] Animals with LOS also have enlarged and edematous placentae.[76] Some die at birth or shortly thereafter.[77]

LOS is also common (but less severe) among cattle and sheep conceived through IVF.[78] This has led scientists to surmise that LOS may be related to rough handling of eggs and embryos in the lab or culture conditions that are less than optimal.[79] It is thought that the molecular root of LOS lies in the abnormal expression of genes in the organism and placenta – particularly genes that are *imprinted*.[80]

To explain, a mammal ordinarily has matching pairs of chromosomes, along with one pair of sex chromosomes. One chromosome in each pair is inherited from the father and the other from the mother.[81] In the case of a cloned animal, all chromosomes are inherited through the donor, but the donor transmits chromosome pairs inherited from its father and mother.

Imprinted genes on the chromosomes are modified with chemical marks that ensure the genes are expressed on either the paternal or maternal copy, but not both.[82] Scientists believe imprinting evolved to regulate the competing interests of the mother and father: genes expressed from the paternal copy encourage the transfer of maternal resources via the placenta to the fetus, whereas genes expressed from the maternal copy conserve resources to keep the gestating mother healthy. If this balance is out of order, the fetus will not develop properly.[83]

Some scientists believe that cloned animals have LOS because embryo culture or some other aspect of the process interferes with reprogramming of the donor DNA or expression of imprinted genes.[84] Some research does link abnormalities in cloned animals to faulty gene expression.[85] However, we do not yet have clear proof that improper expression of imprinted genes is responsible for LOS in cloned animals.[86]

We do know this: cloned cattle and sheep often have placentae that are abnormal in size, structure, and function.[87] Indeed, one scientific team has found that all placentae of cloned cattle, even those that appear normal, have altered gene expression profiles.[88]

Malfunctioning placentae may fail to transmit adequate nutrition or oxygen to the fetus or allow buildup of toxic wastes.[89] This, in turn, may cause the high rates of miscarriage, morbidity (including LOS), and mortality found among cloned ruminants.[90] Some scientists have suggested the term "large offspring syndrome" should be replaced with "large placenta syndrome" or "abnormal placenta syndrome."[91]

Placental malfunction appears to be common in other cloned species. Cloned swine do not suffer from LOS; however, they can suffer from intrauterine growth restriction and end up smaller than normal.[92] Placentae of cloned swine often exhibit morphologic and gene expression abnormalities, implying that cloned fetuses receive improper nutrition during development.[93] Similarly, cloned mice often have abnormal, oversized placentae.[94] Even when the mice themselves have a normal pattern of gene expression, their placentae may not.[95]

An experiment conducted in China underscores the importance of placental function in cloning. Starting with a cloned mouse embryo, researchers removed the outer layer of trophoblast cells (which ordinarily would have become a placenta) and aggregated the inner cell mass of the clone with two tetraploid embryos.[96] A tetraploid embryo has four rather than two copies of each chromosome; as a result, it can only make a placenta and does not contribute to the organism.[97] Thus, the researchers found a means of providing a viable placenta while at the same time ensuring that only the inner cell mass of the cloned embryo could develop into a baby mouse. This ingenious cloning method boosted birthrates to 14–15 percent.[98] The researchers concluded that faulty placentae are the main cause for the poor development of cloned mice.[99]

2. The Health Profile of Animals Born Through Cloning

Given this evidence of LOS and malfunctioning placentae, it may seem hard to believe that animals born through cloning could ever be healthy or normal. Indeed, some scientists have taken that position.

In 2001, when the United States Congress held hearings to determine whether human cloning should be banned, one key witness was a biologist who clones mice. Dr. Rudolf Jaenisch testified that there were probably no normal cloned animals. Even those that appeared normal must be flawed at the epigenetic level.[100] Media accounts of the hearings drove the point home with a photo of a cloned mouse that appeared normal until it reached adulthood and became obese, for what its creators believed were epigenetic reasons.[101]

ANIMALS BORN THROUGH CLONING ARE ORDINARY

Other researchers disagreed. In 2002, a Japanese team reported that it had examined mice cloned from somatic cells (both adult and fetal). Despite the low 2.8 percent birthrate, 92.9 percent of the mice that did survive to birth were healthy and active. Moreover, when the team tested the expression of several imprinted genes, it found the genes were properly expressed in cloned fetuses (but not in placentae – more about that shortly).[102]

Additional studies indicated that cloned mice were reaching developmental milestones, such as ear twitching and eye opening, within the normal time frame for mice. Their activity patterns, motor control, muscle strength, and balance were all normal. The cloned mice were able to negotiate mazes as easily as controls, indicating normal learning and memory skills.[103]

Livestock producers also stepped forward to defend the normalcy of animals born through cloning. In 2001, scientists associated with Advanced Cell Technology, Inc., reported data on somatic cell cloning in Holstein cattle. Transfer of 496 cloned blastocysts resulted in 110 pregnancies; consistent with the relatively high rate of pregnancy loss that is common in cattle cloning, 80 of those pregnancies aborted spontaneously.[104] Thirty calves developed to term. Six died shortly after birth; five of those six deaths were due to cardiopulmonary problems caused by placental inadequacies.[105]

These high rates of miscarriage and neonatal death were discouraging, but the scientists also had something exciting to report: the twenty-four cattle that survived the immediate postnatal period were still alive one to four years later.[106] Moreover, the cattle had been tested and found to be normal in physical condition (including weight), blood and urine chemistry, immune function, fertility, reproduction, social interaction, and conditioned responses.[107] Some of the cows had experienced pulmonary hypertension and respiratory distress at birth; however, they did not have genetic defects, gross obesity, immune deficiencies, or other severe abnormalities.[108]

In 2002, Keith Campbell (who helped clone Dolly) joined some of the same scientists in publishing a review of experiments involving cloned cattle, sheep, goats, pigs, and mice. Concluding that 77 percent of live-born cloned animals were healthy,[109] they opined that most miscarriages, stillbirths, and neonatal deaths could be traced back to abnormal placentae and resulting malnourishment. Newborns were often stabilized within hours through simple measures such as additional oxygen and glucose.[110]

3. Cloned Burgers, Anyone?

Meanwhile, the Food and Drug Administration (FDA), which regulates food in the United States, faced a decision: should it allow producers to sell meat and milk derived from cloned cattle, swine, and other food animals? Moreover, once the cloned livestock mated and had offspring, should the FDA allow producers to sell meat and milk derived from those offspring?

In 2001, the FDA asked producers to voluntarily refrain from introducing meat or milk from cloned animals and their offspring into the food supply while it reviewed the potential risks to humans and animals.[111] In 2008, following years of study, the agency announced that meat and milk from cloned cattle, swine, and goats were as safe to eat as meat and milk from conventional[112] animals. The FDA declined to comment on the safety of food products derived from cloned sheep on the ground that it had insufficient data. However, it declared meat and milk from the offspring of any cloned food animal safe to eat.[113]

The U.S. Department of Agriculture (USDA) supported the FDA's assessment. It lifted the voluntary moratorium on milk and meat from the offspring of cloned animals. (By the time you read this book, you may have eaten such food products.) The USDA asked technology companies to continue to voluntarily refrain from marketing food products derived from cloned animals while it worked with producers, processors, retailers, and customers to transition such products into the marketplace.[114]

These decisions were made in reliance on a massive report from the FDA's Center for Veterinary Medicine (CVM). In "Animal Cloning: A

ANIMALS BORN THROUGH CLONING ARE ORDINARY   21

Risk Assessment,"[115] the CVM reviewed scientific literature through 2007 on cloned cattle, swine, sheep, and goats[116] as well as data submitted by private companies that produced cloned animals. It used this information to evaluate food safety in two different ways.

First, the CVM reasoned that meat and milk derived from cloned animals would not pose any additional food safety risks if it did not differ significantly from meat and milk derived from conventional animals.[117] The CVM studied compositional analyses and found that the milk of cloned cattle and meat of cloned cattle and swine did not differ in any biologically relevant way from the milk and meat of regular animals.[118]

Second, the CVM reasoned that healthy animals would produce safe food.[119] The agency declined to address the question of whether cloned animals were "normal."[120] Nevertheless, its report, which reviews ten years of cloning literature and data, is highly relevant to our discussion. Outcomes for cattle, swine, and goats will be briefly summarized here.

The CVM reviewed extensive data on cloned cattle. It stated that an average of 20 percent of newborn calves died. Among those animals born with abnormalities, the risk of disease and death persisted during the first six months of life. Estimates of mortality during this juvenile period ranged from 14 to 42 percent.[121] These sick or abnormal animals did not concern the CVM, for it reasoned that existing laws and regulations prevented their carcasses from entering the food supply.[122] Most of the 58–86 percent of calf clones that survived the juvenile period seemed healthy and exhibited normal growth and development, including ability to sire, conceive, and bear offspring that appear healthy and normal.[123]

In an appendix to the report, the CVM reviewed unpublished data obtained from Cyagra, Inc., a company that specializes in cattle cloning. The data included blood chemistry assays, hormonal assays,[124] blood counts, and urinalyses comparing cloned cattle with age-matched comparators produced through artificial insemination or mating.[125] At birth, cloned calves were already quite similar to comparators, with 90 percent of their hematology and clinical chemistry values falling within the values of the comparators. At one to six months of age, 95 and 96 percent of the hematology and clinical chemistry values, respectively, were consistent with those of comparators; and by six to eighteen months, clinical chemistry and hematology values for cloned cattle were virtually indistinguishable from those of comparators.[126]

The CVM presented more limited data on cloned swine. Most experiments reported healthy and normal newborn piglets, although birth weights tended to be lower than those of conventional swine.[127] For juvenile and older cloned swine, the CVM relied primarily on two sources. First, a pair of related studies reported that weights, blood chemistries, and behavior of juvenile cloned swine were similar to those of conventional animals.[128]

Second, Viagen, Inc., a company that produces cloned cattle and swine, shared with the CVM its unpublished data on seven cloned swine. These animals gained weight more slowly and weighed less at slaughter than comparators; the CVM attributed this outcome to the immune challenge the swine faced upon leaving the lab at 50 days of age and entering a regular swine facility.[129] Viagen also sampled blood at birth and again right before or after the cloned swine were slaughtered at six months, and assayed blood hematology, clinical chemistry, and urine values. Hematology and clinical chemistry values started out close to those of comparators and became more similar as the cloned swine aged.[130] The CVM also reviewed data indicating that cloned swine were fertile. Offspring of cloned swine did not differ from conventional swine.[131]

Finally, the CVM presented data on cloned goats that was sparse but favorable. Live-born goats did not have LOS or other significant abnormalities, appeared to grow and mature normally, were fertile, and had offspring that also appeared normal.[132]

For all animals born through cloning, the CVM summarized the evidence before it as good news:

> Most animal clones that survive the critical perinatal period appear to grow and develop normally. Even animals with physiological perturbations, including less severe manifestations of LOS, seem

to resolve them, usually within a period of weeks. More severe complications of LOS may persist into the juvenile period, but clones do not appear to develop any additional health risks unrelated to those that were observed during the perinatal period. Clones that reach reproductive age appear to be normal in all of the measures that have thus far been investigated, and appear to give rise to healthy, apparently normal progeny. Mature clones appear normal and healthy, and are virtually indistinguishable from their conventionally bred counterparts.[133]

The CVM's conclusions regarding the offspring of cloned animals deserve special emphasis here, for two reasons. First, scientific teams around the world have confirmed that when cloned cattle, swine, sheep, mice, and other species are bred via methods of sexual reproduction, they generate offspring that look and act normal.[134] These results buttress the USDA's decision to lift the voluntary moratorium on food products derived from offspring of cloned animals.

Second, genetic defects are heritable, but *epigenetic* defects may not always be. As the CVM explained, "Passage through the process of creating the cells that ultimately become ova and sperm naturally resets epigenetic signals for gene expression, and effectively 'clears' the genome of incomplete or inappropriate signals."[135] Thus, the existence of healthy offspring reinforces the notion that the abnormalities observed in some cloned animals result from errors in the expression of genes in their bodies or the placentae that once nurtured them.

However, the epigenetic variation observed in animals born through cloning is not always problematic. As the CVM noted:

Studies that evaluated epigenetic reprogramming in live, healthy clones indicate that although there is some variability between clones and their sexually-derived counterparts, these clones have undergone sufficient epigenetic reprogramming to carry out the coordinated functions necessary for survival and normal functioning. Molecular analyses reveal relatively small methylation differences, and either the animals are tolerant of such differences, or the epigenetic differences are below the threshold that poses observable adverse health outcomes.[136]

In other words, nature tolerates some epigenetic variability. Cloned animals can look and act normal, even if reprogramming is imperfect and their gene expression deviates from that of animals that are not cloned.[137]

We also have evidence that at least some epigenetic anomalies can resolve themselves over time. Scientists studied the epigenetic status of cloned mice and found that 3 out of 2,000 genomic sites were improperly regulated in newborn mice.[138] To their surprise, however, adult mice had only one abnormal site and aged mice had none.[139] The scientists concluded that the bodies of the cloned mice were probably eliminating malfunctioning cells over time.[140]

4. Role of the Placenta

This leaves a nagging question: how can animals born through cloning be healthy and functional members of their species when the placentae that nourished them during gestation are so often patently abnormal?

First, as an embryo develops, its cells take on different functions: the outer layer of cells turns into extraembryonic tissues, such as the placenta, while the inner cell mass becomes the organism.[141] Some scientists have suggested that cells within a cloned embryo that express genes properly may have a selective advantage: these normal cells may become the organism; abnormal cells are directed to the task of forming extraembryonic tissues.[142] In other words, when faced with epigenetically abnormal cells, nature may deal with them in a manner that protects the normalcy of the organism.

Second, the effects of placental dysfunction can sometimes be ameliorated after birth. In a recent survey of data from three countries, the main cause of death in cloned calves that showed no other sign of abnormality was respiratory distress, which could stem from oxygen

ANIMALS BORN THROUGH CLONING ARE ORDINARY   25

deprivation. Leading causes of death in the first sixty days were enlarged umbilical cords (also related to placentae), hyper or hypothermia, and failure to stand. Researchers operated to close enlarged umbilical vessels and administered oxygen, cool baths, and antibiotics; these simple actions helped many calves survive.[143]

Nevertheless, some scientists speculate that malfunctioning placentae may have long-term consequences. Cloned animals that were malnourished as fetuses could suffer from metabolic diseases later in life.[144] More research is required to test this theory.

5. Summary

Although some cloned animals have physical defects or health problems, most do not. Most that survive birth and the initial adjustment to life outside the womb are healthy and functional members of their species. They eat, grow, sleep, and engage in behaviors that are common to their species. They reach developmental milestones (including puberty), mate, gestate, give birth, and raise healthy offspring. Upon analysis, cloned animals are often indistinguishable from others of their species, right down to the composition of their meat.

These results refute the artifact fallacy. Sexual reproduction does not appear to be a prerequisite for membership in a species, because asexual reproduction is capable of producing an animal that falls within the usual range of appearance and behavior.

However, if one considers any epigenetic deviation an abnormality, one may insist that all animals born through cloning are abnormal, no matter how normally they behave. Perhaps this viewpoint has a psychological dimension. If something looks like a sheep, acts like a sheep, and yet people persist in believing that it cannot be a normal sheep, what lies behind their reasoning? This book will explore that question in Part II.

2 Animals Born Through Cloning Are Unique Individuals and Have Their Own Lifespans

WHEN DOLLY TROTTED ONTO THE PUBLIC stage, many people misconstrued her as a copy of the sheep that had donated the DNA for the cloning procedure. This persistently misleading idea – namely, that an animal or person born through cloning possesses the same physical, intellectual, psychological, or behavioral traits as others who share the same nuclear DNA – will be described in this book as the *identity fallacy*.[1]

In a variation on this theme, other observers conceptualized cloning as a means of reclaiming a lost life. Scientists inadvertently bolstered this notion by suggesting that Dolly had inherited the age of her DNA donor. These, too, are scientific errors. The notion that an animal or person born through cloning extends or adopts the life of her donor will be described in this book as the *resurrection fallacy*.[2]

This chapter is devoted to debunking the identity and resurrection fallacies. The first section explains the biological reasons for the individuality of every animal. The second discusses fifteen years of research that prove animals born through cloning can be independent of donors in appearance and behavior. The third establishes that cloned animals do not inherit their donors' age and are not extensions of their donors' lifespans.

A. Influences on Phenotype

To kick off the discussion, consider this thought experiment. Imagine a mammal you have known, of any species: cat, dog, cow, rat, horse, or primate. What you see with your mind's eye is not some Platonic ideal, but rather an individual animal with a unique *phenotype* comprised of observable physical and behavioral characteristics. What biological and environmental forces created that particular animal with that unique phenotype?

1. Genetic Influences

The animal you are imagining has two types of DNA in its cells. First, the *nucleus* of each cell holds nuclear DNA that the animal inherited from its mother and father. As mentioned in Part I, genes are discrete segments of nuclear DNA that ultimately code for precise linear sequences of amino acids bound together as links of a chain.[3] These amino acid chains then fold up into unique three-dimensional shapes to form active proteins that carry out myriad cellular functions necessary for life.[4] These proteins are then assembled into complex three-dimensional structures that build macroscopic tissues, and ultimately bodies.[5]

Second, in the cytoplasm of each cell are *mitochondria*; that is, energy-generating and processing structures the animal inherits through its mother and her egg. These structures have their own DNA, known as *mitochondrial DNA*. Together with nuclear DNA, mitochondrial DNA comprises the *genome* of the animal.[6]

Most people who have studied biology know that the genes found in nuclear DNA can affect the phenotype of an organism. Mitochondrial DNA's influence on an organism's phenotype is less well-known, but the efficiency with which cells produce and use energy can also affect the behavior and body of an animal. Therefore, both types of DNA contribute to the phenotype of the animal in your thought experiment.

2. Epigenetic Influences

Although genes play an undeniable role in shaping phenotype, they are not the only factor. In recent years, scientists have come to realize that what matters is how those genes are expressed.

Thus, as discussed in Chapter 1, epigenetic modifications operate upon the genes and associated proteins of the animal in your thought experiment, influencing the degree of gene expression and how much protein is made (or not made). For example, fur is composed of fur cells because the genes that code for fur are exposed and transcribed; other genes are silenced through epigenetic marks. These marks are maintained as each fur cell divides and creates daughter cells through a process known as *mitosis*. This perpetual silencing is a good thing; otherwise, an animal could end up with heart or bone cells where its fur should be.

Also explained in Chapter 1, there is another category of epigenetic modification known as the imprint. Carried in eggs and sperm, imprints are inherited by embryonic organisms. The imprints control key developmental genes so that they are expressed only from the paternal or maternal copy.[7] Properly functioning imprints protect the mother from the hazards of carrying an oversized fetus, and the fetus from acquiring developmental defects.[8]

These are just the basics, however. From the time an individual animal is conceived, it continually interacts with the environment around it. These interactions can lead to epigenetic changes that alter gene expression.[9] In other words, the animal's epigenetic state is not static; it can change over the animal's lifetime and in response to environment.

Two experiments illustrate this point. To understand the first one, consider that rats vary in the amount of maternal care provided to their young. Some mother rats lick and groom their pups and offer more arched-back nursing than other mothers. The care the pups receive during the first week of life has a lifelong impact on their behavior. Those who receive a lot of licking, grooming, and arched-back nursing (high-care) are less fearful and exhibit a lesser hormonal response to stress than those who do not (low-care).[10]

To test whether this effect is primarily caused by genetic or environmental factors, researchers switched the pups of mother rats at birth. The results are clear: environment trumps genetics. If a pup is born to a low-care mother rat but is switched to a high-care foster mother, the pup develops the mellow personality type of its foster mother rather than the more anxious personality of its biological mother.[11]

Researchers wondered why the effects of one week of maternal care last a lifetime. They hypothesized that maternal care changed the expression of genes that govern an individual rat's response to stress. Through a series of ingenious experiments involving more fostered pups, they showed that different styles of maternal care did indeed have an epigenetic effect. In the brains of high-care pups, the promoter for a gene that regulates hormonal response to stress was in a permissive epigenetic state. In other words, methyl groups existed within specific sites on the promoter sequence in a pattern that rendered the promoter open to transcription and caused its downstream gene to be expressed. By contrast, in the brains of low-care pups, the same promoter was silenced. In other words, a different pattern of methyl groups altered DNA structure in a way that prevented transcription proteins from binding to the promoter. This *methylation* of the promoter suppressed downstream gene expression.[12]

The researchers had one more question. What would happen, they wondered, if they infused the brains of adult rats with a chemical that encourages gene expression?[13] The results were profound: when anxious, low-care rats were infused with this chemical, their methylation pattern, gene expression, and hormonal response to stress changed and became more like those of calm, high-care rats.[14]

This experiment shows precisely how one gene can respond to the environment through the mediating influence of epigenetic marks. Moreover, as the researchers speculated, such epigenetic regulation of behavioral responses may be the result of natural selection. Perhaps maternal care primes rat pups to respond to the environmental conditions they can expect to face upon maturity.[15]

A second experiment offers even more dramatic results. As background, consider this: a particular type of mouse carries the viable yellow *agouti gene*, which produces different phenotypes depending on epigenetic controls. If the gene is switched on in all cells, you get a mouse that has yellow fur, obesity, diabetes, and a predisposition to tumors. If the gene is switched off, you get a lean mouse with agouti fur (black at the tip, yellow in the middle of the shaft, and brown at the base). If the gene is switched on in some cells and off in others, the mouse is an epigenetic mosaic and will display a mix of the two phenotypes.[16]

Scientists discovered that they can manipulate expression of this gene. Certain nutrients, such as folate or vitamin B12, are known *methyl donors* – that is, they contribute to methylation and suppression of genes. If you mate a dam to a sire carrying the dominant agouti gene and feed her mouse chow laced with these nutrients, you switch off the gene for yellow fur and get more baby mice that have agouti fur (first-generation offspring). In this way, the gestational environment has a biological impact on the phenotype of the organism.[17]

Moreover, when a first-generation mouse with agouti fur grows up and reproduces, even if she receives no nutrient supplements, her own babies will also have agouti fur (second-generation offspring). Apparently, the nutrients the first-generation mouse receives as a fetus alter the epigenetic profile of her eggs. In this manner, epigenetic states can be passed from one generation to the next through sexual reproduction.[18]

Taken together, these two experiments with rodents drive home the importance of epigenetics. The environment an animal experiences in the womb or even after birth can alter its biology at a molecular level, leading to changes in its appearance or behavior, and possibly impacting the appearance or behavior of future generations.

3. Environmental Influences

Environment can also affect phenotype in nonbiological ways. Imagine, for example, that the animal in our thought experiment is a dog. If it is a poodle, its owner may have shaved some of its fur in preparation to show her pet at a dog show. Perhaps she also trained the poodle to follow voice commands at the show. The appearance and behavior of this animal will differ from those of other poodles that are not show dogs.

Or imagine a cat that will eat only a certain brand of cat food, or sit only in a particular spot on the couch. These habits may have been engrained through long-standing routines of the animal or its owner. These habits affect behavior, and thus are a part of the cat's observable traits, or phenotype.

This sort of environmental influence is easy for most of us to imagine because we have experienced it in our own lives with pets or other animals. However, at first glance, it might seem as if such influences are more ephemeral than genetic or epigenetic ones. For example, after the dog show is over, if the poodle is not shaved again, its fur will grow back. Habits and other behavior can also be altered through changes in circumstances. If the cat is given to a new owner who can afford to purchase only a lesser brand of cat food, the feline will eventually get hungry enough to eat the new offering.

Still, even such seemingly random factors may themselves have long-term biological consequences. For example, what if the food that the cat once ate had a high fat content? If the cat became obese, the expression of its genes could be altered, leading to a change in metabolism that the new food might not entirely reverse. The possibilities for interactions between an animal and its environment are endless, and science is only beginning to explore the epigenetic consequences of those interactions.

To summarize, the animal you see in your thought experiment is the sum of more than its parts. Its phenotype is the product not only of genes, but also of environmental factors that had epigenetic effects upon those genes. Environment (such as training or habits) may also have influenced patterns of behavior – which, in turn, may produce further epigenetic effects. To replicate all of the multifarious events that ultimately yielded the living, breathing creature standing in front of you would be impossible.

B. The Individuality of Animals Born through Cloning

Let us take these biological basics and apply them to animals born through cloning. This section considers genetic, epigenetic, and environmental influences that affect the phenotypes of such animals.

1. Genetic Influences

We know that genes – and any traits associated with them – can be transmitted from generation to generation via sexual reproduction. Paternal and maternal genes encapsulated in sperm and egg are united to form a new set of chromosomes that become the offspring's nuclear DNA. The mitochondrial DNA that is present in the egg becomes the mitochondrial DNA of the new organism.

Genetic transmission occurs in cloning also, but in a different manner. The nuclear DNA contained in the donor cell used for the cloning becomes the nuclear DNA of the new organism. This direct transmission of nuclear DNA often leads observers to the false conclusion that the donor and cloned animal have the same genome. Yet this is not entirely true, for the egg used to conceive the donor will not be the same as the egg used to conceive the cloned animal. Unless the eggs derive from the same female in both cases, the mitochondrial DNA of the donor and cloned animal will differ.[19] Because mitochondria process energy, body parts that require a lot of energy such as the eye, heart, muscle, or brain could function differently in a donor and cloned animal.[20]

Variations in phenotype are also possible if the nuclear DNA used for cloning has mutated. Some interesting examples come from experiments with mice and cats. In the first case, researchers cloned a mouse with a tail. Two cloned mice were born. One had a normal tail but the other had a short, stubby tail. The short-tailed mouse mated and produced a litter of mice with tail lengths varying from normal to stubby. When normal-tailed mice from this first generation mated, they produced a second generation that also had a range of tail lengths.[21] Since sexual reproduction did not eliminate the tailless phenotype, it was genetic, rather than epigenetic in origin. The researchers could not tell whether the donor cell used to clone the first stubby-tailed mouse had mutated prior to or during the cloning.[22]

In a second case, scientists harvested immature Sertoli cells from newborn male mice and used them as donor cells in cloning. Twenty-seven cloned mice were born and developed into adults. All of the mice should have been male – because the donor cells came from males – but surprisingly, one mouse had female genitalia. The researchers mated the strange mouse; it gave birth to several litters of mice, proving that it was fertile and female.[23] Chromosomal analysis revealed that the mouse had a single X chromosome. The researchers hypothesized that the mouse had been cloned from a donor cell that had lost its Y chromosome, probably while in the body of the donor.[24]

In a third case, researchers started with a white Turkish Angora cat with one gold and one blue eye. They cloned the cat and produced a kitten with white fur and blue eyes. Next, the researchers cloned the blue-eyed kitten and generated four more kittens. Three of these second-generation kittens had blue eyes, but one had one gold eye and one blue eye, like the original donor cat.[25] The researchers did not know why eye color varied in the first and second generations of cloned cats. They speculated that donor cells might have mutated when being cultured prior to cloning. They also raised the possibility that the donor cells had mutated in the body of the donor prior to the cloning, although they considered that less likely.[26]

Fortunately, such dramatic genetic mutations in live cloned animals appear to be unusual. There are few such accounts in the cloning literature.

ANIMALS BORN THROUGH CLONING ARE INDIVIDUALS   35

2. Epigenetic Influences

To continue the discussion, let us try a second thought experiment. Imagine a calico cat standing before you. Now, alongside the cat place a kitten cloned from the adult cat. Assume the donor cell used in the cloning had no mutations. You might expect the cat and kitten to at least look alike, and perhaps act alike, too. You might visualize the kitten as a miniature version of the donor, right down to the pattern of her fur.

As it turns out, however, the first kitten to be cloned did not resemble her donor.[27] Ironically named Cc (for carbon copy), the kitten had a coat of gray stripes over white fur. Her nuclear donor was a calico with orange and gray patches over white fur.[28]

If the kitten had the same nuclear DNA as the donor, how could it look so different? It all comes back to epigenetics. As explained in Chapter 1, a female mammal has two X chromosomes, but only one is switched on in each cell. The pattern of activation and inactivation is random, and is established early in the life of the organism. The genes for fur color in cats reside on the X chromosome. Thus, when X chromosome inactivation occurs anew in a cloned embryo, the result is a kitten that does not resemble the donor.[29] Ten years after her birth, Cc is healthy and happy and living the life of a beloved pet in Texas. She mated the usual way and produced three healthy kittens.[30]

Other cloned animals have been born with coat patterns that vary from each other. In one experiment, scientists cloned ten calves from a black-and-white Friesian donor cow. The patterns of black and white varied from donor to calf, and calf to calf.[31] Observing that such variation was also observed in genetically identical calf twins, the scientists stated that environmental influences during gestation caused variation in the number and location of melanocytes that governed pigment production in the skin.[32]

Not only coloring, but size can change. Multiple cattle cloned from the same donor have been found to vary considerably in weight.[33] In one litter of cloned pigs created at Texas A&M University, Big Bertha was

40 percent larger than Tiny Tina, the runt.[34] Even Ian Wilmut found that when he cloned a set of four rams, the animals varied in size.[35]

What might account for such results? The uterine environment, including the placenta, regulates the transmission of nutrients and waste to and from the fetus. As we have seen earlier in this chapter, early influences on a fetus can have lifelong epigenetic effects. When it comes to gene expression, an animal born through cloning will differ from its donor because the two are gestated in different wombs.[36] Multiple animals cloned from the same donor but gestated in different wombs will differ from each other for the same reason.[37] And even two cloned animals gestated at the same time in the same uterus could experience different microenvironments and develop different phenotypes if their placentae and vascular systems differed in efficiency.[38]

3. Environmental Influences

Going back to our imaginary cloned kitten, let us consider her personality and behavior. To the extent such traits are genetic, we might expect the kitten to have a personality like that of the donor. However, this was not true of the kitten Cc; she was lively and her donor was reserved.[39]

We don't know for sure how or why Cc and her donor diverged. Epigenetic variation might have played a role. However, it is also important to recognize that environment can have a psychological impact. Perhaps the handling and events this very special kitten experienced after she was born differed from the handling and events in the life story of her donor, leading to differences in character.

Cc is not unusual in this regard. Other researchers have noted differences in the behavior of animals cloned in a set from the same genetic line. Big Bertha the cloned pig was more aggressive than her sister, Tiny Tina.[40] Three of the rams Ian Wilmut cloned were much more aggressive than the fourth.[41]

Perhaps the most striking proof that cloned animals are not copies comes from Texas. Chance was an enormous, 1,000-pound Brahman

ANIMALS BORN THROUGH CLONING ARE INDIVIDUALS

bull with meter-wide horns. Despite his fearsome appearance, Chance was tame. His owners, Sandra and Ralph Fisher, had him pose for photographs with children at rodeos and county fairs, but Chance was old – twenty-one years of age. Shortly before he died, the Fishers accepted an offer from scientists at Texas A & M University to clone their pet.

At first they were delighted with their new bull, dubbed Second Chance. He looked the same as Chance, ate in the same manner, and even favored the same spot in the front yard. However, the illusion was dispelled when Second Chance threw Mr. Fisher on one occasion and gored him on another. He was a dangerous animal, not the placid pet they had owned before. Although Mr. Fisher hoped the bull might mellow with age, Second Chance never had that opportunity. He died at age eight of a stomach disease unrelated to cloning.[42]

C. Animals Born Through Cloning and Resurrection

The story of Second Chance raises another interesting issue related to identity and thus best discussed in this chapter. Just as some people expect animals born through cloning to be copies, others imagine them to be a resurrection of their DNA donors. For example, some bereaved pet owners have commissioned the cloning of their departed cats and dogs.[43] When Second Chance was new, his owner insisted that her new bull was not a son or twin brother of Chance, but rather Chance himself.[44]

The individuality of animals born through cloning should go a long way to dispel such poignant beliefs. If every animal is an individual due to genetic, epigenetic, and environmental factors, then it is impossible to use cloning to resurrect the dead. It may be that pet owners are beginning to realize this; one of the first companies to offer pet cloning services went out of business for lack of orders.[45]

There is more to the resurrection fallacy than failure to recognize the individuality of animals born through cloning. The idea that cloned animals are much older than they appear – perhaps even as old as their

DNA donors – resonates with the resurrection fallacy. The rest of this chapter refutes that idea.

1. Animals Born Through Cloning Are Babies

Science fiction stories often portray cloned humans as full-grown adults ready to continue the life of an "original."[46] Such portrayals are fantasy rather than fact. As Chapter 1 explained, cloned animals begin as embryos and are transferred to the uterus of a gestational mother. There they develop through the embryonic and fetal stages until they are born into the world as infants of their species. These infants then develop to adulthood according to the usual timetable for their species.[47]

2. Telomeres

Science fiction aside, where did the public get this peculiar idea that cloned animals are born prematurely old? As first mentioned in Part I, the story of Dolly the sheep holds a partial answer to the question.

Telomeres are repetitive DNA sequences that occur at the ends of chromosomes.[48] They protect chromosome ends against degradation and facilitate *mitosis* (a process whereby cells divide into fresh daughter cells). When cells are cultured in the laboratory, telomeres shorten with every division, until they can no longer support the process and the cells stop dividing.[49] However, the relationship between telomeres and aging in living organisms is less clear. Older animals have shorter telomeres,[50] but it is not known whether such telomeres trigger cell-division arrest or cause physiological aging.[51]

In 1999, Dr. Wilmut and his research team measured Dolly's telomeres and reported them to be shorter than the norm for a Finn Dorset sheep of her age. Noting that her telomere length was consistent with the age of her DNA donor, the team inferred that cloning failed to reset telomere length. Although the team emphasized that Dolly was healthy and typical of a sheep of her breed,[52] the media interpreted the data

ANIMALS BORN THROUGH CLONING ARE INDIVIDUALS 39

as reflecting premature aging.[53] Eventually Dolly contracted a common respiratory virus, leading her keepers to euthanize her.[54] There was never any evidence that her telomeres contributed to her demise.

Research on telomeres makes sense on a scientific level. If cloning is ever to be used to generate replacement tissues or organs, society must be confident that those tissues or organs are healthy and not subject to premature degeneration.[55] However, the media and public fascination with the true age of animals born through cloning goes beyond safety. The notion that telomere length might be transmitted – and cellular or physiological age along with it – fits all too neatly with a false perception that cloned animals are continuing the lives of others, rather than functioning as unique individuals in their own right.

It is now sixteen years since Dolly was born. What do we know about telomeres today? The majority of research indicates that telomeres of animals born through cloning can be similar in length or even longer than those of age-matched control animals.[56] Scientists believe these results are due to *telomerase*: an enzyme active in early embryos that extends telomeres.[57]

This extension of telomere length can occur even when donor cells have been cultured for an extended period in the lab and are nearing the end of their lifespan. In one experiment, researchers cloned cattle from aged cells and produced blastocysts and pregnancies at rates similar to those achieved when cloning from younger cells.[58] Six calves were born; all were alive and healthy seven to twelve months later, when the researchers reported their results. The telomeres of these calves were longer than those of age-matched control animals.[59]

Scientists have also succeeded in *serial cloning* (i.e., the cloning of animals from animals that were themselves cloned). They have cloned cattle for two generations,[60] cats for two generations,[61] and swine for three generations.[62] However, the biggest successes with serial cloning have come with mice.

As early as 2000, scientists reported that they had cloned mice for six generations.[63] The mice had telomeres of normal or extended length.

Moreover, when it came to age-related behaviors such as learning ability, strength, agility, activity levels, and coordination the cloned mice were comparable to age-matched controls.[64] More recently, another group of scientists used chemical treatments to boost reprogramming efficiency and ended up producing fifteen generations of cloned mice.[65] If each generation assumed the cellular age of its predecessor, such serial cloning would be impossible.

To be sure, these results are not universal. Since Dolly was cloned, a few other experiments have found that in some (but not all) cloned animals, telomere lengths were shorter than in age-matched control animals.[66] Although the reasons for shortened telomeres are unclear, one speculation is that certain donor cell types may be less responsive to telomerase than others.[67]

Nevertheless, cloned animals with shortened telomeres can still be healthy and function within normal parameters for their chronological age. In one striking study, cattle cloned from oviduct epithelial cells had shorter telomeres than aged cows. If telomere length truly was a marker for old age, these animals should have been unable to function consistently with their chronological age. Yet the cattle that survived the perinatal period were healthy, and their growth, reproduction, and milk production were all normal.[68] Such outcomes indicate that telomere length does not necessarily drive physiological aging.[69]

More importantly for purposes of this analysis, even if a few cloned animals have short telomeres, many more have normal or elongated telomeres. This undercuts any false notion that cloned animals continue the lives of their DNA donors at the cellular or physiological level.

3. Longevity

Normal telomeres imply that animals born through cloning can expect long lives; but is there direct evidence of their longevity? Unfortunately, there is little data available for cloned cattle and swine. Such species can have long lifespans, and cloning is a new technology. Moreover, producers do not keep livestock once they are no longer useful, so most cloned females are slaughtered when their fertility declines and well in advance of their natural death.[70]

Mice, however, have naturally short lifespans and thus make good study subjects. Cloned mice can survive as long as other members of their species. Cumulina, the first mouse cloned from an adult (cumulus) cell, had a two-year life expectancy but survived for two years and seven months. Other strains of mice cloned from cumulus cells have also enjoyed normal lifespans.[71]

Sometimes a study involving mice cloned from immature Sertoli cells of the B6D2F1 strain is cited as evidence that cloned animals age prematurely. The mice suffered from liver failure and severe pneumonia that may have been related to poor immune systems, and died younger than control mice did. However, the researchers who created the mice noted that their untimely demise could have been due to dysfunctional organs rather than premature aging as such.[72]

Thus, although data on longevity is sparse, what we have so far suggests that animals born through cloning can live as long as conventional animals. This strengthens the inference from telomere studies that such animals do not assume the lives of their DNA donors.

D. Summary

Cloning has come a long way since 1996, when Dolly was born. Through fifteen years of experimentation, we have obtained hard proof that animals born through cloning are far from the carbon copies many expected. Genes, epigenetic factors, and environmental influences work together to shape the unique bodies and behavior of all animals, including those that are cloned.

The individuality of cloned animals also shows that the technology is not a means of resurrection. The body of a cloned animal is not an empty vessel into which the personality or soul of the donor can be poured. Moreover, cloned animals can have normal telomeres and lifespans, dispelling any false notion that they continue the lives of their DNA donors.

3 Humans Born Through Cloning Will Be Unique Individuals and Have Their Own Lifespans

N 1997, PUBLIC INTEREST IN HUMAN GENETICS WAS surging. The Human Genome Project had been initiated with the goal of sequencing the more than 3 billion base pairs in the human genome.[1] Scientists and the public alike hoped that the study of our genes would usher in a new era in human biology, including individualized medical treatments and a better understanding of our species.

When Ian Wilmut and Keith Campbell announced that they had cloned a sheep from the DNA of an adult animal, the public was shocked. The potential application of the new technology to our own species raised many disquieting questions. Many feared scientists were poised to usher in an era of duplicates, triplicates, and more. The media presented humans born through cloning as copies of DNA donors and emphasized the challenge that cloning supposedly posed to our unique identities.[2] Such concerns call to mind the identity fallacy discussed in Chapter 2.

On a more metaphysical level, people pondered the question of what cloning portended for a mortal species. Could cloning produce warm bodies ad infinitum to house the soul? Could it resurrect dead loved ones – or, more menacingly, dictators and psychopaths?[3] These questions reflect the resurrection fallacy discussed in Chapter 2.

Critics also raised concerns about the unnaturalness of conceiving a child through an asexual process.[4] Others perceived a vital distinction between the begetting of human life via sexual intercourse and the manufacture of babies to predetermined genetic specifications via cloning.[5] Such arguments are reminiscent of the artifact fallacy discussed in Chapter 1.

Many years have passed since these concerns were first raised. Genetics research continues, but the hot new science is epigenetics. The first genome-wide maps of DNA methylation in human embryonic stem cells and fetal fibroblasts were published in 2009,[6] and the International Human Epigenome Consortium plans to map 1,000 reference epigenomes within the coming decade.[7] Awareness of the importance of epigenetics is seeping into the public consciousness thanks to popularizing books and articles written for lay persons.[8] We also have hundreds of cloning experiments to draw upon in evaluating the characteristics of animals born through cloning.

Thus, this is a good time to reexamine arguments against cloning. Building on prior chapters, this chapter will evaluate humans born through cloning in light of everything scientists have learned from the time Dolly was born.

A. The Science of Human Cloning

Chapters 1 and 2 presented the results of experiments in animal cloning. Have we learned anything from human cloning experiments? Despite occasional false reports, no cloned humans have been born yet.[9] We do not have direct evidence of the phenotypes, personalities, or health that humans born through cloning will have. However, scientists around the world have cloned human embryos for research. Their hope is that *human research cloning* will make it possible to create stem cells for research and medical treatment.

For example, suppose John Doe has a disease. Scientists would take a skin cell from him and use it to clone an embryo that carried his nuclear DNA. Next, they would create a stem cell line from that embryo. The scientists could test a new medicine for John's disease on the DNA-matched cells in the Petri dish. Or if John needs new tissues, the scientists might direct the stem cells into becoming DNA-matched tissues that are compatible with his immune system, lowering the chances of rejection.[10]

Although such stem cells are not yet available, two experiments give the reader a sense of how far research cloning has already come.[11] First, in 2008, a California company called Stemagen teamed up with an infertility clinic. Some infertile women were already planning to undergo IVF at the clinic using eggs donated by young, healthy women. Since the donors produced more eggs than the patients needed, they shared the excess eggs with the researchers, who enucleated the eggs and added DNA from adult men. Twenty-one reconstructed embryos resulted. Five of those, or 23 percent, developed to the *blastocyst stage* (i.e., became advanced embryos containing hundreds of cells).[12] This success rate is impressive; even in standard IVF cycles, only around 40–60 percent of fertilized eggs develop into blastocysts.[13]

The researchers and other participants in the California experiment sought only to create cloned embryos for research, and had absolutely no intention of producing a cloned baby (which would have been illegal in California).[14] Their work was intended to pave the way for derivation of stem cell lines from cloned human embryos.[15]

Second, in 2011, a New York-based research team took another big step toward the goal of producing stem cells from cloned human embryos.[16] Because payment to egg donors is legal in New York, the researchers were able to recruit young, fertile women to donate high-quality eggs for their research. The researchers were unable to create cloned blastocysts using standard cloning methods; embryonic development stopped at the six to ten-cell stage.[17] The researchers next attempted cloning with a twist: instead of enucleating each host egg, they left its nucleus (bearing twenty-three chromosomes) intact and fused it to an adult male fibroblast (a somatic cell with forty-six chromosomes). Thirteen of sixty-three reconstructed eggs, or 21 percent, developed to the blastocyst stage.[18] However, these blastocysts were abnormal, bearing a load of sixty-nine rather than the usual forty-six chromosomes.

Amazingly, the researchers were still able to derive two pluripotent stem cell lines.[19] For each line, the researchers tested the genome of the donor cell and found that it had been reprogrammed.[20] Based on this experiment, some scientists believe that an unidentified factor related to the egg nucleus is needed to reprogram the DNA in the donor cell and generate blastocysts and stem cells.[21]

The New York stem cells cannot be used as disease models or sources of tissue because they have too many chromosomes.[22] However, progress in research cloning will continue. Scientists are motivated to learn how to create cloned human blastocysts that are genetically and epigenetically normal, for only then will they be able to derive stem cells that are useful in research and therapy. Once scientists learn how to create healthy cloned blastocysts, they will disseminate this information through their publications.

Human reproductive cloning – that is, the cloning of babies – will then become scientifically possible for this reason: embryos that reach the blastocyst stage are only a day or so away from being ready to implant into the lining of a uterus.[23] All that is required is incentive for doctors to create cloned embryos and transfer them to female patients, who will gestate the embryos in their uteri and give birth to the first wave of cloned babies.

What could possibly motivate doctors and patients to engage in such an enterprise? Consider what cloning accomplishes: it passes genes from one generation to the next without sexual reproduction. This feat could make cloning useful to persons who wish genetic offspring but find sexual reproduction difficult or undesirable.

For example, scholars and commentators have anticipated that cloning may serve as an alternative fertility treatment for severely infertile men and women who lack viable sperm or eggs.[24] Gays and lesbians may also benefit from the technology, which could allow them to procreate within their marriages or partnerships without involving the nuclear DNA of third parties.[25] Single women might find cloning an appealing alternative to the genetic roulette of the sperm bank.[26]

Whether one approves these uses or not, it is important to recognize that none of them involve the science-fiction goals ordinarily associated with cloning: narcissistic duplication of self, the quest for immortality, or creation of a superior race. Indeed, as this chapter unfolds, it should become increasingly clear to the reader that it is impossible to achieve such goals through cloning.

B. Humans Born Through Cloning will be Individuals

Therefore, the remainder of this chapter will assume that human reproductive cloning becomes scientifically possible and finds a market niche as an alternative method of assisted reproduction. A hypothetical case will be presented to illustrate the potential effects of genetic, epigenetic, and environmental influences upon the physical, mental, psychological, and behavioral characteristics of a person born through cloning.

Imagine a woman with brown hair and green eyes. She is short (five foot two), has a college degree in mathematics, and works as an accountant. She is healthy and medaled in gymnastics events when she was in college. Unfortunately, she is also infertile because her eggs are dysfunctional. Wishing to conceive genetic offspring, she travels to an offshore clinic to obtain cloning services.

A fertile woman donates her eggs for the procedure. The doctor enucleates the eggs and inserts nuclear DNA harvested from the cells of the infertile patient. Several days later, the reconstructed eggs have matured into cloned blastocysts. The doctor transfers one of these blastocysts to the uterus of the infertile woman and she becomes pregnant. Nine months later, she gives birth to a baby girl who shares her nuclear DNA.

1. Genetic Influences

Because cloning is asexual reproduction, it transmits nuclear DNA from a single parent to her offspring. Thus, the mother's genes will surely influence the phenotype of her baby. Will the baby necessarily have green eyes and short stature, just like her mother? Will she inherit mathematical talent or prowess in gymnastics? The answers to these questions are complicated, for a number of reasons.

a) Mutations

Genes are known to affect eye color and height,[27] but the nuclear DNA in a donor cell may mutate before or during cloning. In Chapter 2, we saw that an odd-eyed cat with one blue and one gold eye produced a cloned kitten with two blue eyes, perhaps as the result of such a mutation.[28] Similarly, suppose that the DNA harvested for our hypothetical cloning procedure has undergone a change in a gene associated with eye color. Our mother with green eyes could have a cloned daughter with brown eyes.

What about mathematical or gymnastic ability? Genes may influence qualities that facilitate achievement in those fields, such as intelligence or flexibility, but such complex qualities could be the product of multiple genes operating together.[29] If a single one of these genes is subtly altered before or during the cloning procedure, the output may change. So, for example, the girl may exhibit skill in mathematics (particularly since her mother is available to share her enthusiasm and knowledge, as discussed below) but may never score quite as high on math aptitude tests as her mother.

b) Copy Number Variations

A person may have more or fewer copies of a particular block of DNA than a standard reference genome has.[30] Such *copy number variations* can affect one or more genes and alter the amount of protein generated. Copy number variations can also alter the expression of nearby genes.[31] Certain copy number variations are associated with disease or disorders, such as autism or schizophrenia,[32] but the full extent of their biological impacts is as yet unclear.[33]

Some biologists employ *monozygotic twins* to study copy number variations. Produced when a fertilized egg splits in two, monozygotic twins share the same nuclear and mitochondrial DNA.[34] In theory, their genomes are identical, which is one reason people call them identical twins. However, studies show that monozygotic twins can have copy number variations and thus different genomes.[35] How is this possible? Although copy number variations can be inherited from parents, they can also occur on their own during mitosis (the process whereby cells divide and create daughter cells).[36] If copy number variations arise in the developing body of one twin and not another, that could lead to differences in protein production and phenotype.

Moreover, copy number variations do more than create differences between individuals. Scientists also believe that copy number variations arising from mitosis can cause nuclear DNA to differ from one tissue to another within a single individual.[37]

Copy number variations have two implications for our hypothetical. First, by selecting a cell to be used in cloning, a doctor may have more of an impact on the phenotype of the daughter than he realizes. If the infertile patient has nuclear DNA that varies from one tissue to another, his choice of donor cell may determine whether the daughter exhibits a particular trait that the mother has, for good or bad. Advances in microarray technology may soon enable doctors to screen donor cells for copy number variations linked to diseases or otherwise known to be harmful.[38] However, the impact of many copy number variations, particularly those that have more subtle effects, could remain unknown for some time.

Second, even if the doctor screens out donor cells with major copy number variations, there is no guarantee that the nuclear DNA taken from the mother will stay the same in the body of the daughter. Indeed, if twin studies are any indication, the opposite is true: the process of cell division will produce copy number variations that may generate phenotypic variation between mother and daughter.

c) Mitochondrial DNA

Chapter 2 explained that mammalian cells include mitochondria – that is, structures that generate and process energy. Therefore, mammals, including human beings, have two kinds of DNA in their bodies: nuclear and mitochondrial.[39]

Our hypothetical mother inherited her mitochondrial DNA from the egg of her own mother. Had she conceived sexually, her fertilized egg would have passed the same mitochondrial DNA to her child. In other words, she and the child would have had the same mitochondrial DNA.

Instead, because she was infertile, the mother reproduced asexually, using eggs that another woman donated. Therefore, her daughter will carry the mitochondrial DNA of the egg donor.[40] As a result, the bodies of this mother and daughter may generate and process energy differently, leading to further phenotypic variations, particularly in tissues and organs that require a lot of energy to function.[41] For example, although the mother had muscles that were powerful enough to win her medals in gymnastics events at the collegiate level, the daughter may not.

2. Epigenetic Influences

Every mammal (including a human) is more than the sum of its genes. As discussed in Chapter 2, epigenetic factors affect the expression of genes and thus the phenotype of an organism. If a gene is silenced, traits associated with it may be lost (or added, if the gene ordinarily functions to repress traits).

Epigenetic influences upon phenotype begin to accumulate as soon as an embryo is cloned. This section will consider influences that operate at embryonic, fetal, and postnatal stages.

a) X Chromosome Inactivation

In Chapter 2, we met a female kitten whose striped fur differed from that of her calico donor. This deviation resulted from a process known as X chromosome inactivation.[42]

To recap the basic science, a female embryo carries two X chromosomes. To avoid a deleterious double-dose of genes, the early embryo must undergo an epigenetic process that randomly silences one of the X chromosomes in each cell.[43] Experiments have shown that cloned embryos undergo X chromosome inactivation,[44] and the plethora of female cloned animals now in existence provides further evidence that the process must often succeed. However, the donor of nuclear DNA and her cloned offspring always experience this process at different times and independent of each other, and thus necessarily exhibit different patterns of active and inactive X chromosomes.[45]

Since our hypothetical mother is female, we would expect her daughter to have undergone the process of X chromosome inactivation as an embryo, and independently of her mother. Therefore, the mother and daughter will each exhibit a different mix of active and inactive X chromosomes in the cells of their bodies.

The full impact of such differences is unclear at present. However, inferences can be drawn from monozygotic twins. As noted above, monozygotic twins share the same nuclear DNA, including the same X chromosomes. If the fertilized egg splits before X chromosome inactivation has begun, however, each twin will undergo the process independent of the other and have a cellular mix of active and inactive X chromosomes that differs from that of her sister. The results can be dramatic: one twin may have a disease or condition linked to expression of the genes on one of her two X chromosomes. The other twin may have silenced most copies of that malfunctioning X chromosome early in development and be perfectly fine.[46] As scientists learn more about genes on the X chromosome, other differences may emerge.

b) Gestational Factors

Chapter 2 explained how simple changes in the diet of pregnant mice can silence a key gene, thereby altering the color and body type of offspring. This research has implications for humans: the food we eat today could impact physical or other characteristics of our children.[47]

Similarly, studies in humans have shown that when pregnant mothers experience famine, the developmental fate of their unborn children can be altered. For example, in one study of the Dutch Hunger Winter of 1944–45, fifty-year-old women who had been exposed to the famine as fetuses in the early stages of gestation had higher body weight, body mass index, and waist circumference than control subjects.[48] In another, middle-aged women who had been exposed to the Great Chinese Famine of 1959–61 as fetuses in gestation had lower body height but greater body weight and body mass index than members of the control group.[49] The nutrition a developing fetus receives (or does not receive) can have a strong impact on human phenotype.

Twin research provides further proof that uterine environment affects phenotype. Despite their shared DNA, monozygotic twins can differ in size. Each twin also has his or her own individual fingerprints and brain-fold patterns. These variations occur because, even though twins share a womb, their pre-birth experiences are never precisely the same. Subtle variations in the flow of nutrients, wastes, and even viruses make an impact.[50]

Consider the hypothetical in light of these facts. When the infertile woman was a fetus, her mother ate certain foods, breathed air that included (or did not include) contaminants, and was exposed to a variety of environmental influences. Any or all of these factors might have affected the woman's phenotype (and could even be the reason she is infertile if her eggs were affected).

Decades later, when the infertile woman became pregnant through cloning, she ate different foods, breathed different air, and provided a different, unique uterine environment to her daughter. Such variations in the developmental environment could lead to changes in her daughter's epigenetic programming and consequent phenotypic differences.[51]

Based on twin research, the daughter would have different fingerprints and brain-fold patterns than her infertile mother. Based on the famine research, she could be fated to grow shorter or taller, slimmer or fatter than her mother depending on uterine factors that could induce differential expression of genes related to metabolism, height, and weight. This supposition is reinforced by research showing that cattle cloned from the same genome can vary widely in size.[52]

c) Postnatal Factors
Embryonic and uterine events are not the only factors that would create phenotypic variations between the hypothetical mother and daughter. Consider a recent study. A group of scientists set out to explain why monozygotic twins, who share a genotype, exhibit phenotypic differences. The scientists assembled twin pairs of varying ages and experiences and studied various chemical modifications of their genomes.[53] The scientists found that twins who were young (age three), spent their lives together, or had similar health and medical histories had similar epigenetic marks; however, twins who were older (age fifty), had spent less of their lifetime together, or had different health and medical histories exhibited epigenetic marks that diverged significantly.[54] Such epigenetic deviation resulted in different gene expression profiles.[55] The scientists suggested that external factors, such as diet or physical activity, could have caused some of these epigenetic variations. However, they also noted that small errors in the transmission of epigenetic information might accumulate over time.[56]

These experimental results allow us to draw inferences about the biological similarities – or differences – between our hypothetical mother and the daughter she conceived through cloning. Decades earlier, the mother was subjected to environmental factors that forged her unique epigenetic profile. But her daughter would be born into a different era, place, and family, and thus would be subject to different environmental factors. Like monozygotic twins who have spent little time together, the mother and daughter could be expected to show divergent patterns of epigenetic modification and gene expression. As the data concerning older twins suggests, this divergence would only increase over time, as the daughter grew up, left home, and established her own independent lifestyle.

3. Environmental Influences

Chapter 2 presented Cc, the cloned kitten, whose lively personality differed from that of her reserved DNA donor; Ian Wilmut's four cloned rams, who shared the same nuclear DNA but varied in aggression; and Second Chance, the cloned bull who was more aggressive and dangerous than his docile and pet-like predecessor, Chance.

Two inferences can be drawn from these results: cloned animals can have distinct personalities of their own; and DNA is not the only factor that determines personality in animals. However, whether such personality differences in cloned animals stem from epigenetic or environmental factors is unclear.

When it comes to human beings, we have better evidence that environment can have a strong influence upon who we are. Some of this evidence is commonsensical: we all know that other people, events, and experiences have helped shape our intellects, personalities, values, and beliefs. Plentiful research supports this commonsense point.

In general, genetic differences account for about 60 percent of the variation in intelligence quotients (IQs) observed among adults. Shared environments (such as family habits or experiences) have some impact on IQ, but their influence diminishes as people get older. Non-shared events and experiences are more important, accounting for around 30 percent of IQ differences in adults.[57]

Although we do not have data comparing the IQs of humans born through cloning and their donors, we do have information regarding monozygotic twins. The IQs of the individuals within a monozygotic twin pair tend to be very similar: in a measure of relatedness where 1.0 means that two different sets of IQ scores correspond exactly, a typical correlation for the IQ scores of monozygotic twins is .86.[58] Even when monozygotic twins are raised apart, their IQs are still more alike than the IQs of *dizygotic twins* (that is, fraternal twins conceived from two different eggs).[59] Such results underscore the importance of genetics to intelligence. Yet even monozygotic twins do not have identical IQs, indicating that shared and non-shared environments also contribute to their intelligence.

Turning to personality, researchers believe that around 20–50 percent of individual differences in personality are genetically determined.[60] Flip that around, and one finds that 50–80 percent of personality differences are not so determined. What else plays a role? Research comparing monozygotic twins raised together with monozygotic twins raised apart shows that shared environments have only a slight impact. Non-shared events and experiences account for the remainder of individual personality differences.[61]

Because a human born through cloning will experience a different family, place, era, and generation than her DNA donor, she will be exposed to many events and conditions that vary from those her donor experienced as a child. These non-shared environmental influences should cause her developing intellect and personality to diverge from that of her donor, despite their common genes.[62]

Applying these insights to the hypothetical, the daughter could be exposed to her mother's enthusiasm for mathematics and accounting. This environment could encourage her to study math and follow a similar career path. However, the daughter might have a different personality than her mother – one that was less suited to the patient and meticulous number work that accounting requires. Also, the society she lived in and the jobs that were in demand could affect her choices. For example, in a future where alternative energy supplies are needed and valued, the daughter might be encouraged to redirect any analytical abilities she has to solar power engineering.

Last but not least, the daughter might also deliberately reject her mother's choice of education and career, just for the sake of rebellion. This could occur as a part of normal adolescence, but it also seems plausible that a person living in a prejudiced society that regarded her as a copy would be motivated to refute such stereotypes and forge her own path.[63]

To summarize this section, genes do matter. A human born through cloning is likely to have some traits in common with her donor and others cloned from the same source. However, it is important to remember that she will not have the exact same DNA as her donor (or any others cloned from the donor), due to genetic mutations, copy-number variations, and differences in mitochondrial DNA. Moreover, epigenetic and environmental influences also contribute to the unique characteristics of any human being. Based on research with monozygotic twins and cloned animals, we have reason to expect that epigenetic and environmental influences will cause a human born through cloning to develop individualized characteristics that distinguish her from the donor and others who may have been cloned from the same DNA.

C. Humans Born through Cloning Will Not Be Resurrections of the Dead

Perhaps the most poignant application of human reproductive cloning that has yet been envisioned is the re-creation of a lost loved one, particularly a child lost to an untimely death.[64]

For example, Mark Hunt, whose infant son died after heart surgery, paid hundreds of thousands of dollars to create a lab for a doctor who promised to clone his lost child. The money was spent in vain; the doctor delivered press interviews but no child. Hunt withdrew his financial support and shut the lab at the request of the U.S. Food and Drug Administration (FDA), which claimed authority over human cloning experiments.

Many would say Hunt should have known better; he had a law degree and had served in his state legislature. Yet, his education and sophistication were not enough to protect him against the age-old dream of resurrection. Unable to accept the death of his son, he wrote an anonymous letter that the doctor in question shared in her testimony before the U.S. Congress. In that letter, Hunt drew an analogy to Christ raising Lazarus from the dead and spoke of cloning as a means to overcome death.[65]

Unfortunately for all of us who have lost loved ones to the Grim Reaper, attempts to re-create them through cloning are doomed to fail.

To be sure, a person cloned from the nuclear DNA of a lost loved one may share some of his traits. However, as the previous section explained, a human born through cloning will be a unique individual with his own body, mind, and personality.

Moreover, a human born through cloning will not pick up life at the point where a loved one left off. As discussed in Chapter 2, experiments indicate that cloned animals are born as babies of their kind and follow a normal developmental trajectory. Extrapolating from this data, we can expect that cloning will result in an infant and not a full-blown adult, even if an adult donates the DNA for the cloning procedure. This infant should exhibit a pattern of development that is consistent with the same timeline and milestones that apply to all human beings.

Also in Chapter 2, we learned that the individual lives of cloned animals are reflected in their telomeres, which generally fall within the normal range as established by controls of the same chronological age. Even animals with shortened telomeres function in a manner consistent with their chronological ages, rather than those of their donors. Although data on longevity is limited, cloned mice have been shown to have normal lifespans. Such results refute the idea that a human born through cloning could continue the life of his or her donor at the cellular or physiological level. In short, there is no reason to expect that human cloning can ever turn the resurrection fallacy into resurrection fact.

D. Humans Born through Cloning Will Be Ordinary Members of Our Species

The last topics to address are the health of humans born through cloning and their status as members of the human species. There are no credible reports of cloned humans, or even cloned pregnancies, leaving this book without any direct physical evidence to discuss. Indeed, it may take many years of experiments before scientists learn to create healthy cloned blastocysts to serve as the basis for stem cell lines – and years beyond that before competent fertility specialists are confident enough in the normalcy of those blastocysts to implant them as the seeds of a new generation. In particular, it may be necessary to develop screening processes to ensure that the DNA selected for cloning has not mutated in harmful ways.

Until then, the best evidence of what we can expect comes from experiments in animal cloning. Contrary to initial expectations and predictions, not all cloned animals are sick, deformed, or dying. As discussed in Chapter 1, cloning technology has already improved to the point where most cloned animals that are born and survive the initial period of adjustment to life outside the womb are healthy. They develop to maturity within the usual time frame, mate, and produce healthy offspring. They exhibit body chemistries and behaviors that fall within the normal ranges for their species. In addition, food animals generate meat and milk that are compositionally indistinguishable from that of naturally bred animals. Even if cloned animals harbor some deviations in gene expression, they are far from the abnormal freaks that many expected or claimed them to be.

Every healthy and functional cloned animal that has been born in the last fifteen years challenges the supposed unnaturalness of asexual reproduction. It appears that sexual reproduction need not be a prerequisite for membership in a species, since asexual reproduction can produce animals that are indistinguishable from others of their kind. Nor is there any evidence that cloned animals are akin to manufactured things simply because scientists selected their DNA and created them. Their bodies and behaviors fall within the usual range for their species. Significantly, efforts to generate identical copies have failed.

The existence of healthy cloned animals increases the odds that humans born through cloning can also be healthy. Healthy or not, however, they will possess a human genome. When coupled with the copious evidence of ordinary development and function in cloned animals, this fact gives reason to anticipate that humans born through cloning will develop and function much the same as other human beings do. To put it another way, despite their supposedly unnatural conception via asexual reproduction, people born through cloning will be just as human as people born the old-fashioned way. There is no biological reason to classify them as objects manufactured to genetic order, particularly given the evidence indicating that cloned animals are unique individuals.

SUMMARY OF PART I

PART I PRESENTED DATA ACQUIRED FROM FIFTEEN years of scientific experimentation in animal and human cloning. These multitudinous experiments have revealed the following key facts about animals and humans born through cloning.

First, although animal cloning is not yet perfected, its efficiency is improving. Birth rates can reach as high as 20 percent in sheep, cattle, and even mice. Miscarriages and neonatal deaths occur, and cloned sheep and cattle are prone to large offspring syndrome. However, such problems may be due to malfunctioning placentae rather than defects in the animals themselves. Most animals that survive birth and the initial weeks of life are healthy. They grow at a developmentally appropriate pace and exhibit normal bodies and behaviors. The body chemistries and meat composition of cloned livestock are comparable to those of other animals. Contrary to the artifact fallacy, animals born through cloning can be functional members of their species, rather than inherently flawed technological products.

Second, although animals born through cloning share nuclear DNA with their donors, they are not carbon copies. Genetic factors, epigenetic factors, and environmental influences give each animal its own physical, psychological, and behavioral traits. Many don't look like their donors or siblings cloned from the same DNA. Behavior and personality can also vary. Contrary to the identity fallacy, animals born through cloning are unique individuals.

Third, animals born through cloning are born as babies rather than adults. Development follows the usual timeline for the species. Most have telomeres that are the same or longer than age-matched control animals. Many cloned ruminants are slaughtered before they reach the natural end of their lifespans, but data on cloned mice show that normal lifespans are possible. These facts contradict the common belief that cloning is a means of extending life or resurrecting the dead. Contrary to the resurrection fallacy, animals born through cloning do not inherit or take over the lives of their genetic predecessors.

Finally, no humans have been born through cloning yet. However, scientists have cloned human embryos to the blastocyst stage, which is close to the point when embryos implant in the uterus. Thus, human reproductive cloning seems possible in principle. Lessons learned from studies of human genetics and epigenetics, monozygotic (identical) twins, and cloned animals all point to the same conclusions. Humans born through cloning will be ordinary human beings and not manufactured things. Their physical, intellectual, and psychological traits will differ from those of their donors and others who share their nuclear DNA. They will be born as babies and have their own lifespans. In other words, the artifact, identity, and resurrection fallacies will prove just as false for humans as animals.

In sum, the science of animal and human cloning has come a long way since Dolly the sheep was born. We have learned enough about cloned mammals to lay several common falsehoods to rest. Unfortunately, however, these falsehoods persist in the human cloning debate. Part II will examine ways in which psychological perception trumps scientific fact.

PART II THE COGNITIVE PSYCHOLOGY OF CLONING

TURNING NOW TO HUMAN CLONING IN POPULAR culture and politics, this book starts with one telling feature of the debate: although liberals and conservatives strongly disagree on the morality of cloning embryos for stem cell research, these ideological adversaries are absolutely unified in their opposition to any attempt to transfer these embryos to the womb. All agree that reproductive cloning – that is, cloning of human babies – must be stopped.[1]

This raises the interesting question of why opposition to reproductive cloning is so consistent across the political spectrum. Undoubtedly, some cloning opponents are sincerely concerned about safety. Animal cloning experiments have not always gone well. Miscarriages have occurred; some newborn animals have sickened and died. No one (including prospective parents) wants to see children suffer from serious health problems or die young.

However, opposition to human cloning also derives from scientific fallacies. Part I described several of these fallacies and explained how experiments with animals have proven them wrong. In brief, animals born through cloning are not copies of other animals (the identity fallacy); rather, they have their own individual phenotypes. Animals born through cloning are not reanimations of deceased animals (the resurrection fallacy); rather, they have their own lifespans. Animals born through cloning are not man-made objects (the artifact fallacy); rather, they exhibit the same developmental and behavioral patterns as other members of their species.

Although there are no humans born through cloning to study at present, we have excellent biological reasons to expect that similar conclusions will hold true for them. Yet, as this Part explains, the identity, resurrection, and artifact fallacies feature prominently not only in discussions of animal cloning, but also in the debate over human cloning. The debate also includes a fourth fallacy: the concern that humans born through cloning will be doppelgangers capable of stealing our assets, jobs, loved ones, and individuality (the *impostor fallacy*).

The unanimity of public opposition to reproductive cloning suggests these four fallacies have a root source common to all humans. Thus, before we evaluate cloning, we should evaluate the evaluators.

A. Psychological Essentialism

We humans pride ourselves on our capacity for logic and rational thinking. However, life is fast-paced and not every decision can be the well-considered fruit of hours of reflection. To a large extent, we rely upon heuristics: that is, mental rules of thumb that may not be entirely accurate, but which exist so that our brains can provide us with a quick and dirty assessment of problems or situations that we face.[2] One such heuristic that has drawn a great deal of research interest from cognitive psychologists and other academics during the past two decades is *psychological essentialism*.[3]

In the classic formulation of psychological essentialism, the brains of human beings intuit that certain categories possess an intrinsic nature or essence. This essence is deep-rooted and cannot be observed directly. It gives individual members of the category a stable identity and causes the similarities among them.[4]

This heuristic may sound dangerously close to a discredited philosophical theory, also known as *essentialism*, in which an object is conceptualized as having an underlying true character or nature. The problem with this as a philosophical theory is that the supposed essence of the object is not independent of the human act of describing the object. Description makes multiple essences possible and undermines the theory at its core. However, even if philosophical essences do not exist, people might think and act as if they do, and that is what cognitive psychologists have proposed.[5]

To introduce a simple example, suppose a pedestrian walking through a neighborhood observes a large creature with an orange and black-striped coat, claws, and long tail slinking through a stand of trees. Her brain intuits from these observable traits that the creature carries the essence of tiger. Operation of the mental module allows her to infer other characteristics that she cannot see: the creature probably eats meat. It could be dangerous.

Some readers might be tempted to respond that the creature in this hypothetical does carry a true essence in the form of the DNA of its species. However, this intuition is inconsistent with modern biology, which classifies species in terms of the characteristics of entire populations and not individual members. It is not possible to locate the DNA of a species in a single animal. Moreover, because species evolve over time, even a population has no fixed essence.[6]

The fact that there is no such thing as essence of tiger, philosophically or biologically, doesn't matter as long as the heuristic serves its purpose and saves the pedestrian's life. Essentialism works pretty well in some situations, but there are other situations in which it leads us astray. A key thesis of this book is that essentialist intuitions have distorted the way in which we humans perceive animals or humans born through cloning. This Part explores that possibility.

Chapter 4 focuses on how we conceptualize things that are alive. Starting with a discussion of the essentialism of living kinds (types of animals or plants), the chapter moves on to consider the role of essentialism in guiding our intuitions about racial and ethnic groups and occupational kinds. It explains how essentialist intuitions related to living kinds and social kinds contribute to the identity fallacy.

Chapter 5 shifts to the realm of man-made objects, such as tables, chairs, or cars. It discusses essentialist accounts of such artifacts. Next, it explains how intuitions about the nature and uses of artifacts have bled over into the cloning debate, leading to erroneous ideas about the nature and purposes of humans born through cloning. These ideas are reflected in the artifact fallacy and, to some extent, the identity fallacy also.

Chapter 6 presents another shift, this time from kinds to the individual. It explains how the brain uses essentialism to render intuitive judgments about individual identity. Next, it discusses the impostor fallacy and documents its role in popular culture, media accounts, and government reports. The chapter explores the possibility that essentialism lies at the root of the impostor fallacy.

Finally, Chapter 7 builds on the information presented in Chapter 6 about essentialism and the individual. It discusses the resurrection fallacy and explains how essentialist intuitions support that fallacy.

B. Evidence

Throughout Part II, this book will present three kinds of evidence that link the cloning debate and its fallacies to psychological essentialism. First, it will discuss science fiction films and television episodes in which human or alien duplicates are created. Although most of these stories refer to cloning, few accurately portray somatic cell nuclear transfer. Indeed, many present cloning as a machine rather than a biological process. However, these stories are valuable precisely because of their errors. The stories play a dual role in the analysis to come, providing direct evidence of cloning fallacies in popular culture and indirect evidence of the cognitive modules that underlie the fallacies. Producers must make a profit, and they do so by dishing up stories that push our preexisting psychological buttons and give us a thrill.[7]

Second, this book will take a hard look at how the media have reported on human cloning and the prospect that babies could be born through the technology. Misleading news and magazine stories, along with provocative visuals, reveal the omnipresence of cloning fallacies. Like science fiction, such accounts are also useful as indirect evidence of the cognitive modules that support the fallacies.

Third, this book examines government reports that summarize concerns about human cloning. These reports are a valuable repository of academic and expert thought. Too often, however, the concerns stated in these reports turn out to be sophisticated versions of the same fallacies that are expressed more blatantly in popular culture or media accounts. Thus, such reports also provide direct evidence of the fallacies and indirect evidence of the heuristics undergirding them.

At the end of Part II, the reader should not only have a better understanding of opposition to human cloning but also be able to identify the roots of that opposition in essentialism.

4 Identity and Essentialism

THIS CHAPTER BEGINS WITH AN OVERVIEW OF psychological essentialism as it applies to animals, plants, and humans, discussing common applications and possible sources of this cognitive phenomenon. It then turns to the identity fallacy. Here, the fallacy stands for the proposition that a human born through cloning is a physical, mental, and psychological copy of the person who donates the DNA for the cloning procedure. This chapter describes various cultural and political representations of cloning that reflect the identity fallacy. It then explores ways in which essentialism supports the identity fallacy.

A. Psychological Essentialism: Animals, Plants, and Humans

As originally formulated by Douglas Medin and Andrew Ortony in 1989, the concept of psychological essentialism was simple: humans often conceptualize a category of things as if the category possesses some underlying reality or essence. This essence, which is deep-rooted, causes the surface properties and similarities that things within the category have.[1]

What is this mysterious essence? It doesn't matter. Indeed, no essence need exist. As Medin and Ortony pointed out, in order for the heuristic to function, we need only a placeholder – that is, an empty slot that the human mind can fill with beliefs about the essence of a thing.[2]

Medin and Ortony speculated that human senses and cognition had evolved to be particularly sensitive to surface properties that were likely to be causally linked to deeper, core properties. Such adaptation was particularly likely with respect to *natural kinds* – that is, things encountered in nature.[3]

Before moving to examine this concept in more detail, the reader may find a brief comment on terminology helpful. As used in discussions of psychological essentialism, "natural kinds" includes not only *living kinds*, such as animals and plants, but also nonbiological natural substances, such as water or gold.[4] This chapter focuses on research concerning animals, plants, and human beings, and not inert substances; thus, it will refer to living kinds and human kinds. The term natural kinds will be used only when describing sources that apply that term.

In 2003, psychologist Susan Gelman published a book on psychological essentialism that reviewed countless experiments she and other academics had conducted with young children and adults. In her book, she identifies several cognitive tendencies which, when taken together, comprise an intuitive essentialism that manifests itself in early childhood, particularly with respect to the natural world (including living kinds).[5] What follows is a brief summary of the research underlying this conclusion.

First, Gelman cites evidence that not only adults but preschoolers perceive natural-kind categories as having rich inductive potential.[6] In other words, research subjects frequently use membership in such a category as a basis for drawing inferences about hidden or nonobvious traits.[7] Second, experiments show that research subjects sense an underlying core to living kinds. Preschoolers understand that the identity of animals can be stable across transformations, including growth and development.[8] Adults treat living kind categories as having strict boundaries, at the same time recognizing that atypical members can belong to a kind (*e.g.*, penguins can be birds).[9] Adults and preschoolers rely on what they construe as the interior of a creature when determining the identity and function of living kinds.[10]

Third, adults and preschoolers view certain categories, including animal species (and human racial and ethnic groups), as having inborn traits that are passed down from parent to offspring,[11] implying a belief in the transmission of essence. Fourth, consistent with essentialism's core assumption, causation matters to categorization. When asked to judge whether a thing belongs to a category, adults and young children rely more on traits that cause other properties than traits that are effects.[12] Both adults and young children are not only strongly motivated to search for causes of events or trait clusters, but in the case of living kinds, likely to settle upon causes that are inherent and hidden inside the organism.[13]

As Gelman notes, not all of these cognitive tendencies are necessary in order for humans to employ psychological essentialism.[14] Nor do they amount to direct proof of the heuristic. However, psychological essentialism is consistent with and unifies these tendencies, while also making sense of the human tendency across cultures to appeal to explicitly essentialist accounts of elements such as the soul, spirit, or (more importantly for this book) DNA or genes.[15]

Gelman's account of essentialism focuses on young children, who have little education and scientific training and thus are more likely than adults to provide untainted evidence of human cognition.[16] However, as indicated in the discussion above, her book also discusses many corroborative experiments involving adults. Her belief is that essentialism continues past childhood and into adulthood – perhaps not in quite such a naïve form, but as a powerful framework for organizing knowledge of the world.[17]

Assuming Gelman is correct, and psychological essentialism is real and persistent, let us return to the classic formulation of essentialism and consider how it might apply to the hypothetical introduced in Part II. If a pedestrian walking through a neighborhood notices a large creature with orange and black-striped fur, claws, and a long tail slinking through a stand of trees, those phenotypic clues may cause her to assume that the creature carries essence of tiger. From there, she can infer other properties that she cannot see. For example, the creature probably eats meat.

The pedestrian need not consciously reason in terms of essence of tiger. Nor need she be capable of explaining what exactly constitutes essence of tiger. Depending on her education and culture, she might ascribe the role of tiger essence to elements as diverse as DNA or the soul[18] (more about that later). The important thing is that the heuristic still allows her to draw the useful conclusion that she should go indoors and remove herself from danger.

What distinguishes psychological essentialism from simple categorization? Simple categorization might lump together all objects with orange fur and black stripes without regard to their other characteristics. For example, suppose the pedestrian strolls past a vintage Mustang, peers through the window, and sees a car seat cover printed with a faux tiger-fur pattern. Based on the color and stripes, she could class this seat cover together with the creature she observed slinking through the trees. This type of categorization does not allow the drawing of useful inferences, however.[19] A car seat cover in bad taste is dangerous only to the pedestrian's sensibilities.

By contrast, essentialism is causal. The tiger essence explains why the orange and black-striped creature has certain characteristics. This gives the heuristic versatility; it can address phenotypic variants that still carry the tiger essence. So, for example, if our pedestrian sees a large creature with white and black-striped fur, claws, and a long tail, she still obtains enough clues to assume the creature possesses essence of tiger and infer that this atypical variant is just as dangerous as orange and black-striped tigers.

What if this large striped creature is pregnant, nests in a wooded area, and bears a litter of cubs? The tiny and helpless newborns bear little resemblance to the adults they will one day become. Because the cubs are born of a tiger, however, the pedestrian can further infer that the cubs bear tiger essence, even if they don't look like dangerous predators yet.[20]

This tiger tale may seem far afield from human cloning. Indeed, if psychological essentialism occurred only in evaluations of animals or plant species, it would be of little value to the forthcoming analysis in this chapter. However, the heuristic has a much wider range of applications, one of which may be relevant to the issues investigated in this chapter.

All human beings around the world constitute a single species and a single living kind. Nevertheless, some social scientists have found that adults and children use essentialism to make sense of social categories such as racial and ethnic groups. We act as if the group has an underlying essence that all of its members share, allowing us to draw inferences regarding the supposedly innate physical, mental, and behavioral traits of group members.[21] This form of essentialism can encourage socially destructive behaviors such as stereotyping and racial prejudice.[22]

B. What is the Origin of Psychological Essentialism?

Social scientists hold a variety of theories regarding the origin of psychological essentialism and the extent of its reach into different *domains* (that is, content areas).[23] Here, I summarize theories that are most relevant to the issues investigated in this chapter.

As Medin and Ortony suggested, it could be that the cognitive mechanisms that cause humans to view the world in essentialist terms are the result of evolutionary adaption.[24] A heuristic that facilitates the drawing of rich inferences about predators, prey, plants, and perhaps even other human beings could have enhanced survival in the ancestral environments humans once inhabited.[25]

Consider *folk biology* – that is, a layperson's working knowledge of the biological world.[26] Anthropologist Scott Atran points out that folk biology exhibits striking similarities across cultures. One common element is *folk-biological taxonomy*: classification of animals and plants into groups (taxa) that are sited within a framework of ranked categories, such as white oak/oak/tree.[27] Taxa corresponding to biological species or genera predominate in folk-biological taxonomies.[28] Folk throughout the world consider groupings at this level to have an underlying essence,[29] and experiments have shown that people from different cultures consider such groupings to be the most potent source of inference about shared properties.[30]

Given this anthropological evidence, and the importance of evaluating animals and plants in the human ancestral environment, Atran has concluded that folk biology is an evolved cognitive module, of which essentialism is a key part.[31] If essentialism evolved to deal with animal and plant species, however, why should humans also apply the heuristic to racial and ethnic groups? These are not biological species, or even subspecies within *Homo sapiens*.

Race, in particular, is a biologically empty concept. Biologists have found that there is more genetic variation within races than between them. Nor does the concept of race capture useful information about clusters of genetic traits, because races are not separate reproductive populations within humanity. Even physical traits do not result from membership in one race or another. Rather, because race is socially defined, traits are simply a part of the definition. Choice of trait drives the racial category, and not the other way around.[32]

Some have answered that human beings as a whole are a natural kind. Perhaps this explains why people tend to treat social categories such as race and ethnicity as natural kinds.[33] Similarly, Atran has suggested that physical and possibly linguistic traits of some human groups may be distinctive enough to trigger operation of the living-kind module. Thinking of humans as kinds and drawing inferences about them reinforces essentialist habits of the mind.[34]

Anthropologist Lawrence Hirschfeld has presented a different theory, in which essentialism works together with culture to produce attitudes on race. Based on research with preschool children, he theorizes that our brains include a cognitive module for folk sociology. This module searches for human kinds that appear to have innate essence and inductive potential.[35] Equipped with this cognitive architecture and eager to make sense of their world, young children readily respond to verbal and social cues (and to a lesser extent, visual cues) that point them toward the racial categories considered relevant in their culture.[36] Although Hirschfeld acknowledges that historical, political, economic, and cultural forces have produced many different forms of racial thinking, in his view all of these forms are rooted in a cognitive architecture that makes racial thinking intuitively appealing.[37]

Hirschfeld does not argue that humans have an evolved cognitive module devoted to the domain of race per se.[38] His argument is that the brain is wired to conceptualize a wide variety of human kinds in essentialist terms. Physical, emotional, or behavioral traits – any one or all of these can be the hub around which members cluster to constitute a human kind.[39] Thus, his folk sociology module encompasses more than racial and ethnic groups. For example, he notes that some foreign cultures view occupation as intrinsically related to caste, that is, a religiously defined class of persons. In such a culture, if you know a person's occupation or occupation-related behaviors, you can infer his caste or kind.[40]

Linking of occupation and identity is not limited to foreign cultures. Hirschfeld conducted experiments in Ann Arbor, Michigan, with subjects aged three, four, and seven to test how children understood growth and heredity. Most children in all three age groups considered race to be more predictive of identity across lifespan and generations than occupation or body build.[41] Thus, Hirschfeld concluded that even preschoolers perceived race in essentialist terms (*i.e.*, as an immutable trait associated with family background and consistent with biological causality).[42] Intriguingly, however, a significant proportion of the three-year-old subjects in the experiment consistently picked occupation over race.[43] A follow-up experiment revealed that three, four, and seven year olds considered occupation more central to male identity over lifespan than female identity over lifespan.[44] In other words, the young mind intuitively perceives occupation as a good way to think about different kinds of people in the world.[45]

Finally, Gelman presents what may be the most flexible theory. In her view, several cognitive predispositions that evolved for varying purposes converge into a general essentialism that manifests differently in different domains.[46] Ability to distinguish appearance from reality encourages us to think about nonobvious properties or essences and classify objects – even ambiguous ones – according to their identity.[47] The assumption that clusters of traits signal more traits leads to the belief that there must be essence-based categories in the world that permit such induction.[48] The insight that traits have causes encourages one to search for additional traits associated with those causes.[49] The ability to track the identity of a person or thing over time rests on two realizations: that historical path (including origin) lies at the core of identity; and that outward appearances are not determinative.[50] Deference to experts (including, for a child, any adult) encourages acceptance of labels and the belief that essentialist categories are real.[51]

Gelman does not see psychological essentialism as solely an evolved cognitive module. She strikes a middle ground in which cognitive biases exist in the brain, but language guides and reinforces those biases.[52] So, for example, common nouns (*e.g.*, "cat" or "dog") guide children by signaling which categories are living kinds and which items belong to those categories.[53] Generic noun phrases (such as "cats like to drink milk") are also important, conveying that kinds have rich properties.[54]

To summarize: the materials in this section raise the intriguing possibility that twenty-first century attitudes toward not only animals and plants, but also humans (as groups and individuals), are unconsciously driven by cognitive mechanisms that evolved tens of thousands of years ago in response to the human ancestral environment.

However, it is important to acknowledge that not everyone believes essentialism is a product of cognitive evolution. Other academics have declared that essentialism is an artifact of Western culture, politics, and science (*e.g.*, the study of DNA), or of certain elements of language, such as names or labels that tend to imply an underlying sameness to members of categories.[55]

IDENTITY AND ESSENTIALISM

Before psychological essentialism can be verified as an evolved phenomenon, social scientists have much research to perform.[56] Relatedly, whether psychological essentialism is a universal phenomenon, culture-specific, or the joint product of human cognition and culture remains a matter for further research.[57]

This book is about human cloning in American culture, politics, and law. For purposes of its analysis, what matters most is that the psychological essentialism theorized by Medin and Ortony has been documented within our own culture. It is not necessary to resolve the academic debate over the origins or universality of psychological essentialism. Still, the theories raised in this section are interesting and will be discussed to the extent they can offer useful insights.

C. The Identity Fallacy and Essentialism

Turning now to cloning, this chapter sets the stage by restating the identity fallacy first identified in Part I: namely, that a person conceived through somatic cell nuclear transfer possesses the same physical, intellectual, psychological, or behavioral traits as the nuclear DNA donor and any other persons conceived from the same nuclear DNA.

As Chapters 2 and 3 explained, this is not true of animals born through cloning, and there is no reason to believe that it will be true of humans born through cloning. Nevertheless, the identity fallacy has been a persistent thread in public and political discussion of human cloning. Indeed, popular culture has long presented humans (or humanoid aliens) born through cloning as copies. So let us begin there.

1. The Identity Fallacy in Popular Culture

Biologist Lee Silver has traced the origin of the word "clone" back to 1903, when it was invented to refer to a colony of organisms created asexually from a single ancestor.[58] This basic meaning still held true in 1968, when *Webster's New World Dictionary* defined clone as a noun describing a group of plants directly descended from a single individual.[59] Interestingly, as originally defined, the term "clone" refers to large numbers of organisms.

In 1970, Alvin Toffler published his blockbuster book *Future Shock*.[60] Silver blames Toffler for perverting the original meaning of "clone" by predicting that man would use cloning to copy himself.[61] In Silver's view, after *Future Shock* popularized this erroneous interpretation of cloning, the public adopted the term "clone" to refer to all things copied, from computers to people.[62] Today, a free online dictionary includes the original definition of "clone" but also uses the term to describe a person who seems to be a copy of an original.[63]

A close reading of *Future Shock* shows that the book did even more harm than Silver claims. Toffler suggested cloning could be used to create multiple copies of Einstein, but also multiple copies of Hitler.[64] He presented the absurd claim that cloning might escalate if society learned that it was easier for a person to communicate with another of the same genotype.[65]

Future Shock was an influential nonfiction book, but it did not corrupt public understanding of cloning on its own. Science fiction has also done its part to spread the identity fallacy. Many films and television episodes have presented people born through cloning as identical copies of their DNA donors and/or each other. Table 1 provides a representative list. In all of these tales, the sameness extends to physical appearance at a minimum, and often to personality, behavior, or occupation, as well.[66] Stories in which these copies occur in large numbers are particularly relevant to this analysis and are marked with an asterisk.

An in-depth description of all of these stories would exceed the scope of this book. Fortunately, one film from a well-known series serves as an excellent example: George Lucas's *Star Wars II: Attack of the Clones*.[67] The following description does not relate the entire plot of the movie, but focuses on scenes related to cloning. When discussing this movie, this chapter will follow the convention employed in the movie and use the word "clone" as a noun.

IDENTITY AND ESSENTIALISM

Table 1. *Cloning Is Used to Create Copies*

Movies

Movie Title	Distributor	Year
2001: A Space Travesty	Columbia/TriStar	2000
Alien: Resurrection	Twentieth Century Fox	1997
**Anna to the Infinite Power*	Scorpion Releasing	1983
* *The Boys from Brazil*	Twentieth Century Fox	1978
* *The City of Lost Children*	Sony Pictures Classics	1995
**Cloned*	National Broadcasting Company (NBC)	1997
The Clones	Filmmakers International	1973
The Fifth Element	Columbia Pictures	1997
Godsend	Lions Gate Pictures	2004
**The Island*	DreamWorks/Warner Brothers	2005
**Moon*	Sony Pictures Classics	2009
**Multiplicity*	Columbia Pictures	1996
Replicant	Artisan Entertainment	2001
Repli-Kate	Twentieth Century Fox	2002
The Resurrection of Zachary Wheeler	Gold Key Entertainment Film Ventures	1971
The Sixth Day	Columbia Pictures	2000
Starman	Columbia Pictures	1984
Star Trek III: The Search for Spock	Paramount Pictures	1984
**Star Wars II: Attack of the Clones*	Twentieth Century Fox	2002
**The Third Twin*	CBS Broadcasting, Inc.	1997
**Xchange*	Trimark Pictures	2000

Television Episodes/Series

TV Series	Episode	Distributor	Air date
Eleventh Hour	"Resurrection"	Granada Television	January 19, 2006
Eureka	"Many Happy Returns"	The Sci Fi Channel	July 25, 2006
Star Trek: Deep Space Nine	"A Man Alone"	Paramount Television	January 17, 1993
Star Trek: Deep Space Nine	*"Ties of Blood and Water"	Paramount Television	April 14, 1997
Star Trek: Deep Space Nine	*"Treachery, Faith, and the Great River"	Paramount Television	November 4, 1998
Star Trek Next Generation	*"Up the Long Ladder"	Paramount Television	May 22, 1989
Star Trek Next Generation	"Rightful Heir"	Paramount Television	May 17, 1993
X-Files	*"Eve"	Fox	December 10, 1993
X-Files	*"Herrenvolk"	Fox	October 4, 1996
X-Files	*"Colony"	Fox	February 10, 1995
X-Files	*"End Game"	Fox	February 17, 1995

* Indicates multiple copies are made of same person

Jedi warrior Obi-Wan Kenobi searches for an assassin who tried to kill Senator Padme Amidala. He arrives at the Kamino system, only to find that the aliens who live there have been working for the past ten years to generate a clone army for the Republic. The Kaminoan leader explains to Kenobi that 200,000 clone soldiers are ready and another 1 million are in progress. The soldiers undergo accelerated maturation and combat education and training programs. They take any order without question because they have been genetically altered to be less independent than the nuclear DNA donor, described as a bounty hunter named Jango Fett.[68]

Throughout this discussion, the movie provides visuals of the clone soldiers: first as countless babies growing in arrays of artificial wombs; next as rows of children being trained; again as identical men eating in a mess hall; and finally as armored soldiers donning helmets and performing drills in large formations.[69]

Shortly thereafter, a Kaminoan introduces Kenobi to Jango Fett and his son Boba. Fett has the same body build, face (albeit with a few added scars), and hair as the clone soldiers depicted in the mess hall. Boba is a clone of Jango Fett, but unlike the clone soldiers, he was not subjected to accelerated maturation, so he appears as a young boy.[70]

Kenobi suspects that Fett is the assassin he seeks. When the Fetts attempt to leave Kamino in their spaceship, Kenobi attacks. A fight ensues. Jango Fett displays impressive fighting skills: he is agile and strong, and bests Kenobi (a Jedi) in the fight. By the time Kenobi recovers, Jango is safely on his ship and Boba is piloting it away.[71]

Based on this description, four themes stand out. First, at each stage of life, the clone soldiers look alike. Babies are shown growing naked in vast collections of clear-sided artificial wombs; although we cannot see their faces, the sameness of the wombs represents the sameness of the babies. Children undergoing training look alike and are dressed alike. Men in the mess hall not only wear the same red uniforms, but also have the exact same body size and build, facial features, and hair. Soldiers drilling in formation wear the same white helmets and body

IDENTITY AND ESSENTIALISM   81

armor, underscoring their sameness. Second, all of the clones have a single nuclear DNA donor named Jango Fett. This genetic link presumably explains why all the clones look like Fett and each other.

Third, Jango Fett has key traits that go beyond his physical appearance. He is described as a bounty hunter, signifying that he is a violent man who fights and captures others for a living. The extended fight scene testifies to his agility, strength, and cunning. We are also told that his clones had to be genetically modified to ensure they would not inherit his independent spirit. Finally, the movie stresses through its dialogue and visuals how innumerable the clones are: hundreds of thousands ready now, more than 1 million to be delivered later.

These themes reoccur later in the film. Informed of the existence of the clone soldiers, the chancellor of the Republic exercises his emergency powers to authorize the creation of a clone army to counter a separatist coalition of civilizations. Clone soldiers then join Yoda in a bid to rescue Jedi warriors being held hostage by the separatist coalition. Although we never see the faces of these soldiers, their helmets and body armor convey sameness, and they prove to be effective fighters. One of the final scenes in the movie shows battalion after battalion of the clone soldiers, marching into battleships under the command of the chancellor.[72] Here again, the movie emphasizes sameness. The clone soldiers not only look alike in their uniforms, but appear to have a common ability to fight well. The movie also continues to emphasize just how numerous the soldiers are.

Putting this all together, *Star Wars II* presents a classic expression of the identity fallacy. Jango Fett and the men generated from his DNA share an identical appearance, physical strength, and the ability to fight well. These traits are preserved across hundreds of thousands of soldiers, with 1 million more to come.

2. The Identity Fallacy in Media Accounts

After Ian Wilmut and his scientific team announced the birth of Dolly, the media unleashed a flood of newspaper, magazine, and television stories speculating about the prospect of human cloning. As Professor Patrick D. Hopkins has noted, the media coverage had a dual effect: it reflected concerns that the public held regarding cloning, but it also created and fixed those concerns in the public mind.[73]

One concern dealt with the threat that cloning supposedly posed to human individuality. Media accounts frequently labeled humans born through cloning as copies or described them as identical.[74] The visuals that accompanied these accounts reinforced the message by showing multiple, identical images of the same person (or artifact that resembles a person, such as a doll). In this manner, humans born through cloning were initially presented to the public not only as identical copies, but as identical copies that could be mass produced in large numbers.[75]

More than one observer has noted a peculiar cognitive dissonance to these stories. The stories hook the reader with unsettling talk and images about copies; however, at the same time, they quote various experts to the effect that humans born through cloning will not be copies at all.[76] Interestingly, many serious nonfiction and academic books on cloning repeat this pattern. Covers depict identical humans (or artifacts that resemble humans)[77] or offer mirror-image visuals,[78] even when the content inside the book refutes the identity fallacy.[79]

Why should anyone understand cloned humans as identical and innumerable? One ethicist has argued that the media draw upon films and other elements of popular culture that are already established in the public imagination.[80] To put it slightly differently, the media resort to identical images because they have become a visual trope for cloning – one that viewers are expected to grasp quickly and intuitively. This may be true, but if so, it simply pushes the question back one level. Why has popular culture imagined these copies long before a single human has been born as the result of somatic cell nuclear transfer?

Granted, *Future Shock* was a popular and influential book, but this still leaves the question of why the public found Toffler's description plausible enough to embrace. Similarly, producers, scriptwriters, and others involved in the film business are not creating at random. They are

IDENTITY AND ESSENTIALISM

attempting to craft stories and images that will sell, and science fiction convinces best when it holds a kernel of truth.

To dig deeper, let us consider what the average person knows about cloning. No babies have been born through cloning yet, so there is no direct evidence of what they will be like. People who follow the news are likely to know that cloning involves the sharing of nuclear DNA, but this fact does not necessarily imply the creation of even one duplicate, let alone dozens of them.

There is another source of information, however. The population includes naturally occurring monozygotic twins (popularly known as identical twins). As explained in Chapter 3, such twins are created when an embryo splits; thus, the members of a monozygotic twin pair share mitochondrial and nuclear DNA. Nancy Segal, a leading expert on twins, describes monozygotic twins as clones.[81]

Monozygotic twins occur in 1 out of 250 births[82]; in other words, they are rare, but not vanishingly so. Most people have seen a monozygotic twin pair, in film or on television if nowhere else, and have experienced the visual impact of seeing two persons of the same age who appear identical (particularly if they are wearing the same clothes). Many (although not all) people understand that monozygotic twins share DNA. These facts suggest a reason why popular culture and the media often present humans born through cloning as identical persons of the same age; we are accustomed to viewing monozygotic twins that way. Toffler also analogized cloned humans to monozygotic twins.[83]

Monozygotic triplets are far rarer, occurring in 1 out of 62,500 births; monozygotic quadruplets occur in 1 out of 15,625,000 births; and monozygotic quintuplets occur in 1 out of 3,906,250,000 births.[84] Not as many people have viewed these higher-order multiples in person, but the occasional news story or photograph provides confirmation that they do exist. The Dionne quintuplets, born in Canada in 1934, are the most notorious case. They starred in movies (thereby exposing many people to their similar appearances),[85] and many films, books, and articles have been written about them, some decades later.[86] So the public knows it is possible for more than two persons of the same age to share DNA and look very much the same.

For genetic, epigenetic, and environmental reasons, humans born through cloning are likely to differ from their DNA donors and each other more than monozygotic multiples do. Nevertheless, it is plausible that a public familiar with monozygotic multiples and the principle of shared DNA could believe (incorrectly) that cloning is a means of producing large numbers of identical bodies.

The next question is harder to answer: why should authors such as Toffler and filmmakers such as Lucas find creative and financial success by promoting a flawed vision of humans born through cloning? Evolutionary psychologist David Buss has suggested that people enjoy art, music, literature, or movies when the content of these cultural products artificially activates mechanisms of the mind that evolved for different purposes. Stories of lust, sexual competition, reproduction, survival in the face of life-threatening danger, and the like push our mental buttons in ways we find exciting and pleasurable.[87] Buss has speculated that cultural products might teach us as much or more about human psychology than planned experiments.[88]

In other words, when seeking the reasons that popular culture presents humans born through cloning as identical and numerous, we should consider whether aspects of human cognitive architecture facilitate such conceptualizations or render them titillating in some way. Before we fully engage this analysis, we must complete our review of the ways in which the identity fallacy has manifested itself in the cloning debate.

3. The Identity Fallacy in Government Reports

The debate over human reproductive cloning has included scientists, academics, politicians, and many others. Well-educated people who should know better have shown a tendency to slip into language that marks humans born through cloning as copies. For example, President Bill Clinton proclaimed: "Each human life is unique, born of a miracle

IDENTITY AND ESSENTIALISM

that reaches beyond laboratory science. I believe we must respect this profound gift and resist the temptation to replicate ourselves."[89] When Ian Wilmut and Rudolf Jaenisch published an editorial opposing human reproductive cloning, they spoke against the copying of a person.[90]

As powerful as individual voices can be, pronouncements coming from groups carry even more weight. Government bodies have taken testimony from experts in various fields and issued reports for the specific purpose of advising lawmakers on cloning legislation. These reports are important both as summaries and (in some cases) endorsements of anti-cloning positions. Three will be discussed here.

The National Bioethics Advisory Commission (NBAC) issued the first report (NBAC Report) at the behest of President Bill Clinton shortly after the birth of Dolly was announced.[91] Following a lengthy review of scientific, religious, ethical, legal, and policy issues, the NBAC recommended Congress place a three to five year moratorium on reproductive use of the new technology. The NBAC based its conclusion primarily on its sense that reproductive cloning was not yet safe for use in humans, but also declared that there were unresolved concerns relating to potential psychological harms to humans born through cloning and impacts on moral, religious, and cultural values of society.[92]

When George W. Bush became president several years later, he created a new President's Council on Bioethics and staffed it with his own experts.[93] This Council issued a report on human cloning in 2002 (Council Report). The report recommended that Congress ban human reproductive cloning – not just for safety reasons, but also due to the moral threats cloning posed to children, families, and society.[94]

Finally, when the California State Legislature placed a five-year moratorium on human reproductive cloning in 1997, it called upon the California Department of Health Services to create a committee to advise it on cloning issues.[95] The California Advisory Committee on Human Cloning issued a report in 2002 (California Report) recommending the Legislature make the ban on reproductive cloning permanent. Although the Committee rendered its judgment primarily on the ground that cloning was unsafe, its members were also persuaded by social and political concerns.[96]

In sum, these blue-ribbon panels of experts recommended that human reproductive cloning be prohibited, not just because they considered the technology unsafe, but also for a slew of other reasons that had nothing to do with safety. Moreover, only the NBAC Report recommended a short prohibition of three to five years. Five years after the birth of Dolly had been announced, attitudes had hardened to the point where the Council Report and California Report recommended outright bans with no sunset clauses or other provisions for reconsideration if the technology became reasonably safe.[97] Thus, going forward, the analysis will assume that non-safety concerns were significant factors behind the decisions to recommend cloning bans.

This chapter focuses on the identity fallacy. A reader of these government reports finds four manifestations of the identity fallacy: assertions that humans born through cloning will suffer from diminished individuality; fears that human cloning will be employed for eugenic purposes; concerns that human cloning will reduce the genetic diversity of our species; and worries that human cloning will create troubled and dysfunctional families. In the following subsections, each of these concerns is analyzed in turn.

a) Diminished Individuality

Some fear that reproductive cloning could impair identity and individuality. The argument goes something like this: even if a human born through cloning is not a copy per se, she will share too much with her genetic predecessor (or others cloned from the same DNA) – physical appearance, intellect, and personality traits. This could lead her to question the uniqueness of her own identity and suffer psychological damage.[98]

The Clinton-era NBAC Report gave this concern a respectful hearing, but rejected what it viewed as "gross misunderstandings of human biology and psychology," such as the prospect of clone armies.[99] By contrast, the Bush-era Council Report urged that problems of identity and individuality were real, especially if the technology was used to "produce multiple 'copies' of any single individual, as in one or another of the seemingly far-fetched futuristic scenarios in which cloning is often presented to the popular imagination."[100]

However articulated, these concerns about identity and individuality are overblown for two reasons. First, experience with monozygotic twins contradicts the concerns. As explained at length in Chapter 3, monozygotic twins share nuclear (and mitochondrial) DNA. They often strongly resemble each other in physical appearance, and may have similar IQs or even personality traits. Yet, no one questions their unique identities.[101] Moreover, as twin expert Nancy Segal notes, twins are not overrepresented as psychiatric patients.[102] Even in this extreme case, where twins share multiple traits, they do not suffer from diminished individuality.

The Council Report attempts to distinguish monozygotic twins on the ground that they are born at the same time, so that one does not loom as a prophecy for the other.[103] However, this distinction is specious. Monozygotic twins who grow up together are exposed to a barrage of information about the traits and talents associated with their shared genome. Yet, twins retain their individuality.[104]

Second, concerns about identity and individuality rest on the false assumption that a person born through cloning will closely resemble her DNA donor. For example, consider this passage from the Council Report:

> Everything about the predecessor – from physical height and facial appearance, balding patterns and inherited diseases, to temperament and native talents, to shape of life and length of days, and even cause of death – will appear before the expectant eyes of the cloned person, always with at least the nagging concern that there, notwithstanding the grace of God, go I.[105]

This creepy prophecy is at odds with the data we have from fifteen years of experiments with cloned animals. These animals have their own appearances, sizes, behaviors, personalities, and lifespans. Some look nothing like their donors, and others who do look the same act differently. Based on this evidence, we can expect humans born through cloning to differ from their donors more than monozygotic twins differ from each other. Like all children, they can anticipate some overlap with genetic parents, but not to the extent predicted in this passage. Perhaps the government reports overstate the potential for diminished individuality because they did not have enough experimental data to work with. All three reports were issued within the first five years after the birth of Dolly was announced and are seriously out of date. Whatever the reason, the government reports have succumbed to a softer version of the identity fallacy – one in which humans born through cloning are not copies but resemble their genetic predecessors too closely for their own good.

Even if cloning does not produce copies, however, many people believe that it does. Could the identity fallacy itself wreak havoc upon the hearts and minds of cloned children? Might they suffer, not because they share too many traits with their donors, but because they believe that they do?

Cloned children will benefit from their own life experiences, which should make their individuality clear to them from an early age. However, to the extent the children could misunderstand and be harmed, the reports erred in recommending cloning bans that seek to eliminate the children themselves. When inadequate information is the fundamental problem, less drastic alternatives are available. For example, as Professor Elizabeth Price Foley has suggested, the government can sponsor counseling to ensure that no cloned child holds such unreasonable expectations for himself.[106] If the problem is that others may refuse to accept cloned children as individuals, then the government can mount a vigorous public education campaign aimed at debunking the identity fallacy. Further, civil rights legislation can be amended to prohibit unjust discrimination against humans born through cloning.

b) Eugenic Cloning

All three government reports associate cloning with eugenics.[107] Some fear public eugenics: that is, governments utilizing cloning to create masses of individuals with specific physical, intellectual, or psychological traits.[108] However, as Chapter 2 explained, cloning is not a reliable means of replicating traits due to genetic variations, epigenetic factors, and environmental influences. Because eugenic programs cannot succeed, governments have no incentive to undertake them.

The Bush-era Council also voiced concerns about private eugenics. In theory, if enough parents replicate children from superior DNA that has been enhanced via genetic engineering, their cumulative choices could end up altering human nature.[109] However, such an outcome is extremely unlikely for three reasons. First, as explained above, cloning cannot replicate traits, and the first few attempts will reveal that fact to prospective parents. Second, as the Council conceded in a later report on assisted reproductive technologies, genetic engineering is not likely to occur in the foreseeable future.[110] We simply don't have the information necessary. A single gene can have multiple effects, making it hard to know what adding or subtracting one might do to a baby. Many human traits are *polygenic* – that is, the result of numerous genes working together – and not all of these genes have been identified.[111] Third, most parents will balk at the expense, effort, and risk involved in conceiving offspring through cloning and genetic engineering. Billions will reproduce through the simpler method of sex and add billions of babies with random gene assortments to the population. This constant replenishment will protect the species against significant alteration.[112]

Still, this association of human cloning with eugenics is interesting in and of itself. It assumes the mass production of cloned humans in numbers that are large enough to make an impact on society. We imagine a rogue government cloning millions of super-strong soldiers, or parents cloning thousands of children from the DNA of a movie star or professional athlete. Such scenarios resonate with science fiction films,[113] but they are also consistent with news stories that persistently display large herds of humans born through cloning.

c) Reduced Genetic Diversity

Relatedly, some worry that if a government or parents choose to clone from certain superior DNA for eugenic reasons, the resulting children will reduce the genetic diversity of the human species and impair its ability to adapt to disease or environmental changes.[114] However, this fear rests on the assumption that cloning can produce thousands, hundreds of thousands, or even millions of individuals with the same traits. As cloning cannot do that, governments will have no incentive to use it for eugenic purposes. Nor will parents have any incentive to clone thousands of children from the same movie star or athlete.[115] Moreover, with billions reproducing through sex, there is little chance that cloning could make a dent in the genetic diversity that already exists.[116]

Although invalid, the argument that cloning would reduce genetic diversity is still fascinating. Like the eugenic concerns to which it is related, it assumes human replication on a massive scale. It is yet another manifestation of the identity fallacy in the cloning debate.[117]

d) Dysfunctional Families

A fourth concern is that cloning will produce dysfunctional families. For example, all three reports raise the possibility that parents might use cloning in an effort to create children with specific traits or skills. Such behavior implies a lack of unconditional acceptance for the child, and could lead to conflict should the child disappoint parental expectations.[118]

As Chapters 2 and 3 have explained, cloning cannot even guarantee a specific appearance, let alone more sophisticated characteristics such as intelligence or artistic talent. If parents really did hold unrealistic expectations for their children, those expectations would be another manifestation of the identity fallacy, in which cloning is perceived as a form of copying.[119]

The Bush-era Council also suggested that cloning could lead to familial conflict, anticipating that a parent might react to a person cloned from a spouse as if he or she were the spouse. If the marriage was a bad one, this could lead to turmoil; if the marriage was good, that might be even worse: "The problems of being and rearing an adolescent could become complicated should the teenage clone of the mother 'reappear' as the double of the woman the father once fell in love with."[120] Of course, there is no biological reason to equate a cloned son or daughter with a spouse. Rather, the view that cloned humans are copies lies at the heart of this concern.[121]

Of course, because there are no cloned children yet, the government reports can only speculate as to what might go wrong. These speculations are fascinating in and of themselves. Ordinarily, parents love and value their children. However, when it comes to cloning, the reports seem predisposed to believe parents will treat their children like copies or misunderstand their role within the family.

If lawmakers believe cloning may lead to dysfunction within families, there is a viable alternative to imposition of a flat ban on the technology. As Professor John Robertson has suggested, regulations can mandate psychological counseling for prospective parents.[122] Moreover, even in the absence of such regulations, existing principles of informed consent will require fertility doctors and clinics to explain all the relevant medical facts before providing cloning services.[123] As cloning is a reproductive technology, these facts should include the individuality, unpredictability, and autonomy of a cloned child.[124]

The California Report considers various forms of regulation, but rejects them all due to the many concerns raised about cloning around the world.[125] Its comments on counseling are most pertinent here. The Report complains that parents may receive counseling but still decide to clone for bad reasons.[126] The Report also speculates that parents with good motives could develop bad motives after a child is born. Its reasoning is telling:

> It is possible that parents who at the onset say that they will cherish their child no matter how he or she turns out may react differently when they see a child *who cannot be distinguished physically from an existing individual.* Faced with this close resemblance, parents may develop strong expectations that they could not predict and therefore did not discuss during prenatal counseling.[127]

Once again, the identity fallacy rears its head. Human cloning will produce babies, not carbon copies of adults. Distinguishing a baby from an adult DNA donor should be easy. Moreover, the animal experiments discussed in Part I demonstrate that even multiple animals cloned at the same time from the same DNA differ from each other in physical appearance, behavior, and personality. Family life will yield many opportunities to observe the individuality and autonomy of a cloned child, making it likely that unreasonable expectations will decrease, rather than increase, over time.

It is possible that a few would-be parents, despite all the counseling in the world, may cling stubbornly to their false expectations. Even then, it does not follow that prohibition is an effective solution to the problem. As Chapter 8 will explain in more detail, parents will circumvent cloning bans through travel or underground services. Once children are born, the bans will do nothing to lessen unreasonable parental expectations. All they can do is further harm cloned children by stigmatizing them as unworthy of existence.

4. Making Sense of the Identity Fallacy

The foregoing discussion has documented the pervasiveness of the identity fallacy in popular culture and media accounts. Humans born through cloning are often portrayed as identical to DNA donors in physical, intellectual, psychological, and behavioral traits. Scenarios involving multiple cloning also present the resulting human beings as identical

IDENTITY AND ESSENTIALISM

to each other. Even government reports have expressed concerns that are rooted in the identity fallacy, such as the claims that cloned children will suffer due to diminished individuality. What is the source of the identity fallacy? Why do people believe in it?

Biology cannot be blamed. To be sure, genes do affect physical, intellectual, and personality characteristics; if a doctor clones a particular person, he increases the probability that the resulting baby will share traits with that person. However, the popular vision of the cloned human as duplicate is inconsistent with biological fact. As Chapter 3 explained, genetic, epigenetic, and environmental influences will ensure that any human born through cloning will be a unique individual and not a copy of the DNA donor or anyone else.

Monozygotic twins and other multiples cannot be blamed. Although such persons can be strikingly similar in appearance, the public does not view them as duplicates. Rather, it seems to be generally understood that such multiples have their own personalities and are individuals.

If everyone from movie-goers to authors of government reports misunderstands humans born through cloning, perhaps we should look inward. Is there something about the human brain that predisposes us to believe in the identity fallacy? In this section, I argue that the fallacy is consistent with psychological essentialism.

a) The Metamorphosis from Individual to Kind

Analysis begins with the conceptualization of humans born through cloning as identical and multitudinous. This nightmare vision appears in science fiction, media accounts, and even government reports.

The California Report offers a good example in its discussion of the use of cloning for eugenic purposes:

> Cloning not only offers the power to select a desired genetic phenotype, but also the power to produce *multiple copies of such persons*. If cloning is combined with such forms of genetic selection, some fear that science fiction images of the *mass production of individuals* with particularly desirable genetic traits could one day become a reality.[128]

Similarly, in commenting on the individuality of humans born through cloning, the NBAC Report stated:

> It is easy to understand why identical twins hold such fascination. Common experience demonstrates how distinctly different twins are, both in personality and in personhood. At the same time, *observers cannot help but imbue identical bodies with some expectation that identical persons occupy those bodies, since body and personality remain intertwined in human intuition.* With the prospect of somatic cell nuclear transfer cloning comes a scientifically inaccurate but nonetheless *instinctive fear of multitudes of identical bodies*, each housing personalities that are somehow less than distinct, less unique, and less autonomous than usual.[129]

In this passage, the NBAC captures several aspects of common thought regarding humans born through cloning. First, there is the intuition that body and personality are intertwined, so that identical bodies imply identical personalities. Second, there is the instinctive fear of multitudes of identical bodies. Third, the passage captures the fascination and horror that the average person experiences when contemplating multiples. However, the NBAC did not explain the reasons for these intuitions, instincts, or fears. This unresolved puzzle cries out for analysis.

A specific fact pattern would facilitate analysis. However, there are no actual multitudes of identical humans for this book to discuss. In lieu of real-life examples, I will focus on *Star Wars II: Attack of the Clones*. This movie is a good choice for three reasons. First, readers are likely to be familiar with the *Star Wars* series and thus will be able to track the analysis. Second, the movie offers a classic example of the identity fallacy, as has already been shown. Third, the canard about clone armies is so widespread and persistent in the cloning debate that it demands attention.

Folk biology: Humans apply principles of psychological essentialism when evaluating living kinds of animals and plants. Similar principles are applied when evaluating human kinds, such as racial and ethnic groups. Although experts disagree on the reason for this, Scott Atran has argued that our brains apply principles of folk biology by analogy when confronted with a group of humans that appear to share common physical traits.

Let us evaluate *Star Wars II* to see if its vision of the clone army is more consistent with modern biology, or the essentialism of folk biology.[130] The members of the clone army are numerous: 200,000 strong, with 1 million more under development. They eat, train, and grow up together in a location situated far away from the rest of the imaginary *Star Wars* universe. All the clones are identical in their appearance at every stage of life. All the grown clones are effective fighters.

As the NBAC recognized, the notion of multitudes of identical persons is scientifically inaccurate. If anyone tried to clone an army, genetic mutations and epigenetic variation would ensure that the soldiers varied in size, build, and possibly hair color and facial features. Intellect and personality would also vary. Moreover, the attempt to impose a uniform environment through common training and living quarters would likely miscarry. As twin expert Nancy Segal has noted, even within the same family, children encounter different social microenvironments and have a tendency to carve out their own niches.[131] Some members of the clone army might accept the training and become fine soldiers. Others might not have an aptitude or taste for fighting, and might reject the training altogether.[132]

However, when considered in light of folk biology, the movie's portrayal makes weird sense. There are enough cloned soldiers together in one place for them to appear as a class of organisms. Their obvious physical similarities could trick the mind into perceiving the clone army as if it were a living kind and applying principles of essentialism.

Essentialism predicts that the members of this clone kind share an essence that causes their physical similarities. Consistent with this, the movie conveniently tells us what this essence is: all of the soldiers are cloned from the DNA of Jango Fett. The principle of rich induction predicts that other traits may be linked to the genetic essence of Jango Fett. Indeed, the structure of the movie is consistent with this principle. Jango

Fett is not portrayed as a teacher, doctor, or anyone else who is likely to be kind, benevolent, and peaceful. Rather, he is made out to be a bounty hunter, a violent man who fights and captures others for a living. He is also shown to be a capable fighter who can hold his own against a Jedi warrior. All of the soldiers cloned from him appear to share his fighting prowess and aggressive personality. The only trait the soldiers do not share with Fett is independence. The movie attempts to explain that deviation by stating that the Kaminoans engineered independence out of the soldiers' genetic profile.

In short, *Star Wars II* presents a world in which persons created through cloning are copies of each other and the DNA donor. Evaluated in light of biological principles, this identity fallacy is incoherent; evaluated in light of essentialism, it is coherent. In a bizarre twist, a mental heuristic that may once have been useful in the human ancestral environment as a means of quickly assessing the traits and dangers of animal or plant species turns out to be compatible with belief in a clone army.[133]

Folk sociology: There is another way in which psychological essentialism may facilitate belief in a clone army. As discussed earlier in this chapter, Lawrence Hirschfeld has postulated that the brain includes a folk sociology module primed to search out human kinds. The members of a human kind are perceived as sharing a common essence that makes it possible to draw inferences about their traits.

In *Star Wars II*, the members of the clone army share the hair color (black), skin color (light brown), and facial features of Jango Fett. The movie does not identify the race or ethnicity of Fett and his clones. By steering clear of such information, the movie avoids exploiting the folk sociological tendency to essentialize racial or ethnic groups. However, it does emphasize traits associated with occupation. The clones have distinctive helmets, uniforms (the white body armor), and weapons. They are trained in battle skills and housed apart from the rest of society. The clones clearly belong to an occupational kind: the soldier.

By presenting the clones as a soldier kind, *Star Wars II* invokes the folk sociology module. In general, invocation of this module encourages the viewer to assume a common essence and infer common traits. *Star Wars II* takes things one step farther, however. It tells the viewer what the common essence is: the DNA of Jango Fett. By identifying the essence as genetic and associating it with Fett, the film encourages the viewer to infer the members of the clone army share the specific traits of Fett, such as his physical appearance, cold-blooded personality, and extraordinary fighting prowess.

Other examples of the association between occupational kinds and humans born through cloning are easy to find. The NBAC Report noted (without endorsing) the fear that cloning could be used to create "armies of complacent workers, crazed soldiers, brilliant musicians, or beatific saints."[134] Similarly, many of the stories in Table 1 portray cloning as a means of creating a group of persons with the same occupation or skills.[135]

Why are these portrayals so common? Folk sociology provides one possible answer. The members of an occupational kind share a common essence. Humans cloned from the same DNA have a shared genetic heritage, making them psychologically plausible in the role of occupational kind. Once humans born through cloning are portrayed as belonging to an occupational kind, however, observers are more likely to infer that they share common traits, or even identical traits. In other words, the portrayals encourage the public to view humans born through cloning as a clone kind.

Labeling: This analysis would not be complete without a nod to the power of language. As Susan Gelman has noted, language can guide and reinforce essentialist habits of mind.[136] A common noun may signal the existence of a kind and encourage the brain to classify individuals as members of the kind.[137] For example, tiger is a living kind for purposes of folk biology. It is also a biological species, which highlights the parallels between folk biology and modern science.[138]

The term "clone" is not as broad – it does not refer to an entire species – but it is a word that was invented to denote a group originated from a single organism. As applied to humans, it implies a group derived from a single person, like the clone army in *Star Wars II*. The word reinforces the essentialist tendency to view humans born through cloning as a living or human kind, rather than individuals.

As discussed previously in this chapter, the word "clone" has also come to mean "copy." This meaning reinforces the essentialist conclusion that shared DNA leads to shared traits.

b) Small Numbers of Humans Born Through Cloning
The identity fallacy is not limited to nightmare scenarios in which thousands of identical bodies are created from a single DNA source. Popular culture and media accounts have often presented humans cloned in much lower numbers, such as one to three. About half of the films and television episodes listed in Table 1 fall into this category. There is a kernel of truth to this presentation: cloning could be used to produce a limited number of offspring, such as a single child for an infertile couple.[139] Let us take that context as a basis for discussion.

Humans apply relational essentialism to kinfolk. In other words, we expect kin to share essence and traits according to the degree of relationship.[140] For example, a parent and child are expected to have more traits in common than first cousins. A person who donated nuclear DNA for cloning and a resulting child would qualify as kin by virtue of their shared nuclear DNA. Whether the pair is characterized as parent/child or sibling/sibling, kinship would predict many common traits but not duplication. Thus, a kinship model of cloning would come close to reflecting biological fact.

However, popular culture and the media consistently favor the copy trope over the kinship model. Even government reports assume parents will view a cloned child as a copy and rear him in an abusive manner. This obsession with copying seems odd. After all, a DNA donor and single cloned child would constitute a pair, and not a kind of the sort that is ordinarily processed through essentialist modules.

One possible explanation is that the essentialist tendency to spot biological or sociological kinds is so powerful that it spills over into contexts

IDENTITY AND ESSENTIALISM

where it doesn't fit. Once the mind accepts nuclear DNA as an essence that produces identical traits in multiple bodies, it may apply that same reasoning when dealing with cases in which a single human being is born through cloning. To put it another way, the intuition that a cloned child would be a copy of his parent may be an instance of folk biology or folk sociology writ small.

An example drawn from *Star Wars II: Attack of the Clones* illustrates these points. Jango Fett has a son named Boba Fett who was cloned but not growth-accelerated. Based on the time when the clone army was commissioned, Boba is about ten years old. Because he is not the same age as Jango, the movie does not present him as identical in appearance. However, he works in tandem with Jango as they fight to escape Kamino and Obi-Wan Kenobi, showing a very un-childlike ability to fire weapons and pilot a spaceship.

Kenobi tosses a tracer on the ship and follows the Fetts. As the Fetts approach a planet ringed with asteroids, Boba is the one who first realizes that Kenobi is tracking them. When Jango promises to spring a couple of surprises (seismic charges) on the unsuspecting pursuer, Boba responds with an evil laugh. Later, he urges Jango to fire a missile at Kenobi's ship, and exults when it appears that Kenobi has been destroyed.[141]

Thus, *Star Wars II* portrays a ten-year-old child as possessing fighting and piloting skills beyond his years. It also depicts Boba savoring the apparent destruction of one of the heroes of the movie (Kenobi). Even at age ten, Boba is violent and enjoys killing. He is as battle-worthy, bloodthirsty, and evil as his parent.

In common experience, children do not possess such traits. Why, then, do viewers accept this ugly portrayal of Boba? By the time viewers encounter this child, they have already seen the clone army and have been primed to believe that clones of Jango are copies of Jango. However, the believability of the clone army rests upon the viewers' intuition that kinds share an essence (in this case, the DNA of Jango).

Many other films depict individuals born through cloning as physical and psychological copies of their DNA donors.[142] If these individuals possess differing personalities, some added plot element usually explains the deviation. For example, in *Starman*, an adult cloned from the DNA of a woman's dead husband has the personality of the alien that inhabits the body.[143]

There is an alternative to the possibility that the essentialism of kinds has spillover effects. Perhaps the brain is geared to view individuals in an essentialist light, leading to the intuition that a human cloned from the unique essence of a specific person will share his or her physical, intellectual, and psychological traits. Chapter 6 will explore that alternative in greater depth.[144]

c) Summary

The foregoing analysis provides a plausible explanation for many vexing aspects of the cloning debate. First, popular culture, media accounts, and even government reports have portrayed humans born through cloning as multitudinous copies. Experience with naturally occurring monozygotic multiples gives such portrayals a toehold in reality. Psychological essentialism stretches that reality to the point where it gives way to the identity fallacy.

One or more cognitive modules may be priming our brains to evaluate large numbers of similar individuals as kinds sharing a common essence. The knowledge that cloning involves transmission of nuclear DNA provides a candidate for the essence that unites the group. The rich inductive potential of this faux kind encourages the observer to infer that members share common characteristics, including nonobvious ones such as intellect or personality. In short, the identity fallacy succeeds because it is in synch with a natural mental tendency. Biological science predicts the individuality of humans born through cloning, no matter how many there are, but psychological perception trumps biological reality.

Psychological essentialism also lies behind what the NBAC Report described as an "instinctive fear of multitudes of identical bodies, each housing personalities that are somehow less than distinct, less unique,

IDENTITY AND ESSENTIALISM

and less autonomous than usual."[145] Our brains may be wired to classify individual human beings, but they are not designed to view the individual as a kind in and of himself (or herself). The individual-to-kind metamorphosis involves a paradigm shift, and that makes it deeply unsettling. The resulting cognitive dissonance helps produce that pleasurable shiver down the back that sells movies, television, and popular nonfiction such as *Future Shock*. In real life, however, a technology that makes clone armies seem possible (even though they are not) is bound to cause the public to react with unwarranted shock and fear.

Of course, humans born through cloning need not be multitudinous. Cloning technology could be used to conceive only limited numbers of persons from a particular set of nuclear DNA. Indeed, as Chapter 3 discussed, experts have anticipated that the technology could be employed as a means of family building.

Even in this context, where a kinship model would predict some shared traits but not identity, government reports speculate that children could suffer due to distorted self-image and unreasonable parental expectations. Such concerns are not frivolous. Essentialist intuitions are very powerful, and the conceptualization of cloned humans as faux kinds with a shared genetic essence is widespread. Unfortunately, the reports do nothing to unmask the role of essentialism in the cloning debate, nor do they advocate the public education or counseling that could equip parents to raise healthy children in an informed and fair-minded society. Instead, they recommend cloning bans that would eliminate the issue by eliminating the children. Part III of this book will examine the challenges involved in employing legal prohibitions as the solution to problems that are informational and psychological in origin.

5 Artifacts and Essentialism

CHAPTER 4 APPLIED THE PSYCHOLOGICAL essentialism of living kinds, such as plants, animals, and human beings, to analyze a key fallacy in the cloning debate: the identity fallacy. This chapter takes up the artifact fallacy: that is, the false notion that cloning produces technological products rather than ordinary members of species.

This chapter begins by describing the psychological essentialism of artifacts – that is, nonliving, man-made objects. It contrasts the essentialist account of artifacts with the essentialist account of human beings, who qualify as a living kind. Next, this chapter shows how popular culture, media stories, and government reports have portrayed humans born through cloning as more product than human. Indeed, these accounts have presented humans born through cloning as products that can be designed to match the physical, intellectual, and psychological traits of a progenitor. Thus, these accounts also reflect the identity fallacy. Finally, this chapter explores the ways in which psychological essentialism promotes the artifact and identity fallacies with respect to humans born through cloning.

A. The Essentialist View of Artifacts

Recall the original formulation of psychological essentialism: humans conceptualize a category of things as if the category possesses some underlying, deep-rooted essence that causes the surface properties and similarities that things within the category have.[1] Does essentialism apply to artifacts? On this question, experts differ. Psychologist Paul Bloom argues persuasively that essentialism does apply to artifacts. In his view, the essence of an artifact is the intention of its creator.[2] Psychologists Deborah Kelemen and Susan Carey offer a slightly different take, arguing that humans adopt what they call a "design stance" in reasoning about artifacts.[3] This stance recognizes that a designer intentionally makes an artifact to serve a function. The intended function drives the surface properties, actual uses, and category or kind of the artifact.[4]

To illustrate this, consider an experiment in which research subjects were asked to categorize a newly created artifact according to either its original intended function or current use (by a person other than the creator). For example, subjects were asked to classify an object as either a teapot (as the creator intended) or a watering can (the use to which the object was put by another person).[5] Adults strongly favored original intended function,[6] and so did six-year-old children.[7]

Interestingly, Kelemen and Carey describe the original intended function as the essence of the artifact. However, they stop short of claiming that the design stance is a form of psychological essentialism.[8]

Susan Gelman agrees that a creator's intention serves as a nonobvious, underlying quality that determines the categorization of artifacts.[9] Yet, she finds some elements of essentialism do not apply to artifacts, at least not to the same extent as for living kinds and natural substances (natural kinds).[10] For example, Gelman notes that natural kinds are associated with clusters of nonobvious properties, but artifact kinds have much less inductive potential. In other words, the human mind draws fewer inferences about the underlying characteristics of artifact kinds.[11] This fact has been enough to convince some academics that artifact kinds are not a proper domain for essentialism.[12]

Gelman also cites further distinctions. The essence of a living or other natural kind is inherent, but that of an artifact kind relies on external factors (the creator and his intention).[13] Category boundaries tend

ARTIFACTS AND ESSENTIALISM 105

to be inflexible for living kinds – *i.e.*, an animal is or isn't a tiger – but boundaries expand to accommodate novel artifacts that look like one thing but serve another purpose.[14] Unlike living kinds, for which identity is stable despite growth and associated transformations, artifacts can switch categories when redesigned for new purposes.[15]

One final distinction is particularly significant for purposes of this book. Animals and plants reproduce and pass inborn traits down to their offspring. No such transmission occurs with artifacts.[16]

1. Why Do Humans Treat Intended Function as the Essence of Artifact Kinds?

As Chapter 4 explained, some academics believe that the essentialism of living kinds is an evolved cognitive module.[17] Although humans are a living kind, and artifacts are made by humans, some deem it unlikely that the essentialism of living kinds extends to artifacts.[18] As shown in this chapter, reasoning about living kinds and artifacts differs in significant ways. Neurological evidence backs up the distinction: different types of brain damage impair knowledge of animals or artifacts but not both; and neuroimaging scans have shown that words or images associated with living things produce different patterns of brain activation than words or images associated with artifacts.[19]

Could there be an evolved essentialism specific to artifacts? Evolutionary psychologist H. Clark Barrett doubts such a module would have been selected, given the limited inductive potential of artifact kinds.[20] Names and images of tools do produce a characteristic pattern of brain activation, suggesting that if there is an evolved system, it has more to do with identifying tools or weapons than artifact kinds in general.[21]

Kelemen and Carey argue that children are not born with the design stance, but begin to manifest it around the age of four to six years.[22] Although they do not see the design stance as an evolved module, these psychologists believe that innate cognitive elements underlie it. Specifically, even infants recognize physical properties that make artifacts good tools, and toddlers learn what an artifact does by watching the intentional acts of others.[23]

According to Kelemen and Carey, two other factors support emergence of the design stance. Children develop the capacity to distinguish kinds from mere assortments. Linguistic cues (such as common nouns and generic phrases) and conceptual cues (such as inductive potential) point them to kinds.[24] Moreover, children assume that kinds track the identity of items over time. This fosters an appreciation for the importance of origins.[25] However, it takes some time for children to synthesize all of these elements into a framework in which inferences about artifact properties and kind can be drawn from knowledge of a creator's intention.[26]

Gelman takes a somewhat different tack. As explained in Chapter 4, she believes evolved cognitive elements converge into a general essentialism that functions differently in various domains.[27] Although not all of these elements are involved in reasoning about artifacts, she acknowledges two that are. One is the ability to distinguish appearance from reality, which encourages one to look past the structure of an artifact to the underlying intent of its creator.[28] Another is the ability to track the identity of a thing over time, which relies on the notion that historical path (including origin) lies at the heart of identity.[29]

For purposes of this book, it is not necessary to resolve this academic debate over the origins of reasoning about artifacts. It is sufficient that adults and even children in the United States rely on the creator's intended function in determining the nature and characteristics of artifacts.[30]

B. How Are Human Beings Conceptualized Differently than Artifacts?

Human beings would seem to be the farthest thing possible from artifacts. Because we are animate, we are more similar to the animals and plants processed under the psychological essentialism of living kinds. Moreover, like other animals, we reproduce not through manufacture but through sexual intercourse. From a biological point of view, our offspring are human because they have a human genome; from an essentialist point of view, our offspring are human because they are born of human parents who transmitted a human essence to them.[31]

What, then, does it mean to have a human essence? Although there is no easy answer, a series of experiments from Australia sheds some light on this question. In 2004, social psychologist Nick Haslam and his colleagues asked adults to evaluate a large number of personality traits. The research subjects conceptualized some traits in essentialist terms. Specifically, they interpreted traits such as independence, intelligence, talkativeness, creativity, dominance, and imaginativeness as biologically based, discrete, immutable, consistent, informative (inductively potent), and inherent in the person.[32]

In 2005, Haslam and colleagues asked adults to rate personality traits as part of human nature (core or typical of humans) or as uniquely human (associated with humans but not animals).[33] The research subjects associated human nature with traits involving cognitive flexibility, emotional responsiveness, and warmth. In contrast, they deemed traits involving intelligence, openness, self-control, sociability, and morality uniquely human.[34] The subjects perceived traits associated with human nature as consistent, inherent, and inductively potent,[35] indicating that the mind comprehends human nature in an essentialist manner.[36]

In 2006, Haslam built on this work by theorizing two different modes of dehumanization. In one, a person denies to others traits that are human nature, such as emotional responsiveness, warmth, cognitive openness, individuality, and depth. This conceptualization implies that the dehumanized others are cold, inflexible, lacking in human agency (passive) and individuality (fungible), and superficial – in other words, more machine than human.[37] In the other mode, a person denies to others traits that are uniquely human, such as civility, refinement, morality, rationality, and maturity, construing them as uncultured, coarse, amoral, irrational, and childlike – in other words, more animal than human.[38]

Haslam speculates that slippage between cognitive domains could account for the two different kinds of dehumanization. For example, Scott Atran's theory that the mind transfers principles of folk biology into the social domain might account for the dehumanization of ethnic or other social groups as animallike. Slippage between the technological and social domains could lead to mechanistic dehumanization, in which individuals or social groups are interpreted as artifacts.[39] This theory will be featured in the next section, as it holds the potential to explain a great deal of the opposition to human cloning.

C. The Artifact Fallacy and Essentialism

With this background, the discussion now returns to cloning. Recall that the artifact fallacy paints cloned animals as faulty products, rather than typical members of their species. As explained in Chapter 1, this is incorrect. Cloned animals grow from babyhood to maturity like other animals do, and produce normal offspring. If born healthy, they generally stay that way. Vital signs, body chemistries, and behaviors fall within the usual range for their species.

Extrapolating from animal data, Chapter 3 argued that there is no scientific reason to anticipate that people born through cloning will be products. Instead, they will be human beings with the same basic physical, intellectual, psychological, and behavioral characteristics that all humans share. The fact that DNA must be selected for cloning will not change this conclusion; if animals born through cloning are unique individuals, humans born through cloning will be, too.

Unfortunately, popular culture and the media have presented humans born through cloning as manufactured products. Even government reports have raised concerns that rest on a false vision of human cloning as a manufacturing process. After documenting the existence of the artifact fallacy in the human cloning debate, this section will analyze its psychological underpinnings.

1. The Artifact Fallacy in Popular Culture

Many science fiction films and television episodes have portrayed humans (or humanoid aliens) born through cloning as identical copies of a genetic predecessor. Often these individuals are produced in large quantities, meaning that they are identical to each other also. Chapter 4 discussed *Star Wars II: Attack of the Clones* as a paradigmatic example of this identity fallacy. Bounty hunter Jango Fett is cloned not just once, but more than a million times, and the resulting soldiers are indistinguishable from each other in appearance and abilities.[40]

Such films and episodes do more than impugn the individuality of people born through cloning; they undermine their status as living beings. Since the Industrial Revolution, we have become accustomed to products that are mass-produced and fungible. Films and episodes evoke this manufacturing paradigm when they portray large numbers of bodies with the same appearance. The implicit message of these stories is that those born through cloning are akin to manufactured products, as per the artifact fallacy.

Many films and episodes shift people born through cloning from the realm of living kind to artifact. Table 2 provides a representative list.[41] Several common plot elements are employed to achieve this shift.

First, in a large number of stories, cloned bodies are grown in artificial wombs (vats, glass tubes, plastic sacks) or are made with the aid of machines.[42] This is contrary to biology: any human must be gestated inside the uterus of a woman for nine months and be born of that woman. However, such portrayals are consistent with a view of cloning as manufacture.

Second, cloning is occasionally portrayed as a means of creating a body without any personality of its own. For example, in *The Sixth Day*, manufactured bodies must have memories downloaded into them.[43] Similarly, in *Star Trek III: The Search for Spock*, a planet engineered to create life from inert matter spontaneously clones a new person from

Table 2. *Cloning Is Associated with Manufacture*

Movies

Movie Title	Distributor	Year	Type
2001: A Space Travesty	Columbia/TriStar	2000	A
Alien: Resurrection	Twentieth Century Fox	1997	A
The Clones	Filmmakers International	1973	A
The Clones of Bruce Lee	Newport Releasing	1977	A
Creator	Universal Pictures	1985	A
The Fifth Element	Columbia Pictures	1997	A
The Island	DreamWorks/Warner Brothers	2005	A
Judge Dredd	Hollywood Pictures	1995	A
Moon	Sony Pictures Classics	2009	A
Multiplicity	Columbia Pictures	1996	A
Replicant	Artisan Entertainment	2001	A
Replikator	Aurora Motion Pictures	1994	A
Repli-Kate	Twentieth Century Fox	2002	A
The Resurrection of Zachary Wheeler	Gold Key Entertainment Film Ventures	1971	A, B
The Sixth Day	Columbia Pictures	2000	A, B
Shadow Fury	Pathfinder Pictures	2001	C
Star Trek III: The Search for Spock	Paramount Pictures	1984	B
Star Wars II: Attack of the Clones	Twentieth Century Fox	2002	A, C
Xchange	Trimark Pictures	2000	A, B

Television Episodes/Series

TV Series	Episode	Distributor	Air Date	Type
Star Trek: Deep Space Nine	"A Man Alone"	Paramount Television	January 17, 1993	A
Star Trek Next Generation	"Up the Long Ladder"	Paramount Television	May 22, 1989	A
X-Files	"Herrenvolk"	Fox	October 4, 1996	C

A = Artificial gestation or creation; B = Bodies without personality; C = Lacking human traits

ARTIFACTS AND ESSENTIALISM

Mr. Spock's dead body.[44] This character quickly grows to adulthood but has the mind of a child. He shows no personality and is inarticulate. The movie ends with the mystical reinstallation of Spock's katra (soul) to create a complete person.[45]

Third, in some stories, cloning is used together with genetic engineering to eliminate traits that ordinary humans would be expected to have. For example, in *Star Wars II: Attack of the Clones*, the Kaminoans have altered the clone soldiers to follow orders and be less independent than their nuclear DNA donor, Jango Fett.[46] This lack of independence is the result of genetic engineering, rather than cloning as such. However, the film depicts hundreds or thousands of identical persons as they train, eat, and march in unison. These widely disseminated scenes teach that those born through cloning lack autonomy.

Not every movie or television series depicts cloned characters as objects or things. For example, in *The Island*, the cloned protagonist, Lincoln Six Echo, lives in a compound with others born through cloning. He discovers that he and his companions are destined to be killed for their organs. He escapes the compound, taking a female friend named Jordan Two Delta with him. The company hires an assassin to kill the two escapees before they can reveal the truth, and the chase is on.[47]

Throughout the movie, representatives of the company describe the cloned humans as products. The company brands numbers on their wrists, and initiates a recall (murder) of generations that exhibit abnormal neural activity such as Lincoln Six Echo's. When confronted with his misdeeds, the evil scientist who runs the cloning compound even describes the cloned humans as tools or instruments with no souls.[48]

However, the movie refutes these claims by portraying Lincoln Six Echo and Jordan Two Delta as human beings with emotions and distinct personalities. Indeed, when they return to the compound to save others from being destroyed, their courage and compassion makes them seem more human than their oppressors. However, the fact that the entire story is built around the need to establish the humanity of those born through cloning testifies to the power of the artifact fallacy.

2. The Artifact Fallacy in Media Accounts

Chapter 4 documented that media accounts have framed humans born through cloning as identical copies that can be produced in large numbers.[49] As noted above, any presentation that involves sameness and large quantities associates humans born through cloning with mass-produced and fungible objects.

Media visuals also depict humans born through cloning as artifacts. For example, they show cloned babies coming out of test tubes, laboratory beakers, or machines, rather than the womb of a human mother.[50] Or the visuals display images of identical dolls, marionettes, or other artifacts that only resemble human beings.[51]

3. The Artifact Fallacy in Government Reports

Chapter 4 introduced three government reports on human cloning: the 1997 report from President Bill Clinton's National Bioethics Advisory Commission[52] (NBAC Report); the 2002 report from President George W. Bush's President's Council on Bioethics[53] (Council Report); and the 2002 report from the California Advisory Committee on Human Cloning to the California State Legislature[54] (California Report). These reports are useful because they summarize objections to human reproductive cloning, including some that invoke the artifact fallacy.

a) Human Cloning is Unnatural

One common objection is that human cloning is unnatural because it involves asexual rather than sexual reproduction. The California Report notes that cloning is inconsistent with natural reproduction for mammals (which is ordinarily sexual), and warns that it could render males "reproductively obsolete."[55]

One response to this shift from sexual to asexual reproduction has been to deny that cloning involves reproduction at all. For example, law professors George Annas and Lori Andrews have framed cloning as a form of replication rather than reproduction and argued that constitutional guarantees of reproductive freedom do not apply, even for infertile men and women who have no other means of conceiving genetic offspring.[56]

Another response has been to worry that asexual reproduction via cloning will confuse family relationships.[57] For example, suppose an infertile man uses cloning to conceive a baby boy. If one accepts that human reproduction can be asexual, the baby is the man's son – a characterization that also suits his intention to raise the baby as his child. However, to observers accustomed to the existing paradigm of sexual reproduction, the baby may appear to be more of a twin brother, as the last male and female to procreate were the man's own parents. As the Council Report put it:

> The crucial point is not the *absence* of the natural biological connections between parents and children. The crucial point is, on the contrary, the *presence* of a unique, one-sided, and replicative biological connection to only one progenitor. As a result, family relations involving cloning would differ from all existing family arrangements, including those formed through adoption or with the aid of IVF ... these existing arrangements [adoption, artificial insemination, and IVF] attempt in important ways to emulate the model of the natural family (at least in its arrangement of the generations), while cloning runs contrary to that model.[58]

In other words, asexual reproduction through cloning challenges the sexual reproduction paradigm and its associated models of kinship. This is another way of saying that the technology is unnatural and leads to unnatural results.

That cloning is unnatural is a charge leveled against the technology. It does not address humans born through cloning or their characteristics. Nevertheless, by framing the technology as unnatural, objectors imply that those born through the technology must also be unnatural – that is, abnormal, strange, and artificial.[59] This unfair aspersion runs counter to the evidence presented in Chapter 1 indicating that animals born through cloning (and by extension, humans born through cloning) can be typical members of their species.

b) Human Cloning Is a Form of Manufacture

If those born through cloning are not ordinary members of the human species, what else could they be? The artifact fallacy predicts them to be flawed products. This forecast resonates with a concern featured prominently in the Bush-era Council Report. According to that concern:

> [Cloning involves] the transformation of human procreation into human manufacture, of begetting into making. By using the terms "making" and "manufacture" we are not claiming that cloned children would be artifacts made altogether "by hand" or produced in factories. Rather, we are suggesting that they would, like other human "products," be brought into being in accordance with some pre-selected genetic pattern or design, and therefore in some sense "made to order" by their producers or progenitors.[60]

This passage has two components. First, in describing what has gone before, the Council Report uses the old-fashioned terms "procreation" and "begetting," thereby harkening back to a bygone era when conception could occur only through sexual intercourse.[61] These terms, with their connotations of naturalness, draw an implied contrast with the technological unnaturalness of cloning. Second, the Council Report builds on the dichotomy by describing cloning as making or manufacture. In contrast to human beings conceived through procreation and begetting, those born through cloning are products that are made to order by producers. This rhetoric insinuates that cloning produces not human beings but things.[62]

Granted, the passage quoted above disclaims any intent to claim that humans born through cloning are artifacts made in factories.[63] Yet, in a later passage, the Council Report uses the rhetoric of objectification:

> The problem with cloning-to-produce-children is not that artificial technique is used to assist reproduction....The problem has to do

ARTIFACTS AND ESSENTIALISM

with the control of the entire genotype *and the production of children to selected specifications.*

Why does this matter? It matters because human dignity is at stake. In natural procreation, two individuals give life to a new human being whose endowments are not shaped deliberately by human will, whose being remains mysterious, and the open-endedness of whose future is ratified and embraced. Parents beget a child who enters the world exactly as they did – as an unmade gift, not as a product. Children born of this process stand equally beside their progenitors as fellow human beings, *not beneath them as made objects.*[64]

As if this were not enough, the Council Report frets that cloning – even on a small scale – could cause a market mentality to intrude into human reproduction and dehumanize all of us.[65]

The NBAC Report from the Clinton era does not present humans born through cloning as products, but voices the concern that those who select genes for cloning may treat the resulting children as if they were designer objects. In other words, it presents the fact that many people *believe* in the artifact fallacy as a reason to oppose reproductive cloning.[66] The California Report takes a similar position.[67]

There is no justification in biology for the concerns expressed in the Bush-era Council Report. As Chapters 2 and 3 explained, cloned humans, like cloned animals, will be unique individuals due to genetic, epigenetic, and environmental factors that will distinguish them from genetic predecessors. They can never be products made to order.[68]

As for the NBAC and California Reports, they are right to recognize that the artifact fallacy is powerful. Parents may indeed misunderstand what cloning can deliver and pressure a child to meet their expectations. However, as Chapter 4 discussed, counseling and informed consent can help educate parents and prevent such behavior. Bans will not do the trick; parents who have never been properly counseled will retain their unrealistic dreams and travel abroad or go underground to obtain cloning services. After children are born, the bans will not curb parental expectations but will inflict further damage by stigmatizing cloned children as unworthy of existence.

c) Humans Born Through Cloning Lack an Open Future

The flip side of the argument that parents might treat a cloned child as a product is that the child will view himself or herself as lacking in autonomy. According to this notion, which appears in all three government reports, knowledge of a single genetic predecessor will deprive the child of an open future.[69]

There is little biological basis for this argument. A cloned child cannot be a made-to-order product; therefore, his future will always be open. Genes do count for something, and the cloned child can expect to have some features or traits that echo those of his DNA donor. However, the same could be said of a child conceived through sexual reproduction. Genes link us to our parents in ways great and small. Yet, epigenetic variation, personal experiences, and societal influences allow us to transcend those links and forge our own destinies. The cloned child will do the same.

Still, some worry that the child will believe in the artifact fallacy and feel constrained by everything the predecessor is or does.[70] That seems unlikely. Physical and personality differences between a cloned child and DNA donor should be obvious from the beginning and increase as time passes. It is far more likely that a cloned child would react to the verifiable facts of her own existence and rebel against parental or societal expectations (just as all children and adolescents do). As suggested in Chapter 4, if the child does need psychological support, counseling can provide that.

To be sure, living in a society that believes in the artifact fallacy may pose challenges for a cloned child. He will grow up fighting unfair stereotypes and may face discrimination. However, the same is true of a child born into a society that discriminates against his racial or ethnic group. No government report would dare recommend that racial or ethnic minorities stop reproducing because their children might suffer discrimination. Similarly, no government report should recommend legislating cloned children out of existence; that is blaming the victim. Rather, the reports should demand public education that is designed to dispel the artifact fallacy and the stereotypes it produces. In addition, if governments are truly concerned about the prospect of discrimination, they should amend antidiscrimination laws to add humans born through cloning as a protected class.

To summarize the foregoing analysis, government reports sometimes use rhetoric that comes close to the artifact fallacy. Other times, the reports concede the falsity of the artifact fallacy but assume others will act on it to the detriment of cloned children. This assumption then becomes one more reason to ban reproductive cloning.

Perhaps the experts behind the reports are conflicted. Intellectually, they realize that cloned children will be human beings rather than designer products. Yet, at a subconscious level, they may find the artifact fallacy plausible. That would explain why they are so ready to assume the worst of parents and children and conclude that cloning bans are the solution. This willingness to assume the worst invites a deeper analysis. Accordingly, this chapter turns to examining the psychological roots of the artifact fallacy.

4. Using Psychological Essentialism to Make Sense of the Artifact Fallacy

Stories, images, and arguments that present humans born through cloning as made-to-order products assume the power of nuclear DNA to determine the identity and even the future of a person. To this extent, these accounts are consistent with genetic determinism.[71] At the same time, however, the fact that a cloned person will possess a human genome doesn't count for as much as one would expect. Too often, humans born through cloning are conceptualized as things.

This contradiction is puzzling. Assuming that the human brain is wired to view the world through an essentialist lens, why does it not conceptualize humans born through cloning in the same manner as other human beings, who comprise a special type of living kind?

a) Asexual Reproduction
Finnish scholar Jussi Niemela has noted that in folk biology (and the essentialism that is part of folk biology), sexual reproduction is central to transmission of essence and resulting membership in a living kind.[72] Cats mate and create kittens; dogs mate and create puppies; and so on. Folk biology does not accommodate cloning, which requires only one parent to contribute DNA, rather than the standard two.[73] Therein lies the root of the artifact fallacy as applied to cloned animals.

The media, policymakers, and even some scientists have questioned whether cloned animals can be normal members of their species. Some critics may have genuine concerns about the efficiency and safety of cloning technology. However, as Chapter 1 explained, such concerns are often stated in extreme terms, and good news about the health and function of cloned animals is overlooked or downplayed. This biased portrayal suggests that cognitive psychology is playing a role in the cloning debate. If a person intuits that a cloned animal lacks the essence of its kind, he will not expect that animal to have the usual traits of its kind. Experiments and reports indicating that cloned animals can be typical members of their species may be good biology, but are cognitively dissonant.

Let's extend this reasoning to human beings. Here is what folk biology and essentialism presume: one man and one woman procreate together and beget a human child. Human cloning doesn't fit this model. Cloning makes it possible for women to conceive, carry, and birth daughters who have no biological fathers. It also makes it possible for men to conceive sons who have no biological mothers other than egg donors or surrogates. Science fiction films exaggerate this latter point by imagining that cloning involves artificial wombs, so that those conceived through cloning are not even born of a woman. These elements – reproduction without sex, children with one parent, and artificial

ARTIFACTS AND ESSENTIALISM 119

wombs (which are not real but commonly associated with cloning) – are cognitively dissonant. They may trigger a strong subconscious belief that cloned humans lack human essence and the traits that go along with it.[74] This belief opens the door to an alternative account in which cloned humans can be reassigned from the domain of living kinds into another domain.

b) Manufactured Products

Two factors appear to have shifted humans born through cloning into the artifact domain. One is that scientists select nuclear DNA for cloning and carry out the procedure in a laboratory, which is akin to a factory.[75] The other is that monozygotic twins and higher-order multiples are born at the same time and often resemble each other physically. Thus, people who know that monozygotic multiples share the same nuclear DNA are encouraged to visualize humans born through cloning as age-matched replicates of their DNA donors and each other (if more than one person is conceived using the same DNA). Taken together, these factors may prompt the mind to analogize humans born through cloning to fungible manufactured products.

As explained in the preceding sections, available data from popular culture, the media, and government reports indicates that all too many people are drawing just such an analogy. Films and television episodes show identical bodies decanted from artificial wombs or generated via machines. Media stories not only portray humans born through cloning as identical and numerous, but sometimes illustrate the concept through images of manikins or dolls rather than human beings. Government reports theorize that cloning is wrong because it involves a switch from procreation to manufacture of a designer product – or because the public will perceive it that way.

Stories, images, and rhetoric that shift humans born through cloning from living kinds into the artifact domain may seem harmless. In fact, they are anything but. Based on what we know about the essentialism of artifacts (or the design stance, for those who prefer that theory), it is dangerous to encourage the public to indulge such intuitions. Humans born through cloning could be misunderstood – and possibly mistreated – in four distinct ways.

First, as this chapter has discussed, people believe that a creator's intention determines the properties of an artifact. In the context of cloning, this translates to a belief that a scientist who selects nuclear DNA can determine the physical, intellectual, and personality traits of a cloned human. As indicated in Chapter 4, popular culture, media accounts, and even policy reports have succumbed to this false vision of human copies lacking in individuality. In other words, the essentialism of artifacts contributes to the identity fallacy.

To illustrate, consider a popular film from the 1970s: *The Boys from Brazil*.[76] In this film, the sadistic Nazi doctor Dr. Josef Mengele flees to South America. There he founds a clandestine laboratory and clones from the DNA of Adolf Hitler ninety-four times. With the aid of other Nazis, Mengele adopts the babies out to parents around the world who have the same traits as Hitler's parents, all in an effort to duplicate the dictator's dysfunctional upbringing and recreate Hitler.[77] In essentialist terms, Mengele is the creator. The movie shows that he succeeds in determining the traits, talents, and personality of the young boys, who are uniform in their appearance and cold contempt for others. This fictional portrayal bears little resemblance to the biological reality of cloning, as discussed in Chapters 2 and 3, but the essentialism of artifacts makes it intuitively plausible.

Second, essentialism teaches that the creator's intention determines the use of an artifact. Thus, if a donor of nuclear DNA has a particular occupation or role in society, essentialism could trigger the intuition that a person cloned from that DNA will perform the same occupation or role. Evidence of this intuition appears in government reports that buy into the argument that a human born through cloning will feel constrained to follow in his donor's footsteps and lack an open future.[78] The reports twist this intuition into an argument that humans born through cloning should not exist because they will suffer.

Popular culture provides additional examples of the expectation that a cloned person will function consistently with the intention of his creator. In *The Boys from Brazil*, Mengele's aim is to make a dictator who can lead a reconstituted Third Reich.[79] Although the boys in the story are too young to have become dictators, their contempt for other human beings suits their intended occupation. Moreover, at least one of the boys is murderous: after Dr. Mengele shoots his father, the boy orders his Doberman Pinschers to kill Mengele.[80] This movie illustrates how essentialist intuitions can lead to the conclusion that cloned humans are dangerous. If their creators have evil intentions, they will do evil things.

In another science fiction film, *Anna to the Infinite Power*, a company clones several girls from a scientist named Anna Zimmerman who died just as she was about to invent a profitable food replicator.[81] One of these girls, Anna Hart, is the protagonist of the story. She is born to a family selected for its potential to match the home environment of the deceased inventor, and her mother pushes her to study science and math so that she will be qualified to complete the food replicator. Anna Hart has a nearly robotic personality. She is cold and disagreeable and focused only on science, just as her mother and the company wish her to be. Michaela Dupont, a woman cloned from Anna Zimmerman at an earlier time, attempts to awaken the girl's humanity by teaching her to play the piano with emotion, but Anna Hart struggles to forge her own identity and destiny apart from her parents and the company.[82] This portrayal of a stunted personality is consistent with concerns that humans born through cloning will lack an open future.

Third, according to Nick Haslam, the shift from the social to the artifact domain encourages mechanistic dehumanization.[83] His theory predicts that people will deny human nature to humans born through cloning, perceiving them as inert, cold, inflexible, fungible, passive, and superficial.[84] Science fiction supports this prediction. As indicated in Table 1 (see Chapter 4), many films and television episodes portray characters who are cloned as copies – in other words, as fungible. As shown in Table 2, other films and episodes present cloned bodies devoid of personality – in other words, as inert, cold, and superficial. Essence must be added (in the form of memories or a soul) to humanize them. Finally, Table 2 lists stories that depict characters who are cloned as obedient soldiers or drones – in other words, as passive.

Fourth, if Haslam is correct, once humans born through cloning are dehumanized in this mechanistic fashion, they should evoke indifference from others, as objects do.[85] That would be unfair enough. However, those born through cloning may also inspire stronger negative feelings.

Jussi Niemela has noted that cloning does not fit the usual folk-biological paradigm in which sexual reproduction and birth transmit the essence of living kinds to offspring. This creates the illusion that a person born through cloning lacks a human essence, leading to emotions such as fear and disgust.[86] Unfortunately, there are those who exploit such feelings. Leon Kass, the former chairman of the President's Council on Bioethics, has written a well-known essay opining that the repugnance people feel when contemplating human cloning reflects deep wisdom.[87] His objective may be to attack cloning as a technology, but his rhetoric encourages people to believe that humans born through cloning are also disgusting.

D. Summary

As Chapter 3 explained, if reproductive cloning can be made safe and effective, humans will be born through cloning. These people will be normal members of their species, just as animals born through cloning are. They will not be made-to-order products with their destinies engraved in stone. Rather, genetic, epigenetic, and environmental factors will ensure that humans born through cloning are autonomous individuals.

Nevertheless, the artifact fallacy is widespread in popular culture, media accounts, and government reports on human cloning. Its roots can be traced to psychological essentialism. This cognitive heuristic may be useful as a means of assessing animals or things that fall within traditional folk-biological or artifact paradigms, but it leads to terrible

ARTIFACTS AND ESSENTIALISM 123

misapprehensions when applied to the twenty-first century technology of cloning. Humans born through cloning are shifted from the domain of living kinds into the domain of artifacts, thereby prompting false intuitions regarding their fundamental character and traits. The essentialism of artifacts also contributes to the identity fallacy, by encouraging us to believe that humans born through cloning will conform to whatever their creators intended when selecting their nuclear DNA.

Unfortunately, some have embraced the artifact fallacy, restating it in various forms. For example, government reports sometimes comment on the unnaturalness of cloning, or proclaim that human procreation should never become human manufacture. As Jussi Niemela has suggested, those who make such arguments are either reacting to their own essentialist intuitions, or employing rhetoric in an effort to manipulate the intuitions of their audiences.[88]

Other times, government reports argue that cloning is bad because parents and others will treat cloned children as if they were products. This approach genuflects to the power of essentialism without ever acknowledging the role that essentialism plays in fostering the artifact fallacy. It is disappointing that experts assigned to help forge public policy would blame the victim rather than prescribe public education, counseling, informed consent, and antidiscrimination laws. Cloning bans hold the potential to damage children more seriously, as explained in Part III.

6 Impostors and Essentialism

THIS CHAPTER ADDRESSES ANOTHER misconception regarding human cloning: the impostor fallacy. The impostor fallacy occurs in two versions, one extreme and one subtle. The extreme version is commonly found in science fiction films and television episodes. In these stories, a person born through cloning is a dangerous doppelganger who impersonates the DNA donor in order to steal his assets, job, spouse or partner, and life. The subtle version of the impostor fallacy occurs in media and government reports on human cloning. In these reports, a person born through cloning poses a different kind of threat to his or her DNA donor: the copy takes away some measure of the individuality and uniqueness of the original.

In theory, human cloning could be accomplished with DNA extracted from a single cell. This fact raises concerns that cloning could be done after culling a stray skin cell or other DNA sample from a non-consenting donor. Thus, unlike the identity and artifact fallacies, which have led primarily to discussions of the harms cloning might inflict upon humans born through cloning, the impostor fallacy focuses on the supposed menace that cloning poses to you and me. Fear is a significant factor motivating opposition to human cloning. It is important to test whether the threat is real and break the power of any illusions.

Toward that end, this chapter first describes how psychological essentialism drives common intuitions about individual identity. Next, it addresses the impostor fallacy in popular culture. It explains that essentialism makes cloned impostors seem plausible, but that biology teaches otherwise. The chapter then analyzes the impostor fallacy in media and government reports. It explains why cloning cannot diminish individuality and exposes the essentialist roots of such arguments. Finally, the chapter concludes with a look at how essentialist intuitions about individual identity may also promote the identity fallacy.

A. Psychological Essentialism and the Individual

Chapter 4 discussed the basics of essentialism. As recounted there, essentialism is a heuristic that helps us make quick but effective judgments about the members of a natural kind or social group. In its classical formulation, essentialism is about kinds and not the individual. However, Professor Susan Gelman has written a book on psychological essentialism[1] in which she presents experimental and anecdotal evidence indicating that people also hold essentialist intuitions about the individual. This section reviews and builds upon her work.

1. Historical Path and the Essence of the Individual

Essentialism relies on a *placeholder* – that is, an open place that the mind can fill with various beliefs about what the essence is.[2] Gelman proposes that the *historical path* of an individual may serve as a kind of nonobvious, causal essence that prevails over outward appearance and determines identity.[3] Several pieces of evidence support this proposal.

First, as Gelman notes, practices associated with naming demonstrate the role of historical continuity in conceptualizing the individual. The name that parents assign to a baby at birth remains constant throughout the lifetime of that individual, no matter how much her outward appearance might change due to growth or other factors.[4]

Second, Gelman cites an experiment in which researchers asked college students to evaluate the identity of a person based on descriptions that paired phenotypic traits with personal history. In some of these descriptions, the phenotypic traits were accurate but the personal history was not.[5] For example, students were asked to decide whether a man with the following characteristics could be John F. Kennedy: a youthful and handsome charismatic leader with a Boston accent who was once prime minister of Great Britain. In such cases, students agreed that the name matched the description only 3.5 percent of the time.[6] That is, for this type of pairing, history trumped outward appearance.[7]

This experiment is particularly relevant to impostors. Appearance and behavior can be faked. Thus, the descriptions pairing accurate phenotype with inaccurate history could be representations of look-alike impostors; the refusal of the research subjects to acknowledge the impostors as real could reflect not only the primacy of historical path in identity judgments, but its utility in unmasking impostors.

Third, an experiment conducted after Gelman published her book provides additional evidence for historical path as essence. Working with two identical stuffed toys (*e.g.*, two Winnie-the-Pooh bears), researchers acted out a scenario in which the first toy saw a drawing but the second one did not. Researchers then asked their subjects whether the second toy knew what was in the drawing. Preschoolers and adults alike responded that the second toy did not know what was in the drawing. The researchers took this to mean that both the children and the adults based identity judgments on historical path rather than name or appearance.[8]

Given the focus of this chapter on impostors, the inspiration for the Winnie-the-Pooh experiment is particularly interesting. The researchers had noticed that people often use historical path to evaluate the identity of an individual. For example, in many fairy tales, books, and movies, the hero must prove his identity by recounting past events in his own life.[9]

2. Body Parts and the Essence of the Individual

In her book, Susan Gelman also presents anecdotal evidence of essentialist reactions to organ transplants. She relates the story of Claire Sylvia, a woman suffering from primary pulmonary hypertension. Sylvia received the transplanted heart and lungs of a young man and later wrote a book about her experiences.[10] Here I present some more detailed information from Sylvia's book.

After the transplant, Sylvia believed she could feel the presence of her donor, an eighteen-year-old man who had died in a motorcycle accident.[11] She began to experience cravings for foods that had never been her favorites, such as chicken nuggets, green peppers, candy, and beer.[12] She had much more energy than before and seldom caught colds or other viruses.[13] She also had an increased libido, felt less sensitive, and favored colors she considered masculine, such as green and blue.[14] Three years after the transplant, Sylvia located and visited the family of her donor. They told her he had been a high-energy, healthy person who loved beer, green peppers, and chicken nuggets.[15]

Which of Claire Sylvia's changes can be accounted for biologically? The DNA in the cells of the transplanted heart and lungs would have continued to affect the function of those organs inside her body. If the organs were young and efficient, she would have received more oxygen and had more energy than she did when she was sick. Her immune function and libido might also have improved along with her overall health. Moreover, these biological changes might have triggered psychological changes. For example, if she associated energy and physical strength with masculinity, as many people do, she might subconsciously have felt more masculine and been drawn to "masculine" colors or other traits that she associated with maleness.

Claire Sylvia also had to take powerful antirejection drugs after the transplant. These drugs could have had side effects that affected her body chemistry and emotions.[16] Whether the drugs caused her craving for chicken nuggets (protein and fat), green peppers (hydration), candy (sugar), and beer (alcohol) is unknown. However, with the exception of the green peppers, the items on this list are popular with most people. Such common cravings do not prove a connection with the spirit or essence of her donor, even if Sylvia and the donor's family interpreted them that way.[17]

Claire Sylvia's book also includes stories from other transplant recipients. Those who received new hearts experienced them as "others" with whom they argued or negotiated. Many felt as if they were inhabited by the donor's spirit or life force. Others underwent changes in personality, favorite foods, or activities.[18] Some felt they had acquired the donor's memories. One had an overpowering feeling of déjà vu in an unfamiliar church; another had a vision of how his donor died (before the facts of that event were reported); and yet another was bothered by the clicking of windshield wipers (the last sound before a car crash that killed the donor).[19]

What can account for such beliefs? Gelman argues persuasively that the experiences of transplant recipients are consistent with psychological essentialism. The recipients construe the donor's essence as internal (residing inside the donor and then the recipient) and nonvisible. The essence persists through change (the transfer of the organ from one body to another) and is causal (affecting behavior and tastes). It can be experienced as material (residing in a body part) or immaterial (a spirit).[20] This essentialist interpretation renders the experiences of transplant recipients psychologically coherent, even if the experiences have no basis in biology.

It is worth noting that many of the transplant recipients discussed in Claire Sylvia's book behaved as if the donor's life story had been transferred along with the organ, causing them to manifest the donor's personality, acquired tastes, and memories. In other words, they acted as if the donor's historical path was embedded in his body and capable of persisting in a severed organ.

Formal experiments yield similar results. In a 2004 study from Israel, approximately one out of three heart transplant recipients directly acknowledged that they had considered the possibility that donor characteristics might be transferred to them through the heart.[21] The researchers also found indirect evidence of such fantasies: asked what donor they would prefer if physiological functions were equal, nearly half of the recipients exhibited a religious, racial, or gender preference that reflected their beliefs or prejudices. For example, most of the men in the study rejected a female heart, on the ground that it might be physically incompatible or cause them to take on stereotypically female traits such as sensitivity.[22]

Based on their findings, the Israeli researchers concluded that the recipients experienced their transplants in two different ways. Intellectually, they understood that the heart was only a pump. However, they also indulged magical thinking in which the heart conferred donor traits.[23] In other words, essentialism placed their intuitions at odds with their reason.

3. The Origin of Essentialist Intuitions about the Individual

Chapter 4 discussed the origins of psychological essentialism. Some academics theorize that the heuristic evolved as a means of assessing natural kinds or social groups. Others believe it originated in culture and language. Such category-based theories leave little room for essentialist intuitions about the individual. However, Susan Gelman has a different notion of what essentialism is all about. In her view, several independently evolved cognitive predispositions work together to produce a flexible heuristic that functions differently in different domains.[24]

Two of these cognitive predispositions may promote essentialist intuitions about the individual. First, humans can distinguish outer appearance from inner reality.[25] This ability makes it possible to believe that each person harbors a unique essence that persists despite change – even change as drastic as transfer of an organ to another body. Second, we can track the identity of an individual person or thing over time.[26] This ability rests not only on the appearance/reality distinction, but also on the insight that historical path lies at the core of identity.[27] Experience in tracking specific men and women may foster the belief that the historical path of the individual is a unique essence capable of distinguishing

IMPOSTERS AND ESSENTIALISM   131

him or her from all others, including those of similar appearance such as impostors.

B. Popular Culture and Essentialism

The next challenge is to take this information on the essentialism of the individual and use it to make sense of the impostor fallacy as it applies to humans born through cloning. This section addresses an extreme version of the fallacy that appears in science fiction films and television episodes.

1. The Impostor Fallacy in Popular Culture

Science fiction plots often revolve around the idea that cloning is capable of creating an impersonator who is visually indistinguishable from the DNA donor.[28] A variation on this theme involves the use of cloning to create look-alike multiples who impersonate each other.[29]

Table 3 provides a representative list of films and television episodes that rely on the clone-as-impostor plot device.[30] At a minimum, the characters cloned in these stories look like their victims. Often they also share the memories of their victims up until the point when the cloning occurred – either because they were born with those memories[31] or because their creators implanted the memories after their bodies were cloned.[32] However, the personalities of those cloned often differ from those of their genetic predecessors.[33] Many are evil or have a nefarious agenda, as the act of impersonation implies.[34]

Cloned impostors exploit the confusion of others who encounter them. They steal the assets,[35] jobs,[36] and spouses/partners[37] of their DNA donors or others cloned from the same DNA. Sometimes the theft is comical, as when the protagonist in *Multiplicity* finds that all three of the men he cloned from himself have had sex with his wife.[38] More often, it is frightening, as when the protagonist in *The Clones* finds that his doppelganger has taken all he has.[39] Occasionally, life itself is stolen,

Table 3. *Cloning Is Used to Create Impostors*

Movies

Movie Title	Distributor	Year
2001: A Space Travesty	Columbia/TriStar	2000
The Clones	Filmmakers International	1973
The Island	DreamWorks/Warner Brothers	2005
Invasion of the Body Snatchers	United Artists	1978
Moon	Sony Pictures Classics	2009
Multiplicity	Columbia Pictures	1996
Replikator	Aurora Motion Pictures	1994
Repli-Kate	Twentieth Century Fox	2002
The Sixth Day	Columbia Pictures	2000
The Third Twin	CBS Broadcasting, Inc.	1997

Television Episodes/Series

TV Series	Episode	Distributor	Air date
Eureka	"Many Happy Returns"	The Sci Fi Channel	July 25, 2006
Star Trek: Deep Space Nine	"A Man Alone"	Paramount Television	January 17, 1993
Star Trek Next Generation	"Rightful Heir"	Paramount Television	May 17, 1993
X-Files	"Colony"	Fox	February 10, 1995
X-Files	"End Game"	Fox	February 17, 1995

as when the alien pods in the 1978 remake of *The Invasion of the Body Snatchers* kill their victims while cloning them.[40]

One recent film illustrates these points, but with a twist. The protagonist of *The Island* is Lincoln Six Echo, a cloned man who emerged full-grown from an artificial womb. After he discovers the company that created him harvests organs from cloned persons, he escapes from the compound, taking his friend Jordan Two Delta with him. The two search for their DNA donors in the hopes of revealing the company's crimes to the world.[41]

IMPOSTERS AND ESSENTIALISM   133

The company sends assassins to kill the escapees. While evading the assassins, Lincoln Six Echo flies a futuristic motor scooter even though he is unfamiliar with such vehicles. His surprising facility is explained when he meets his DNA donor. Tom Lincoln designs and owns speed vehicles of all kinds, including a boat that Lincoln Six Echo remembers although he's never seen it before. Tom is also nearly identical in appearance to Lincoln Six Echo.[42]

There, however, the resemblance ends. Tom Lincoln is self-centered and dissolute. He contracted hepatitis from promiscuous sexual activity and is willing to kill for the new liver he needs. He agrees to help Lincoln Six Echo and Jordan Two Delta, but then notifies the company of their location so the assassins can hunt them down.[43] When Lincoln Six Echo realizes that he has been betrayed, he impersonates Tom Lincoln. He slaps his identity bracelet from the compound onto Tom's wrist, and that fools an assassin into killing the donor rather than him. At the end of the movie, Lincoln Six Echo and Jordan Two Delta are shown cruising down the coast in the boat that Tom designed and once owned.[44]

The plot twist in *The Island* is that the cloned man is good and the donor evil, rather than the other way around. The film still suggests, however, that cloned impersonators are capable of destroying their donors and seizing their possessions. That message makes humans born through cloning appear dangerous in the extreme.

2. Making Sense of the Impostor Fallacy in Popular Culture

Upon closer examination, one finds that these stories about cloned impostors are designed to exploit essentialist intuitions. The stories also build upon the audience's familiarity with monozygotic multiples. However, the stories fail to acknowledge the significant differences that exist between monozygotic multiples and humans born through cloning.

a) Historical Path and Severed Body Parts
As noted in Chapter 4, fictional stories are designed to push our psychological buttons in a pleasurable way.[45] Stories about cloned impostors

are a good example. As the impostor tricks his victims, suspense builds; by the end, the victims usually succeed in distinguishing the cloned person from the donor through the use of historical path. This revelation relieves the dramatic or comedic tension.

For example, in the comedy *Repli-Kate*, the protagonist accidentally clones an adult woman from the blood of a beautiful journalist. The two women look identical, leading to mix-ups. The protagonist identifies the cloned impostor based on her historical path: she is only a few days old and cannot name the capital of the United States.[46]

However, historical path is not an infallible means of determining identity, for a couple of reasons. First, historical path is not self-evident. It must be uncovered through diligent investigation, such as interrogation of the impostor or careful observation of his behavior. Any error committed during the course of that investigation may let the impostor get away with his scheme. Second, historical path can be faked. Impostors can rehearse answers to likely questions, dress like their victims, or deliberately exhibit behaviors associated with their victims.

The weaknesses of historical path as a means of discerning identity only increase its value to storytellers. The easier it is for the victims of an impostor to make mistakes about historical path, the easier it is for writers to introduce plot elements that escalate the suspense for their audience. If the truth might not be learned until it is too late, writers can pen stories with dark outcomes – as when Lincoln Six Echo uses his identification bracelet (a relic of his historical path) to fool the assassin into killing his donor.[47]

When it comes to human cloning, essentialist intuitions create an opportunity to ratchet up the suspense yet another notch. As discussed previously, recipients of transplanted organs have reported manifesting the personality traits, acquired tastes, and memories of the deceased donor. These accounts imply belief in a unique essence that permeates the body of the donor[48] and persists even in severed parts or organs. The essence incorporates historical path, as it carries traits, tastes, and memories that are rooted in life events. Potentially, this essence could inhere in even tinier segments of the body, such as a single cell.

Now, consider reproductive cloning. From a biological point of view, a researcher harvests a somatic cell from a donor and fuses it to an egg. Once activated, the egg incorporates the nuclear DNA of the cell and develops into an embryo and ultimately an entire cloned organism. From a psychological point of view, a researcher takes a body part that, no matter how tiny, bears the unique essence of a donor. The researcher then transfers that essence into an egg, and watches as the resulting embryo transmits that essence throughout a developing organism. In this manner, the cloned organism acquires the historical path of the donor.

If a cloned impostor has the same historical path as his donor, investigations of his true origins are more likely to fail. The impostor has no need to learn the answers to likely questions; the memories are already in place. He has no need to mimic acquired tastes or behaviors; he naturally exhibits them. In short, essentialist intuitions encourage audiences to believe that cloned impostors, by their very nature, are particularly hard to detect and thus especially dangerous.

From this skewed perspective, victims have only one hope: after the cloned impostor is born as an adult, his historical path will diverge from that of the donor, creating an opportunity to detect the impostor. *2001: A Space Travesty* illustrates the point: an adult cloned from Bill Clinton fails to impersonate the president because he cannot play a saxophone tune that the real Clinton learned after the impostor was created.[49]

b) Monozygotic Multiples

Essentialism is not the only factor that makes these impostor stories credible. As Chapter 4 explained, the public has seen monozygotic twins and higher-order multiples and is used to same-age look-alikes. The public has also been exposed to many tales in which twins impersonate each other, deliberately or by accident. These stories are often exaggerated for dramatic or comedic effect. Suspense builds as those who encounter the look-alikes struggle to make sense of the situation. Tension is relieved when the twins are correctly identified.

A classic example is *The Parent Trap*.[50] The parents of monozygotic twins divorce, each taking custody of one of the babies. Years later, the eleven-year-old twins attend the same summer camp. Lindsay Lohan plays both: a tomboy from Napa, California, and a proper young lady from London, England. At first, the girls don't get along; a friend of the American girl even refers to the British girl as an evil clone. Hostility turns to friendship when the girls realize they are twins. They decide to swap places and impersonate each other in a plot to reunite their mother and father. Despite efforts to learn all about each other's lives, each girl gives herself away in subtle ways, like using words common in one country but not the other. In other words, historical path trips them up. Even after the truth comes out, the mischievous twins drive off their father's fiancée and bring their parents back together.[51]

Big Business, a film from the 1980s, presents a variation on this theme.[52] A rich New Yorker passing through West Virginia gives birth to monozygotic girl twins on the same night and in the same hospital where a local woman is also birthing monozygotic girl twins. A befuddled nurse swaps the babies, creating what appear to be fraternal twin pairs. One of these faux fraternal twin pairs returns to New York; the other remains in West Virginia.[53]

The film picks up four decades later. The New Yorkers (Bette Midler and Lily Tomlin) run a powerful corporation and plan to sell an unprofitable company in West Virginia. The West Virginians (also Midler and Tomlin) want to save the company so they travel to New York City to oppose the sale. This plot device places both monozygotic twin pairs in the same location. Identical appearances lead to confusion for the twins and their associates. When all four women finally encounter each other, one of the New Yorkers (Midler) exclaims that the West Virginians must be clones, causing the other New Yorker (Tomlin) to question whether the West Virginians are real (as per the artifact fallacy). After the truth is revealed, two of the women persuade the big corporation to keep the local company.[54]

In the end, the Midler twin who should have been a New Yorker all along stays in the city with the ex-husband of her monozygotic twin. Meanwhile, the Tomlin twin who should have been a West Virginian all along accepts the marriage proposal of her monozygotic twin's boyfriend and plans to return to the countryside where she belongs.[55] Thus, the movie sends the message that genes are a more powerful influence upon behavior and lifestyle than upbringing.

Young twins can look alike; thus, it is not unreasonable to have Lindsay Lohan play both twins in *The Parent Trap*. However, studies show that as twins grow older, their appearances diverge.[56] Repetitive expressions (such as smiling or frowning a lot) can alter muscle structure; weight can be gained in the face and elsewhere; hair styles can be changed; and so on.[57] Having Bette Midler or Lily Tomlin play both members of a middle-aged twin pair makes *Big Business* work as a comedy, but is not true to life. If real twins played these roles, the audience would probably not believe that anyone dealing with them could have been misled.

Modern technologies further reduce the risk of twin impostors when it comes to serious matters such as access to valuables, trade secrets, public authority, and the like. Authentication systems can reliably distinguish monozygotic twins from each other based on biometrics, such as fingerprints, irises, and palm prints.[58] These systems work because the environmental factors that a fetus experiences during gestation shape the biometrics.[59]

Nevertheless, the fact remains that many people have been fooled or confused when dealing with the members of a twin pair, whether in real life or when watching movies like *The Parent Trap*. Most people also know that twins owe their similar appearances to their common DNA. Fewer people are familiar with the details of cloning technology; but the one thing everyone seems to know is that cloning involves a transfer of a cell and its DNA from one person to another. This knowledge may encourage viewers to compare humans born through cloning to twins and accept stories that present humans born through cloning as identical persons of the same age. What people seem not to realize is that there are significant biological distinctions between monozygotic twins and humans born through cloning. These distinctions will make humans born through cloning less effective impersonators than twins.

As explained in Chapter 1, cloned animals are born as babies and mature at the usual rate for their species.[60] Likewise, cloned humans will be born as babies and mature over a period of many years. This would be true even if artificial wombs existed (and they do not). Thus, a human born through cloning will not share the chronological age or developmental stage of the person who donated the DNA for the cloning. Moreover, genetic, epigenetic, and environmental influences will cause humans born through cloning to diverge from their donors even after they are grown.[61] Based on animal cloning experiments, we can expect differences in height and weight, and possibly in hair and eye color also.[62]

These scientific facts mean that the deviation in historical path between a donor and a person cloned from him will be immediately observable in their differing bodies. As a result, a cloned impostor can be detected without the need for probing questions or careful observations. There is no chance that the impostor can impersonate the donor successfully. Therefore, we need not fear that humans born through cloning can steal the identities of existing persons.

It is possible that multiple individuals could be cloned from a single donor and born at the same time. Still, if one of these individuals tried to impersonate another, he would be unlikely to succeed. Although matched in age, these individuals would still diverge from each other more than monozygotic multiples do, for two reasons. First, all cells within the body of a donor are not necessarily the same. Cells can harbor genetic or epigenetic variations. Because each individual would be cloned with the aid of a unique donor cell, the members of the group could exhibit differences in appearance, personality, and other traits. Second, each individual would have his own gestational mother. Differences in gestational environment and postnatal influences could cause members of the group to display additional variations in gene expression and phenotype.

Finally, even in those rare cases where several persons cloned from a single donor did appear similar to the naked eye, impersonations would be unlikely to succeed for long. Biometric systems based on fingerprints, irises, palm prints, and the like should be at least as effective in identifying humans born through cloning as they are in distinguishing monozygotic twins.

In sum, humans born through cloning are unlikely to succeed in impersonating anyone, let alone in stealing assets, jobs, and spouses. Nevertheless, essentialist intuitions and experience with monozygotic multiples make science fiction accounts of cloned impostors psychologically plausible.

C. Media Accounts, Government Reports, and Essentialism

Up to this point, this chapter has analyzed the impostor fallacy in its most extreme form, in which cloned impostors steal assets, jobs, spouses, and lives. Media accounts and government reports do not take such impersonation seriously. This makes sense: journalists and academic experts who author stories and reports on human cloning have more knowledge about the subject than the public does, and must realize how hard it would be for a human born through cloning to impersonate a donor.

However, a more subtle version of the impostor fallacy appears in the media. In 1998, Professor Patrick D. Hopkins reviewed news stories in an effort to determine the media's impact on the human cloning debate. He found a common thread: concern that humans born through cloning may undermine the individuality and uniqueness of their originals.[63] Similarly, the 2002 report from the California Advisory Committee on Human Cloning to the California State Legislature (California Report) states: "The person who is the source of the genetic material (if still alive) may experience a loss of self worth [sic] rooted in the knowledge that he or she is no longer unique, but now has a genetic copy."[64] In other words, a DNA donor loses some portion of his or her individuality through cloning.

If this concern seems familiar, it is because we have encountered its flip side before. Chapter 4 debunked the notion that a person born through cloning will suffer diminished individuality due to the existence of a genetic predecessor. That will not happen because people born through cloning will not be copies of their DNA donors, but rather unique individuals.[65] The same logic applies here. It will take many years for a cloned baby to mature. In that time, he or she will develop distinct physical, intellectual, and psychological traits. Thus, there is no biological risk that cloning can diminish the individuality of a donor.

Granted, the impostor fallacy is prevalent in our culture. It may cause some DNA donors to doubt their own individuality. However, just as counseling can help parents understand the individuality of cloned children, counseling can help protect donors against any false sense of diminished individuality. Therefore, it would not be unreasonable for regulators to mandate that donors undergo such counseling before participating in cloning. Moreover, as the California Report recognizes, as participants in a medical procedure, donors are entitled to informed consent.[66] Fertility doctors and clinics can provide information that explains what cloning can produce: not a doppelganger, and not a second chance at life, but rather a fresh person, a unique individual with an open future.

Of course, these solutions do not explain why a donor would believe in the impostor fallacy in the first place. If biology does not supply an answer, we must seek one in psychology.

1. Making Sense of the Impostor Fallacy in Media Accounts and Government Reports

Is opposition to human cloning rooted in fear that the technology could take a person's unique essence – and if so, how would that taking occur? As discussed previously, many people seem to believe that each

IMPOSTERS AND ESSENTIALISM 141

individual has a unique essence that inheres throughout the body and persists in severed body parts, even after those parts have been transplanted into another person. It is easy to see how such intuitions could extend to cloning. The technology begins with a severed body part, that is, a cell that contains the essence of the donor. Once merged with the egg, the cell transmits the unique essence of the donor throughout the developing organism, resulting in a cloned organism with the same essence.

From an essentialist perspective, cloning appears to reduce the original store of personal essence that the donor possessed. Moreover, unlike organ donation, in which the donor is deceased, cloning involves a donor who is still alive. The donor may intuit that he has lost some part of himself, and this feeling may increase if multiple individuals are cloned from his DNA. Although cloning does not diminish individuality, intuition can make it seem as if it does.

Moreover, cloning need not be consensual. It can be accomplished with a single cell harvested clandestinely from a scrape of skin or a fallen strand of hair. Cloning without consent is a common element of science fiction stories,[67] and the California Report characterizes it as a violation of autonomy.[68] In essentialist terms, however, it is more than that. Cloning without consent involves a theft of precious essence, which is then transferred to an undeserving recipient of stolen goods (the person born through the cloning).

A psychological account of cloning as loss of essence suggests an alternative interpretation of science fiction stories in which cloned impostors steal the assets, jobs, or spouses of DNA donors. Such valuables may be the symbolic embodiments of something more precious: the essence that makes a person who he or she really is. In other words, the impostor who steals all that I am steals all that I have.

Although it has not been at the forefront of the cloning debate, the argument that cloning diminishes the individuality of the original should not be underestimated, for it packs a real psychological punch, particularly in the context of non-consensual cloning. Anyone is potentially a victim of this psychological form of identity theft, in which a portion of one's unique essence now belongs to another.

Thus, laws prohibiting non-consensual cloning could do more than preserve the right of autonomous adults to decide whether to reproduce. They could assuage essentialist fears and help calm the public. If fertility doctors and clinics must obtain informed consent from DNA donors in any event, they will have records that regulators can inspect to ensure that cloning services are consensual.

Public education offers yet another means of attacking this problem at its root. Federal and state governments should disseminate the scientific facts of cloning, so that people can see for themselves that the technology yields baby animals (not adults) that are unique individuals with observable differences in phenotype. Governments should also explain to the public that it is only essentialist intuitions that make it seem as if cloning can steal individuality.

Unfortunately, federal and state reports have done little to quell public fears about diminished individuality. Instead, the California Report may have exacerbated such fears by asserting diminished individuality as one more justification for the enactment of a permanent cloning ban in California.

D. Essentialist Intuitions about the Individual and the Identity Fallacy

Essentialist intuitions about individual identity have implications for more than the impostor fallacy. Such intuitions may also account for the identity fallacy as applied to humans born through cloning in small numbers.

To understand this point, recall the analysis presented in Chapter 4. Stories in which cloning produces masses of identical bodies – such as clone armies – are consistent with the essentialism of living kinds or social kinds. The clone kind shares a common essence; thus, the members of the kind have common traits. People accustomed to stories or images of clone kinds may extend their essentialist intuitions to cover instances where cloning is used to create only one person, or perhaps two or three people. In other words, the essentialism of kinds has spillover effects; it induces us to view even a single cloned person as a copy of his cell donor.

This chapter suggests an alternative account of the identity fallacy that does not depend upon the essentialism of kinds. If one imagines every human being to be imbued with a unique essence that persists in severed body parts, one may perceive cloning as a technology capable of transferring a portion of that essence to a new body (or multiple bodies) via a severed somatic cell. Further, as essences are causal, one may expect the new body to acquire the physical traits, personality, behaviors, tastes, and even the memories of the donor who provides the cell. Just as essentialist intuitions about kinds encourage one to believe in a clone army, essentialist intuitions about the individual may encourage one to believe that cloning can replicate the cell donor.

This alternative account of the identity fallacy may explain those science fiction and media stories that assume that one or two or three people cloned from a single donor are copies of that donor and/or each other. These stories do not need to involve clone kinds if all that is required to trigger essentialist intuitions is the severance and transfer of a body part from one person to another.

This alternative account may also explain government reports that focus on the hypothetical woes of humans born through cloning, as discussed in Chapter 4. If cloning really did transmit a donor's essence and traits, the cloned person could indeed suffer from diminished individuality. Likewise, if cloning really did transmit a parent's essence and traits to a child, the family might be dysfunctional. Life as a doppelganger would be no fun at all; but then again, doppelgangers are possible only in the imaginations of those who have been led astray by their essentialist intuitions.

Perhaps these reports mean only to suggest that false perceptions of cloning could lead to cases in which cloned children experience diminished individuality or families become dysfunctional. Unfortunately, the reports do not investigate or identify the psychological sources of those perceptions. Instead, they demand legislative bans on cloning. In so doing, the reports offer a policy of appeasement rather than engagement. As Chapter 4 explained, a combination of public education, parental counseling, informed consent, and child counseling would be more effective in dispelling false perceptions before they lead to unhappy outcomes.

E. Summary

This chapter has focused on the impostor fallacy. Science fiction presents the extreme case: people born through cloning who steal our assets, jobs, personal relationships, and lives. These stories benefit from essentialist intuitions that make it seem credible that a severed somatic cell could transmit historical path from donor to another person. Experience with monozygotic multiples further heightens the illusion by making it seem possible that a person created through cloning could have the same age and appearance as the donor. However, there is no biological basis for these stories. A cloned person will be distinguishable from the donor, who will be much older. Even if multiple individuals are cloned at the same time, science teaches that these individuals will differ from each other in appearance, personality, and behavior.

Media and government reports present a more subtle version of the impostor fallacy, in which humans born through cloning diminish the individuality of their donors. This claim has no biological basis, but it may have a psychological basis in the intuition that a unique essence permeates the body of every individual. From that perspective, cloning looks like a technology that takes the essence of one person and transfers it to another, leading to diminishment of the original store of essence. If the cells used for cloning are stolen, then the technology enables theft of essence.

The notion that each individual has a unique essence may also promote the identity fallacy – that is, the belief that a human born through cloning is a copy of his or her donor. The brain may be predisposed to interpret the transfer of any body part – even one as tiny as a somatic cell – as a transfer of essence along with a cluster of associated traits to a host who necessarily becomes a duplicate rather than original.

If federal and state governments want to play a constructive role in the human cloning debate, they must defuse the impostor and identity fallacies through public education of two kinds. First, as science fiction indicates, people are inclined to view humans born through cloning as duplicative, duplicitous, and dangerous. These fears will dominate public opinion until they are dispelled. An education campaign must alert people to the role that essentialism is playing in shaping their views. Second, an education campaign must offer people an alternative account, one that is based in scientific fact. Cloned animals provide that account. These animals are unique individuals with their own phenotypes and life histories. The better people understand those facts, the more readily they will abandon their belief in cloned impostors and duplicates.

Regulations can also help protect participants in cloning against psychological distress. Mandatory psychological counseling for parents and DNA donors alike can help protect the individuality of both child and donor. Fertility doctors and clinics can further aid all cloning participants by providing them not only with medical facts about the procedure, but also scientific facts about humans born through cloning.

Finally, to the extent that non-consensual cloning is a concern, legislators can enact a law that penalizes those who participate in the cloning of a person without his or her consent. There is no need to adopt a total ban that places cloning outside the reach of infertile couples and others who wish to use the technology to build families.

7 Resurrection and Essentialism

THIS CHAPTER IS DEDICATED TO AN ANALYSIS OF the resurrection fallacy. According to this fallacy, a person can be cloned to extend or resume the life of a deceased genetic predecessor. In other words, cloning is a means of achieving immortality and raising the dead.

The resurrection fallacy is very close to the identity fallacy; it too predicts that a person born through cloning will have the same traits as the DNA donor. In this case, however, that person is less copy than extension. He or she emerges as an adult, ready to reclaim the lost life of the donor.

Part I of this book refuted the resurrection fallacy. Chapter 2 established that cloned animals are born as babies, exhibit their own individual physical and behavioral traits, and enjoy normal lifespans. There is no indication that cloned animals somehow inherit the bodies or physiological ages of their DNA donors. As Chapter 3 discussed, the same should hold true of cloned humans. Based on the available evidence, we have every reason to expect that they will also be born as babies with their own identities and lifespans.

Nevertheless, the resurrection fallacy is a popular theme in science fiction films. This vogue suggests that some people find the fallacy credible. In addition, the media has reported several cases in which people have cloned their dead pets, as well as the heartbreaking story of a couple who spent hundreds of thousands of dollars in a failed attempt to clone their deceased infant son. Even government reports have noted the prospect that bereaved parents might turn to cloning as a means of replacing a lost child.

Thus, the resurrection fallacy merits critical analysis. This chapter begins with a discussion of cultural and political manifestations of the fallacy. It then examines the role of psychological essentialism. Analysis reveals that the resurrection fallacy, like the impostor fallacy, feeds on essentialist intuitions about the individual.

A. The Resurrection Fallacy in Popular Culture

The resurrection fallacy is a staple of science fiction. In the paradigmatic storyline, a person has died but a scientist attempts to resurrect him or her through the cloning of his or her entire body. Table 4 lists some examples of this storyline in films and television episodes.[1]

1. Who Is Resurrected?

Several of these stories present cloning as a means of resurrecting a political or religious leader.[2] The most notorious example is *The Boys from Brazil*.[3] As explained previously in Chapter 5, Nazi doctor Dr. Josef Mengele sets up a lab in South America and clones ninety-four boys from the DNA of Adolf Hitler. These infants are placed with parents whose traits mirror those of Hitler's parents. Mengele does not expect all of these human experiments to recreate the Fuhrer, but he hopes that a few might. After encountering one of these young boys, he declares that Hitler is alive.[4]

Cloning has also been portrayed as a means of recreating men or women whose talents qualify them for particular tasks. Another movie discussed in Chapter 5, *Anna to the Infinite Power*, is based on the premise that girls cloned from a dead scientist can carry on her work and complete the invention of a food replicator.[5] In the film *Alien: Resurrection*, a military base clones a deceased Ellen Ripley because she once demonstrated prowess in fighting aliens.[6]

RESURRECTION AND ESSENTIALISM

Table 4. *Cloning Is Used to Resurrect a Person*

Movies

Movie Title	Distributor	Year
Alien: Resurrection	Twentieth Century Fox	1997
Anna to the Infinite Power	Scorpion Releasing	1983
The Boys from Brazil	Twentieth Century Fox	1978
Cloned	National Broadcasting Company (NBC)	1997
The Creator	Universal Pictures	1985
Godsend	Lions Gate Films	2004
Fifth Element	Columbia Pictures	1997
Morella	Taurus Films	1997
The Sixth Day	Columbia Pictures	2000
Sleeper	United Artists	1973
Star Trek II: The Wrath of Khan	Paramount Pictures	1982
Star Trek III: The Search for Spock	Paramount Pictures	1984

Television Episodes/Series

TV Series	Episode	Distributor	Air date
Eleventh Hour	"Resurrection"	Granada Television	January 19, 2006
Star Trek: Deep Space Nine	"Ties of Blood and Water"	Paramount Television	April 14, 1997
Star Trek Next Generation	"Rightful Heir"	Paramount Television	May 17, 1993

Last but not least, popular culture also presents cloning as a means of bringing back a lost loved one.[7] Thus, in *Godsend*, bereaved parents give in to the temptation to clone their dead child only to find that their new child is genetically altered and has sociopathic tendencies.[8]

2. Scientific Errors in Resurrection Stories

For a resurrection story to work, the cloned person must be a good stand-in for the deceased DNA donor. Looks, personality, and even memories should all be the same. To include those plot elements, producers and scriptwriters must run roughshod over scientific reality.

a) Looks and Personality

The Boys from Brazil offers a good example. The cloned boys have Hitler's dark hair, pale skin, and blue eyes. All are the same size and are visually indistinguishable from each other. More than that, they share a sociopathic personality: cold, rude, contemptuous, and utterly lacking in compassion.[9] However, the idea that Dr. Mengele could create such perfect copies of Hitler is more fantasy than fact. As explained at length in Chapter 3, genetic, epigenetic, and environmental variation will individuate humans born through cloning. Differences in uterine environment, culture, historical era, and random life events would ensure that Dr. Mengele could never recreate Hitler, or even make a set of identical boys.

The Boys from Brazil is realistic in one respect: Mengele clones babies who mature at the normal rate for human beings.[10] Other films violate the rules of biology and show that cloning can create adults.[11] Such plots are unscientific but achieve the desired goal of heightening the visual similarity between the deceased donor and his or her replacement.

b) Memories

Another peculiarity appears in many resurrection stories: vestigial memories are transferred along with the DNA, so that the clone remembers events that happened to the deceased predecessor, but not her.[12] *Anna to the Infinite Power* offers an example.[13] The protagonist, Anna Hart, is a cloned girl who has the same neuroses (lying and kleptomania) that her DNA donor developed when interned in a Nazi concentration camp decades before. Anna also has the donor's memories. She fears flickering lights, because the donor died in a fire; and she fears the song "Reverie" because the donor heard that song when her own mother was chosen to die in the concentration camp. Anna is cured of all this when an understanding neighbor (who also was cloned from the same DNA donor) teaches her to play the piano with feeling (thus tapping into her musical and human side). Anna does develop her own personality in the end, but not without a struggle.[14]

In other science fiction tales, memories do not inhere in the body of the cloned person and must be added through other means. For example, in *The Sixth Day*, cloning creates bodies that must have memories downloaded into their brains.[15] Similarly, in the *Star Trek Next Generation* episode "Rightful Heir," Klingon religious leaders transfer knowledge of religious secrets and sacred texts to a clone of Kahless, so that he knows all that Kahless knew.[16] In *Star Trek III: The Search for Spock*, a Vulcan priestess transfers the katra (soul) of the deceased Mr. Spock into a cloned Vulcan body. Afterward, the cloned Vulcan encounters Captain James Kirk and begins to repeat things that Spock said to Kirk right before he died. He even calls Kirk by his first name (Jim), as Spock would have done. In other words, Spock's memories have been transferred along with the katra.[17]

Whatever their entertainment value, these stories are scientifically inaccurate. Memories are not heritable. A baby born through cloning will have her own mind. As she grows to maturity, she will live her own life and establish her own personality and memories. It is biologically impossible for her to exist as an empty vessel awaiting the technological or mystical transfer of a new persona or memories. Perhaps hypnosis or some other means of brainwashing could be used to remove all of her existing memories and implant new ones. However, this would be a difficult process with uncertain results. Moreover, there is no scientific reason to expect that her origin in cloning would make her particularly susceptible to such methods.

3. Organ Donors

A related strand of science fiction deserves mention here. These stories do not involve the recreation of a person who has already died. Rather, living persons clone themselves as a hedge against disease and death.

Table 5. Cloning Is Used for Spare Body Parts

Movie Title	Distributor	Year
Parts: The Clonus Horror	Group 1 International Distribution Organization Ltd.	1979
The Island	DreamWorks/Warner Brothers	2005
Never Let Me Go	Fox Searchlight Pictures/Twentieth Century Fox	2010
The Resurrection of Zachary Wheeler	Gold Key Entertainment Film Ventures	1971

Organs are forcibly harvested from the cloned bodies so that the genetic predecessors may extend their lifespans indefinitely.

Table 5 lists some of these stories. Representative samples include: *The Resurrection of Zachary Wheeler*, in which a quasi-governmental conspiracy makes zombie-like cloned persons and uses their body parts to repair and resuscitate politicians and other powerful individuals[18]; *The Island*, a similar tale in which a biotech company clones ready-made adult doppelgangers to serve as organ donors for rich clients[19]; and *Never Let Me Go*, a dystopian story in which humans born through cloning are studied during their childhood and harvested for organs upon reaching adulthood.[20] In these gruesome tales, the cloned persons share the DNA and some physical traits of their predecessors, but do not necessarily share the same memories or souls.[21]

There is a kernel of scientific truth in these stories. If a person is cloned, his or her organs will share the nuclear DNA of his or her donor, reducing the chance of immune rejection.[22] However, the films err in supposing that companies could create entire individuals and force them to serve as involuntary organ donors. Anyone born through cloning will be a human being and should have the basic legal rights of a human being. Anyone who steals organs from or murders him or her could be prosecuted and sent to prison.[23]

Family needs could pose a greater concern. The parents of a sick child sometimes induce the child's existing sibling to serve as a tissue or

RESURRECTION AND ESSENTIALISM 153

organ donor.[24] Taking things a step farther, parents can undergo IVF and screen embryos prior to implantation in an effort to conceive a "savior sibling" who is both free of disease and a good immunological match for the sick child.[25] In theory, cloning could provide an alternative means of conceiving a savior sibling; however, it would not be useful in cases of genetic disease, because the cloned child would have the same DNA and suffer from the same disease as the ailing child.

Parental consent may be enough to allow a minor to donate tissue in uncontested cases, but courts have the power to block donation when one parent objects to tissue donation or when a minor is asked to donate an organ (a more dangerous procedure).[26] Some question whether the law does enough to protect underage donors from parental coercion,[27] but there is no reason to expect that humans born through cloning would be any worse off than other children in this regard. In sum, science fiction errs in singling out humans born through cloning as the likely victims of coerced organ donation.

B. The Resurrection Fallacy in Media Accounts

Turning from fiction to media reports on cloning, three themes involving immortality or resurrection can be identified.

1. Dictators Who Never Die

First, immediately following the announcement that Dolly had been cloned, the media ran stories on the possible uses and misuses of the new technology. For example, a *Time* magazine article suggested that a dictator might be able to use cloning to hold onto leadership forever. The article noted that such concerns had been aired in science fiction movies like *The Boys from Brazil* and *Sleeper*.[28]

Similarly, *U.S. News and World Report* published a question-and-answer article to address concerns the public might have. Querying whether a megalomaniac might decide to achieve immortality through cloning, the article answered its own question in the affirmative.[29] Only at the very end did the article clearly explain (in response to a different question on religion) that cloning was not a means of resurrection.[30]

The inclusion of the cloned dictator scenario in these articles might signal nothing more than a desire to educate a public misled by science fiction. If so, the authors could and should have done more to explain why the scenario is false. Throughout history, aging political leaders have passed power down to sons. A cloned son would be no more reliable than any other, and a public exposed to his personality and foibles would quickly realize he was not his father.

2. Cloning Loved Ones

Second, the media have also reported on pet cloning. Such stories tend to focus on pet owners who clone, with two types emerging. Some owners seem convinced that they can resurrect their dead pet. For example, as reported in Chapter 2, the owners of Second Chance the Brahman bull believed at first that they had succeeded in reanimating their old friend, Chance.[31] Only later, after Second Chance had attacked them twice, did the owners realize that cloning did not guarantee the same animal.[32]

Another type of owner is conflicted. Intellectually, she concedes the new pet may not be exactly the same as the old one. Emotionally, she goes the other way, marveling at the physical, psychological, and behavioral commonalities between the original pet and the cloned animal.[33] In other words, the mind acknowledges the new animal as an individual, but something deeper in the psyche insists that the old pet has come home.

A similar conflict is evident in the poignant story of Mark Hunt. As reported in Chapter 3, this educated attorney paid hundreds of thousands of dollars in a failed attempt to clone his dead infant son. On the one hand, Hunt spoke of giving his son's DNA – rather than the son himself – another chance. On the other hand, he appears to have viewed cloning as a means of cheating death and achieving resurrection for his son.[34]

3. Premature Aging

Third, the media have encouraged a controversy over the true age of animals born through cloning. As Part I explained, the media ran many stories suggesting that Dolly inherited the physiological age of the sheep that had provided the DNA for the cloning. Her unnaturally advanced age was supposedly reflected in her telomeres, arthritis, and early death. Such stories implied that Dolly had no independent life of her own and was simply continuing the life of the deceased donor sheep. In other words, she was portrayed as a resurrection of that sheep.

This is nonsense. As discussed in Chapter 2, experiments have shown that cloned animals do not inherit the ages of their DNA donors. They are born as babies and mature at the usual rate for members of their species. Most do not have shortened telomeres, but even those that do mature at a pace consistent with their own chronological age, rather than that of the DNA donor. Finally, cloned animals born healthy stay that way and enjoy lifespans within the usual range for their species.[35]

C. The Resurrection Fallacy in Government Reports

Government reports do not portray the resurrection fallacy as real. However, they present three issues that are related to resurrection or life extension more generally.

1. Cloning Loved Ones

First, and most importantly, the reports speculate that some people may want to clone a lost loved one. The NBAC and the President's Council on Bioethics present this scenario: a tragic car accident claims the life of a young father and mortally wounds his infant child. In response, the mother clones the dying infant. The NBAC Report describes the wife as motivated to raise the biological child of her dead husband.[36] The Council Report assumes the wife acts for three purposes: to preserve a connection to both the husband and child; to create new life in the face of death; and to continue the family name and line of the husband.[37] These reports stop short of suggesting that the wife is attempting to resurrect her dead child.

Similarly, the California Advisory Committee on Human Cloning surmises that parents might clone a child who died too young in the belief that a genetically identical child would help relieve their grief and loss.[38] This scenario stops short of attributing to the parents a desire to resurrect the child. Nevertheless, the California Report does go on to debunk the resurrection fallacy. It correctly notes that a replacement child would not be the same as the one that died, and suggests this type of cloning might not be healthy for parents or child, particularly if the child turns out different than expected.[39]

It is reasonable to worry that bereaved parents might be sad or confused enough to attempt to create a replacement child through cloning. However, there are strategies that government can employ to discourage such attempts. Public education is one. Something as simple as a picture can be worth a thousand words: imagine how different perceptions of human cloning might be if the photographs of Cc (the cloned cat who does not resemble her DNA donor) were more widely disseminated. In addition, as suggested in Chapter 4, mandatory psychological counseling and informed consent can help ensure that prospective parents understand what cloning can and cannot do. In particular, the counseling and information provided must emphasize that a child born through cloning will be a new individual and not a replacement or reincarnation of the donor.

Some might argue that counseling can fail, leaving parents with unhealthy expectations; therefore, cloning bans are preferable.[40] However, cloning bans will not prevent such cases. As Chapter 8 discusses, individuals with sufficient motivation will do whatever it takes to get around cloning bans, even if it means breaking the law or traveling to a foreign country. Indeed, by portraying cloning as a forbidden fruit, the bans may only encourage the bereaved to believe the technology can reincarnate their loved ones. Once children are born and reside in this country, the bans will add insult to injury by stigmatizing them as unworthy of existence.

2. Shortened Telomeres

The government reports question whether shortened telomeres or premature aging will threaten the health of cloned children. The NBAC Report brushes off concerns with an educated guess that telomerase activity in the egg will reset telomeres.[41] However, the Council Report presents premature aging as a risk that a cloned child could face,[42] and the California Report cites shortened telomeres as a potential health risk.[43]

As Chapters 1 and 2 explained, cloned animals that survive the critical neonatal period are generally healthy. Infants and juveniles develop in synch with their own chronological ages. Most cloned animals have telomeres of normal length, but even those with shorter telomeres do not undergo accelerated aging. Finally, the evidence we have today indicates that cloned animals can have normal lifespans. In sum, there is no evidence that cloned animals inherit the age of their DNA donors.

Nevertheless, it is interesting that the Council and California Reports include these speculations about premature aging and shortened telomeres. As discussed in Chapter 2, such speculations are consistent with the intuition that a cloned animal (or human) reincarnates or extends the life of the DNA donor. In other words, even experts may take concerns about premature aging and shortened telomeres more seriously because the concerns align with the fallacious notion that cloning is a means of resurrection.

3. Research Cloning

Finally, all three government reports suggest that scientists may one day clone human embryos for the purpose of generating replacement tissues and organs for sick and dying people.[44] This potential application may have associated cloning with life extension in the public mind. However, stem cell research of this kind would not recreate an entire person. This topic will be explored at greater length in Chapter 9.

D. Making Sense of the Resurrection Fallacy

To summarize the analysis so far, cloning as a means of resurrecting dictators, messiahs, and other powerful figures is a theme in science fiction. Media accounts also show that some people view cloning as a means of reincarnating lost loved ones, and government reports are concerned about such use. This section examines the ways in which the resurrection fallacy is consistent with psychological essentialism.

1. The Essence of the Individual

Psychological essentialism and the belief in a unifying essence holds true primarily for classes or kinds. However, as explained in Chapter 6, the mind also harnesses the power of essentialism in conceptualizing the individual. For example, recipients of organ transplants act as if their donors were present inside their bodies. Some recipients claim to manifest the gender-related characteristics, personality traits, and acquired tastes of their donors. Others claim to know about things that their donors experienced; in other words, the recipients believe they have the memories of their donors.[45]

Based on this evidence, the brain intuits that a unique essence permeates the entire body of an individual. The essence continues to exist after death in severed body parts. Once a body part is transferred to another, the essence in that part has the power to confer the personality, acquired tastes, and even memories of the donor upon the recipient. It is as if the historical path of the donor is embedded in the body part.

2. Essentialism and the Resurrection Fallacy

This information suggests a theory of how essentialism contributes to the resurrection fallacy. Assume the essence that permeates the body of an individual person persists in a severed somatic cell, even after the person has died. If a scientist fuses that cell to an egg, and activates the egg so that it becomes an embryo, the essence contained in the cell is transmitted throughout the developing child. As a result of essentialist intuition, one expects that the child when born will have all traits that the dead person possessed, even those rooted in history such as personality, acquired tastes, and memories. In other words, the child is a resurrection.

The various manifestations of the resurrection fallacy discussed in this chapter are consistent with this essentialist account of cloning. First, consider science fiction. Often, a cloned person is born with the personality and memories of someone who died. In other words, the cell used for the cloning carries much more than genetic and epigenetic information; it carries the essence of the dead person, including elements of his historical path.

Next, consider pet owners who clone after a beloved animal dies. Many talk as if the new animal is the old animal, not only in appearance but also personality and behavior. It is as if the cloned pet carries the essence of the dead pet – an essence that incorporates elements of historical path.

Similarly, consider the story of Mark Hunt, an educated man who lost his infant son. He knew the son could not be revived, yet he spoke of using cloning as a means of cheating death.

Finally, consider reports of premature aging in cloned animals. Time and again, the media presented facts about Dolly in terms of premature aging. For example, although she died of a common infectious disease, the news stories about her death focused on premature aging. Although scientifically misleading, the stories were consistent with an essentialist vision in which Dolly carried within her the donor sheep's six years of life. Government reports that overemphasize premature aging in cloned animals also reflect the same essentialist intuition.

However, a caveat is in order. The intuition that cloning can transmit essence and bring an individual back from the dead is strongly at odds with human experience. Whether animal or human, dead bodies cannot be reanimated. They disintegrate and decay, and personality and memories vanish along with them.

Human experience with death could explain why some screenwriters and movie producers go to great lengths to show how a cloned person ends up with the personality and memories of the deceased. For example, *Star Trek III: The Search for Spock* included a Vulcan religious ceremony to show how Mr. Spock's intangible soul (essence) was transferred to a cloned adult body.[46]

Human experience with death could also account for the cognitive dissonance exhibited by some pet owners who clone. Emotionally, they want to believe the pet has come home. Intellectually, many acknowledge the cloned animal is a new and distinct creature. Nothing else makes sense in the face of death. Nor has there been a rush to clone dead pets. Rather, as noted in Chapter 2, a company that pioneered pet cloning recently went out of business for lack of orders.[47]

The weak market for pet cloning suggests that concerns about parents cloning dead children are overblown. Adults who lose a child are likely to have had some prior experience with death and decay, even if only of a pet. Essentialism is powerful, but so is experience, and there would be many opportunities for family and friends to talk common sense into bereaved parents.

3. Organ Donors

As explained previously, a subgenre of science fiction speculates that people will clone themselves so they can plunder organs from doppelganger bodies and live forever. This type of cloning fiction is rare in that it portrays humans born through cloning as sympathetic individuals who are being exploited.

Consider the two most recent of such films. *The Island* is an American film released in 2005.[48] Lincoln Six Echo learns that the company that created him kills cloned humans for their organs. He and a friend named Jordan Two Delta escape the compound. They search for their DNA donors and find Tom Lincoln. Tom is dishonest, exploitive, and dissolute. He deceives and betrays others, but gets his just reward when an assassin kills him.

By contrast, Lincoln Six Echo is honest, compassionate, and brave. Once he realizes that the company plans to kill the other cloned humans at the compound, he and Jordan Two Delta return to save them from gas chambers, at the risk of their own lives.[49] Despite its many essentialist trappings, the movie conveys the humanity of those born through cloning.

The British film *Never Let Me Go* was released in 2010.[50] Even more so than *The Island*, it highlights the humanity of its cloned protagonists. The movie never depicts DNA donors, and thus never compares physical appearances or personalities. Instead, it focuses on the all-too-human lives and thwarted loves of the protagonists, who grow up together in a cloistered British boarding school. The children are encouraged to create art, and rumors swirl that exceptional creativity or true love can earn them a deferral from the organ harvesting that awaits them upon reaching adulthood. In the end, there is no reprieve: harvesting and death comes to them all.[51]

At first glance, films such as these seem to be attacking a straw man. Once humans are born through cloning, existing criminal laws against battery and murder will protect them against harvest schemes. What, then, is the point of the films?

In 1998, scientists created the first stem cell lines derived from non-cloned human embryos.[52] Although no one has succeeded in creating functional stem cell lines from cloned human embryos,[53] scientists are working toward that goal and could one day learn how to differentiate such cell lines into tissues or possibly organs, as government reports have anticipated.[54]

However, creation of a stem cell line requires scientists to disaggregate and destroy the embryo. For this reason, the morality of embryonic stem cell research has been hotly debated. For many Americans, embryos are human life and just as deserving of protection as babies, children, and adults. From their perspective, the disaggregation of cloned embryos to create DNA-matched organs or tissues is an atrocity.

Chapter 9 of this book examines the controversy over embryonic stem cell research in detail. In the meantime, it is worthwhile to note the parallels between the controversy and the plots of *The Island* and *Never Let Me Go*. For those who view the embryo as a person, a film that depicts sympathetic people being harvested for the benefit of others is not unrealistic at all. Rather, it is a frightening metaphor for research projects that scientists already pursue. The cloned humans in these movies function as stand-ins for embryos in the ongoing debate over the moral value of embryonic life.[55]

Along these lines, a scene from *Never Let Me Go* is particularly telling. After they grow up, two of the cloned protagonists visit the headmistress of their former school. They hope she will give them a deferral from organ harvesting because they are in love. Instead, they learn that there are no deferrals. As the headmistress points out, the school was the last place to study the ethics of the organ-harvesting program. The art the children produced was used to show that they were good as human, but no one listened. No one wanted to go back to the days in which people died of cancer and other diseases.[56]

Much the same will be true of research cloning if it succeeds in delivering DNA-matched organs or tissues for existing persons. Whatever moral value cloned embryonic life might have, it will be swiftly overridden by public demand for life-saving therapies.

E. Summary

Biology teaches that animals born through cloning are individuals with their own phenotypes, personalities, and lifespans. Humans born through cloning will be equally unique.

RESURRECTION AND ESSENTIALISM

Despite these facts, the resurrection fallacy persists in science fiction and media accounts. Government reports do not present the fallacy as real, but express concerns that those who have lost loved ones may turn to cloning for solace.

The resurrection fallacy is likely rooted in psychological essentialism. If one believes that a unique essence permeates the body of a dead person, one may also believe that cloning transmits that essence to a new body via the donor cell. This analysis explains why many people expect humans and animals born through cloning to have not only the same appearance as their deceased predecessors, but also the same personalities, tastes, behaviors, and memories.

However, the market for pet cloning is weak. The reluctance to clone dead pets is a hopeful sign. Dead animals and people stay dead, and most people know it. That hard reality serves as a powerful counter to this particular manifestation of essentialism. Building on this realism, the government can employ public education to drive home the message that animals and humans born through cloning are new individuals and not resurrections. If the government believes it necessary to intervene further, it can require parental counseling and informed consent to discourage attempts to reincarnate loved ones through cloning.

SUMMARY OF PART II

PART I DOCUMENTED THAT ANIMALS BORN through cloning are unique individuals and functional members of their species, and explained why cloned humans should be likewise. Yet, Part II has shown that false beliefs regarding humans born through cloning are pervasive in popular culture, media accounts, and even government reports. Chapter 4 documented the identity fallacy, that is, the idea that humans born through cloning are copies of DNA donors or each other. Chapter 5 demonstrated the prevalence of the artifact fallacy, in which humans born through cloning are conceptualized as manufactured products. Chapter 6 identified the impostor fallacy, wherein humans born through cloning are feared as interlopers capable of stealing the assets, loved ones, or individuality of their DNA donors. Chapter 7 discussed the resurrection fallacy, that is, the idea that a human born through cloning could be a resurrection of a deceased person.

The primary task of Part II has been to find an explanation for widespread belief in these four cloning fallacies. I have argued that the fallacies have their roots in psychological essentialism. Essentialism is a cognitive phenomenon that manifests itself differently in different contexts. Thus, it is not surprising that Part II has identified three different ways in which essentialism promotes cloning fallacies.

Chapter 4 explained how psychological essentialism accounts for the identity fallacy. Encouraged by experience with monozygotic twins and higher-order multiples to conceptualize humans born through cloning as visually identical multiples in unlimited numbers, the brain is tricked into applying a heuristic intended for the evaluation of living kinds or social groups to an apparent clone kind. The brain infers that members of the clone kind possess a wide range of traits in common, ranging from intellect to personality to occupational behaviors. This intuition supplants the more accurate biological account of humans born through cloning as unique individuals who are shaped by genetic, epigenetic, and environmental influences.

Chapter 5 discussed the role of psychological essentialism in promoting the artifact fallacy. Asexual reproduction contradicts the essentialist belief that two parents of a kind mate and procreate offspring of the kind. This contradiction loosens the association of humans born through cloning with living kinds and opens the door to an alternative domain. The fact that scientists work in laboratories encourages the intuition that humans born through cloning are man-made products. The domain shift from living kind to artifact implies that humans born through cloning somehow lack a human essence – an implication that provokes feelings ranging from indifference to disgust. Finally, the domain shift also promotes the identity fallacy by encouraging us to believe that humans born through cloning will have the traits and functions that their scientist-creators intend them to have.

Chapter 6 explored the relation of psychological essentialism to the impostor fallacy. Although essentialism ordinarily is applied to kinds, many humans believe that each individual possesses a unique essence. The nature of this essence varies according to context. When the issue at hand is identification, people rely upon historical path as essence. Furthermore, many recipients of organ transplants believe that a unique essence permeates the body of their donor and causes his or her physical traits, personality, behaviors, tastes, and memories. After an organ has been removed from the donor and transferred to the recipient, this essence persists in the recipient's body and causes the same traits, personality, behaviors, tastes, and memories.

SUMMARY OF PART TWO

Such essentialist intuitions have obvious implications for human cloning. Cloning is similar to organ transplantation in that it involves the transfer of a body part (the somatic cell) from one person (the adult donor) to another (a cloned embryo that can grow into a person). If that analogy holds, then cloning can be interpreted as the transfer of a unique and personal essence from one person to another. Essentialism primes us to intuit that the recipient of this essence acquires the physical traits, personality, behaviors, tastes, and memories of the person whose cell is utilized for the cloning.

Essentialist intuitions fuel crazy stories about cloned doppelgangers who steal the assets, jobs, spouses, and lives of their donors. They also lead to concerns that the existence of a human born through cloning will diminish the individuality of his or her genetic predecessor. Such intuitions also provide an alternative explanation for the identity fallacy as applied to humans born through cloning in numbers too small to constitute the clone kinds discussed in Chapter 4.

Powerful though they may be, such intuitions are at odds with two key facts: humans born through cloning will be born as babies and will differ from donors in appearance, intellect, personality, and behaviors due to genetic, epigenetic, and environmental influences. Contrary to science fiction, cloned impostors should be relatively easy to identify and defeat. Nor do humans born through cloning threaten the individuality of their donors.

Chapter 7 carries the discussion of essentialism and the individual forward into an analysis of the resurrection fallacy. The myth of resurrection through cloning appears in science fiction, media accounts, and government reports. This makes no biological sense, as the dead must stay dead. However, from an essentialist point of view, resurrection via cloning is an appealing idea. A single cell harvested from the dead person seems to transfer the unique essence of that person to the cloned successor, who thereby inherits all the traits associated with that essence, including appearance, personality, behaviors, tastes, and even memories.

It may seem improbable that a single heuristic could produce so many different fallacies. However, as Part II has illustrated, psychological essentialism is something of a chameleon. Although most academics view essentialism as an element of folk biology or folk sociology, essentialist intuitions also play a role in the conceptualization of artifacts and even the individual. As Professor Susan Gelman suggests, essentialism may reflect the convergence of several underlying cognitive predispositions, giving it the flexibility to function in different domains. Thus, it makes sense that essentialism yields multiple misconceptions that depend on the context.

However, when Part I and Part II are compared, one unifying theme does emerge: again and again, biological fact conflicts with psychological intuition. This conflict leads to several conclusions. First, most people are not biologists. They do not know the basic scientific facts of cloning, nor are they familiar with recent advances in the technology. Cloning bans do nothing to improve this situation. Public education, counseling, and other methods of distributing information are better means of rectifying the abysmal state of public knowledge.

Second, most scientists and bioethicists probably do understand the scientific facts of cloning. Journalists interview these experts, and blue-ribbon commissions rely upon their opinions in assembling government reports on cloning. However, news stories and some government reports exhibit cognitive dissonance, debunking and yet reaffirming myths about cloning at the same time. This vacillation between fact and fallacy may reflect an internal struggle between conscious thought and essentialist intuition.

Moreover, even when government reports acknowledge a fallacy as such, they accept its power over the public and recommend cloning bans rather than education, counseling, or other strategies that could challenge the fallacy at its core. Better information about the role that essentialism is playing in the cloning debate could help reorient the experts.

Third, if fact and intuition are in conflict, there is a risk that politicians are making poor public policy decisions. Therefore, it is time to examine the law that presently exists on human cloning in the United States.

Part III describes federal and state laws against human reproductive and research cloning. It explains how the identity, artifact, impostor, and resurrection fallacies have helped bring about the laws. It reveals how both conservatives and liberals have made essentialist arguments without realizing that they are undercutting their own political positions. Finally, it discusses the ways in which cloning bans contradict fundamental American values such as reproductive freedom, scientific freedom, and egalitarianism.

PART III THE LAW OF CLONING

PART I OF THIS BOOK DISCUSSED THE SCIENTIFIC facts of cloning for animals and humans. Animals born through cloning are not copies or extensions of their donors, nor are they manufactured things. Rather, they are unique individuals with their own lifespans who function as ordinary members of their species. Likewise, if humans are ever born through cloning, they will be unique individuals with their own lifespans who function as ordinary human beings.

Despite these facts, many people believe that humans born through cloning can be identical copies, manufactured products, impostors, or resurrections of the dead. Part II discussed how the identity, artifact, impostor, and resurrection fallacies have distorted the debate over human cloning. It revealed that these four fallacies are consistent with psychological essentialism. The fallacies appear to be the byproduct of a cognitive heuristic that our brains ordinarily use for other purposes.

The task of Part III is to examine the consequences of essentialist intuitions about cloning. For clarity's sake, it divides human cloning into two subtopics: reproductive cloning (the creation of babies) and research cloning (the creation of cloned embryos for stem cell research and possibly therapy).

Chapter 8 identifies regulatory actions, bills, and laws that ban reproductive cloning. Drawing upon public opinion polls, government reports, legislative findings, and lawmaker statements, this chapter shows how the identity, artifact, impostor, and resurrection fallacies have encouraged such bans. It also explains how the fallacies link the bans to essentialism.

Chapter 9 shifts the discussion to research cloning. It describes how conservatives exploit cloning fallacies to ban all cloning, and liberals use the fallacies to ban reproductive cloning only. However, as this chapter further explains, the fallacies are double-edged swords that cause politicians to take incoherent positions that undercut their own values. For example, some conservatives have argued that research cloning must be banned lest it lead to the birth of cloned babies who are copies, manufactured products, and so on. In this manner, they have wielded essentialist misconceptions of humans born through cloning as weapons in the political battle against stem cell research. However, by embracing fallacies that dehumanize cloned babies, conservatives have strengthened the liberal claim that cloned embryos are nothing more than fodder for research.

Both Chapters 8 and 9 conclude with the observation that faulty intuitions about humans born through cloning have led public policy astray. Essentialism has encouraged politicians to propose and enact laws that violate American values of reproductive freedom, scientific freedom, and egalitarianism.

The Conclusion brings Part III to a close. It explains that psychological essentialism is a powerful force, but not an omnipotent one. Essentialism has contributed to racism; yet, Americans have learned to question their racial intuitions and work to ensure fair treatment for everyone. Similarly, although essentialism has contributed to false intuitions about humans born through cloning, we can choose not to act on those misleading cues. The Conclusion recommends that scientists active in the fields of animal or human cloning take a leading role in educating the public about the facts. In addition, federal and state governments should sponsor new policymaking reports that update the science of mammalian cloning and acknowledge the role that essentialism has played in bringing about cloning bans. The Conclusion urges politicians to reject cloning bans in favor of public education campaigns and counseling for parents, DNA donors, and cloned children. Fertility doctors and clinics that provide cloning services can support this effort by ensuring that parents and DNA donors are informed regarding the true characteristics of cloned children.

8 Essentialism and the Law of Reproductive Cloning

THIS CHAPTER ANALYZES POLITICAL AND LEGAL responses to human reproductive cloning (i.e., cloning to create human babies). It begins with a discussion of public opinion and goes on to describe regulatory actions, bills, and laws against reproductive cloning. Throughout this discussion, the chapter explains how the identity, artifact, impostor, and resurrection fallacies have swayed the public, regulators, and legislators.

The chapter then proceeds to argue that cloning bans are rooted in psychological essentialism, just as the fallacies are. Finally, it discusses how these bans threaten American traditions of reproductive freedom and egalitarianism.

A. Public Opinion

In our democracy, there is an expectation that elected officials and their appointees carry out the will of the people. Ideally, these public servants will produce regulations and legislation that are consistent with public concerns and goals. Cynics might say that money has a greater influence upon politicians and their actions. Nevertheless, those who are elected must be responsive to public opinion or risk being ousted. Votes do count, and that makes it worthwhile to consider public opinion polls on human reproductive cloning.

In general, public opposition to human reproductive cloning has been clear from the beginning and remained consistent over time. Gallup's website presents data on polls taken from 2001–2010. Asked whether human cloning is morally acceptable or morally wrong, 85–90 percent of respondents declared human cloning was morally wrong. Animal cloning was also viewed with suspicion, with 59–68 percent finding it morally wrong.[1] This string of Gallup polls does not explain why the public opposes human cloning. Some insight can be gleaned from questions and responses to some earlier polls.

1. 1997 Polls

Three public opinion polls were administered either in February or March of 1997, immediately after the announcement of Dolly's birth. The percentage of respondents who opposed human reproductive cloning was 88–93.[2] These polls show that public aversion to human cloning was immediate and instinctive, occurring well before academics, ideologues, and politicians had the chance to spin the issues and come up with intellectual rationalizations for opposition to human cloning.

These polls are also notable for their detailed questions. Cloning was new back then, too new for pollsters to simply ask respondents if it was morally right or wrong. Some level of explanation was considered necessary. For example, in a Gallup Poll, respondents were told that cloning allowed scientists to make exact copies of animals. The respondents were then asked whether human cloning – described as a process that could make exact copies of people – was a good or bad thing. Similarly, in a *Time* poll, respondents were told that cloning could create an exact duplicate of an animal before being asked whether they thought cloning people was a good or bad idea.[3] These questions show that the pollsters did not understand the biology of somatic cell nuclear transfer. Rather, they framed their questions in terms of the identity fallacy, in which cloned animals or humans are copies. Accordingly, the answers reflected opposition to copying more than opposition to cloning.[4]

The identity fallacy also played a role in the sensationalistic news stories that circulated in the wake of Dolly's birth announcement. As discussed at greater length in Chapter 4, Professor Patrick D. Hopkins reviewed those stories and found that many portrayed humans born through cloning as copies and cloning as a threat to human individuality.[5] The stories lent credence to mistaken beliefs that many people already held, thereby reinforcing them in the public mind[6] and creating a warped template for future political discussion.

2. 2001 Time/CNN Poll

Four years later, in February 2001, Time and CNN did an opinion poll on human cloning. The Time/CNN poll is important for three reasons. First, it immediately preceded a concerted effort in Congress to ban human cloning altogether and thus offers a snapshot of public opinion at an important time. (Congressional attempts to outlaw cloning are discussed below in Section B.)

Second, this was a rare poll in which people were asked their opinion about various uses of human cloning. Although 88 percent of respondents said scientists should not be allowed to clone humans,[7] some of that opposition was weak around the edges. For example, 20 percent of respondents thought that cloning was justified to help infertile couples have children without having to adopt. When asked whether scientists should clone specific individuals, 18 percent of respondents approved the cloning of Albert Einstein, 14 percent approved the cloning of Abraham Lincoln and Isaac Newton, and 12 percent embraced the cloning of Ludwig van Beethoven.[8]

Third, the pollsters also asked respondents who opposed human cloning to identify their main reason. A solid 34 percent cited religious beliefs. However, 22 percent stated that cloning interfered with human uniqueness and individuality. Another 22 percent feared that cloning could be used to breed a master race or clone armies. Only 14 percent identified the danger of the technology as their reason for opposition.[9]

As Chapter 4 explained, the concern that humans born through cloning will suffer from diminished individuality is a manifestation of the identity fallacy. The same is true of claims that cloning can create armies of aggressive soldiers or a race of supermen and women, because such projects presume cloning can replicate desirable traits. Thus, one interpretation of the poll is that 44 percent, or close to half, of respondents based their opposition to human cloning upon the identity fallacy.

The artifact fallacy also lurks behind these poll responses. As Chapter 5 explained, the conceptualization of humans born through cloning as man-made objects with designer traits makes it easier to believe that scientists can create multitudinous persons who share identical traits and/or a particular occupation such as soldiering.[10]

Moreover, given the vagueness of the question on human uniqueness and individuality, some of the respondents who answered positively may have been expressing a fear that cloning could interfere with their own uniqueness and individuality. If so, that fear reflects the impostor fallacy, in which humans born through cloning are believed to diminish the individual essence of their DNA donors.

What about the resurrection fallacy, in which cloning is believed to be a means of recreating a dead person? Here the evidence was conflicted. One question asked whether a person cloned from a deceased person would have the same personality as the deceased person. Only 10 percent answered yes; 74 percent answered no.[11] These results suggest that most of the public does not believe in the resurrection fallacy. However, many respondents were willing to clone Einstein, Lincoln, Newton, and Beethoven, all deceased persons who had special talents and made major contributions in their respective fields. It is hard to understand why anyone would support such cloning unless he believed the technology would recreate these lost talents in fresh bodies.

Relatedly, 28 percent of respondents agreed that it was appropriate to use cloning to make copies of humans whose organs could be used to save the lives of others.[12] It is not entirely clear that respondents interpreted this question to mean that organs should be harvested from live human beings (a gruesome prospect). Perhaps some respondents believed the organs might be grown independently. Either way, their responses reflect a willingness to explore cloning as a means of prolonging life.

In sum, public opposition to human reproductive cloning has been overwhelming from the start. The opposition is grounded in several fallacies, particularly the identity fallacy. This chapter next considers how this public opposition has shaped the actions of regulators and legislators.

B. Federal Law

The United States is composed of fifty states, and that makes its legal landscape complicated. Federal regulations and laws apply throughout the entire nation, and state regulations and laws apply only within individual states. This chapter will begin by describing federal regulatory actions, bills, and laws that address human reproductive cloning.

1. Food and Drug Administration

Since 1998, the FDA has maintained that human reproductive cloning cannot be performed in the United States without its permission.[13] At the same time, the FDA has signaled that it is unwilling to grant permission due to concerns about the safety of the technology.[14]

What prompted the FDA to take this position? At the time, the United States was in an uproar over the prospect that a physicist named Richard Seed might succeed in his quest to clone a human baby. Concerned that Congress might ban all human cloning, including the cloning of embryos for research, the Biotechnology Industry Organization encouraged the FDA to assert jurisdiction and block the cloning of babies.[15] Thus, although the FDA gave safety as its reason for halting reproductive cloning, its involvement resulted in part from public hysteria and the fallacies that inspired that hysteria.

Although the FDA has halted reproductive cloning for the time being, its jurisdiction extends only as far as the safety of the technology for mother and child. It has no authority to consider moral concerns.[16] As discussed in Chapter 1, cloning technology continues to improve. It is much more efficient than when Dolly was born and risks to animal mothers and babies are dropping. At any time, researchers working with animals could discover a breakthrough that renders the technology even more efficient and safe. Meanwhile, as explained in Chapter 3, researchers in America and abroad are working to establish a stem cell line from a cloned human embryo. That goal requires them to clone healthy embryos, which is also the first step in achieving reproductive cloning. Finally, although the FDA has blocked attempts to clone babies in the United States, scientists in other countries may be the ones to pioneer reproductive use of the technology and make human cloning safe. Once safety concerns evaporate, the FDA may have no choice but to grant an application to clone a human baby.

Congress is well aware that the regulatory authority of the FDA is limited.[17] To stop human reproductive cloning for reasons other than safety, Congress must act – yet it has not done so. No federal statute specifically addresses the legality of human cloning. This omission is due to political gridlock.

Shortly after the birth of Dolly was announced, congressmen and congresswomen began to introduce bills aimed at corralling the new technology. Two strategies quickly became evident. Conservatives wanted a total ban on human cloning – including a ban on the creation of cloned embryos that would be destroyed in the course of research or the creation of stem cell lines.[18] Liberals wanted to preserve the ability of scientists to clone embryos for research while banning reproductive cloning.[19] In 1998, Senator Trent Lott rushed a total ban to the floor for a vote but was thwarted when Senators Dianne Feinstein and Teddy Kennedy led a filibuster.[20] No law was enacted, but the battle lines for an ongoing political war were drawn.

ESSENTIALISM AND THE LAW OF REPRODUCTIVE CLONING 181

2. Bills that Propose a Total Ban

Conservatives drew first blood in 2001, when the House of Representatives passed a bill that would have made it a federal crime to apply somatic cell nuclear transfer to create a human organism at any stage of development (including embryonic).[21] In other words, the bill prohibited both reproductive and research cloning. Representatives were aware that the vast majority of the public opposed reproductive cloning; one even cited the Time/CNN poll in his remarks.[22] Despite public opposition to reproductive cloning, however, Senate liberals refused to approve any bill that would send scientists to prison for engaging in research cloning.[23] This conservative/liberal scenario repeated itself in 2003. The House passed a total ban, only to watch as the Senate let the matter die once again.[24]

Undaunted, conservatives reintroduced essentially the same proposal to ban all cloning in each subsequent Congress through 2009.[25] None of the later bills made it to the floor for a vote. However, Congress tilted to the right after the 2010 elections and is poised to grow still more conservative in the wake of the upcoming 2012 elections. The total ban could make a comeback along with the conservatives; thus, its most recent iteration is worth considering in some detail.

The Human Cloning Prohibition Act of 2009 was introduced during the 111th Session of the U.S. Congress. It prohibited any use of somatic cell nuclear transfer to create a human embryo, meaning that both research and reproductive cloning would have been criminalized if it had been enacted.[26] It listed fourteen findings in support of a total ban, including several aimed specifically at reproductive cloning.[27] These findings illuminate the motivations of those who wish to ban reproductive cloning and will be analyzed in the paragraphs that follow.

The first finding noted that some individuals had announced plans to clone humans, and the second stated that reproductive cloning was unperfected and unsafe for human use.[28] Perhaps sensing that safety is a temporary argument, the authors of the bill included three additional findings on reproductive cloning.

The third finding stated that "efforts to create human beings by cloning mark a new and decisive step toward turning human reproduction into a manufacturing process in which children are made in laboratories to preordained specifications and, potentially, in multiple copies."[29] This finding contains two fallacies. The claim that cloning is a means of manufacturing designer children is a version of the artifact fallacy, in which humans born through cloning are conceptualized as man-made products rather than normal members of their species. The suggestion that these children can be made in multiple copies reflects the identity fallacy, in which humans born through cloning are imagined to be physically, intellectually, and psychologically identical to their DNA donors and each other.

The fourth finding claimed that "because it is an asexual form of reproduction, cloning confounds the meaning of 'father' and 'mother' and confuses the identity and kinship relations of any cloned child, and thus threatens to weaken existing notions regarding who bears which parental duties and responsibilities for children."[30] This seems to be an argument that asexual reproduction is bad because it upends the existing paradigm of sexual reproduction; in other words, asexual reproduction is unnatural and leads to unnatural relations. This finding resonates with the artifact fallacy, in which humans born through cloning are viewed as products rather than ordinary members of their species.

Notably, the third and fourth findings reflect positions carved out early in the cloning debate. During the House debates of 2001 and 2003, conservative members often appealed to the identity and artifact fallacies to justify opposition to reproductive cloning.[31] In 2002, the President's Council on Bioethics issued its report (Council Report) claiming that cloning transforms procreation into manufacture and confuses family relations.[32]

The fifth finding asserted that "because cloning requires no personal involvement by the person whose genetic material is used, cloning

ESSENTIALISM AND THE LAW OF REPRODUCTIVE CLONING 183

could easily be used to reproduce living or deceased persons without their consent."[33] Although ostensibly concerned with lack of consent, this finding also invokes various fallacies. By using the verb "reproduce" as a synonym for copy, the finding relies upon the identity fallacy. By implying that living people have good reasons to withhold consent to be copied, the finding calls to mind the impostor fallacy, in which humans born through cloning steal not only assets and relationships but individuality itself. Finally, by suggesting that even the dead could be copied, the finding appears to embrace the resurrection fallacy, in which cloning emerges as a technological means of restoring the dead to life.

Had Congress enacted this bill, federal law on cloning in the United States would have been firmly rooted in four ideas that scientific experiments had already proven to be false. It will be interesting to see whether future bills to ban all human cloning incorporate similar findings.

3. Bills that Propose a Ban on Reproductive Cloning Only

Congressional attempts to prohibit reproductive cloning only have been even less successful. For example, in 2001, the House considered a bill to ban all human cloning. Representative James Greenwood (R-Pennsylvania) tried to amend the bill so that it would prohibit only reproductive cloning. In support of his amendment, Greenwood stated: "We all agree that we want to ban reproductive cloning, that it is not safe, it is not ethical to bring a child into this world as a replica of someone else. A child deserves to be the unique product of a mother and father and should not be created by cloning."[34]

Representative David Price (D-North Carolina), who supported the Greenwood amendment, articulated similar sentiments: "Reproductive cloning would threaten individuality and confuse identity, confounding our very definition of personhood, and it would represent a giant step toward turning procreation into manufacture."[35]

Such remarks reflect the influence of the identity and artifact fallacies. Greenwood, however, did not succeed in his attempt to refashion the conservative bill into a measure that scientists and liberals could support. His proposed amendment failed in 2001,[36] as did a similar proposal in 2003.[37]

By 2007, Democrats held the majority in the House. Liberals seized the opportunity to take the initiative on human cloning. Representative Diana DeGette (D-Colorado) attempted to push through a bill that banned reproductive cloning only.[38] The House of Representatives defeated her effort in a vote that broke down largely along party lines, with most Democrats for and nearly all Republicans against.[39] Although the DeGette bill did not include Congressional findings, one can glean insight into the motivations of proponents and opponents from the discussion that took place on the floor of Congress.

DeGette stated once in the course of the discussion that reproductive cloning was unsafe.[40] By contrast, she repeatedly appealed to the political and public consensus in favor of such a ban on reproductive cloning and ended with a plea to "stand up for our constituents."[41] Like any savvy politician, DeGette was trying to follow what she viewed as the will of the people. As public opinion polls indicate, however, the will of the people has been distorted by the identity and artifact fallacies, and probably the impostor and resurrection fallacies also.

Another sponsor of the bill, Representative Zachary Space (D-Ohio), argued: "The development of human life is a natural process that cannot be replaced by scientists in a laboratory. I cannot in good conscience support a world where the chance and wonder of the birth of a child is eliminated in favor of a cold, sterile process."[42]

Space's statement implies humans born through cloning are the unnatural products of an unnatural process, as per the artifact fallacy. His reference to cloning eliminating the chance and wonder of a child suggests that humans born through cloning are designed to order and thus predictable in their character – an insinuation that draws upon both the artifact and identity fallacies.

One representative, Sheila Jackson-Lee (D-Texas), submitted extended comments. Like DeGette, she complained that reproductive cloning was unsafe, but she also supported the bill because "it reinforces

ESSENTIALISM AND THE LAW OF REPRODUCTIVE CLONING

the views and values of the American people. Human beings should be born, not cloned. Bringing a child into this world should be a consecrated act of grace; not a clinical or commercial enterprise."[43]

Jackson-Lee's statement appeals to public opinion, with all the fallacies that undergird it. In addition, by stating that persons who come into being through cloning are not born like other human beings, but are rather the product of a commercial enterprise, she invokes the artifact fallacy.

On the other side of the aisle, Republicans lined up to explain that they opposed reproductive cloning, but would not accept a law that permitted cloned embryos to be created and killed in research. Representative Dave Weldon (R-Florida) put it this way:

> I and millions of Americans like me believe that human life is sacred and we should not be wholesale producing it to be experimented with in the lab and then discarded when the experimentation is done.
>
> Are we really trying to say to the American people we want to make the human embryo the lab rat of the 21st century?[44]

Representative Christopher Smith (R-New Jersey) noted the effect that a ban on reproductive cloning would have:

> As a matter of fact, the [DeGette] legislation makes it a serious crime to allow a cloned human being to survive pass [sic] a certain point.
>
> In other words, this bizarre piece of legislation would make it illegal not to kill a cloned human being; and the penalties are stiff, up to 10 years in prison and a $10 million fine.[45]

Congressional conservatives respect embryonic human life, cloned or not. Their position will be discussed at greater length in Chapter 9, on research cloning. For now, it is enough to say that this pro-life perspective has blocked liberal attempts to ban reproductive cloning.

C. State Laws

Congress has debated; state legislatures have acted. Arizona, Arkansas, Indiana, Oklahoma, Michigan, North Dakota, and South Dakota ban all cloning.[46] In other words, both research cloning and reproductive cloning are illegal there. California, Connecticut, Illinois, Iowa, Maryland, Massachusetts, Missouri, Montana, New Jersey, and Virginia have laws that permit research cloning but prohibit reproductive cloning.[47] In sum, seventeen states (approximately one-third of all states) have made it illegal to use cloning to have a baby. There is a split down the middle, however, on the legality of cloning for research.

The split on research cloning appears to reflect the same political divide that has plagued Congress. In conservative states where many believe the destruction of human embryos is morally wrong, legislatures have preferred the total ban. In states that are liberal or have strong biotechnology industries, legislatures have acted to create a clear legal environment in which research cloning is permitted.

This does not explain, however, why so many state legislatures have vented their wrath on reproductive cloning. Religion alone cannot account for the trend. For example, the Roman Catholic Church teaches that cloning is morally wrong.[48] It also teaches that IVF is morally wrong,[49] yet IVF is legal throughout the United States. This implies that opposition to cloning must be greater than opposition to IVF, and must rest on grounds other than religion.[50]

Similarly, business needs alone cannot account for anti-cloning laws in states that are liberal or have powerful biotechnology lobbies. Research cloning and reproductive cloning are simply different applications of the same technology. One does not necessarily undermine the other. However, biotechnologists fear that a legislature will overreact to the public opposition to reproductive cloning and shut down their research projects.[51] In other words, it is public opposition to reproductive cloning that underlies the business need for a clear legal environment.

Thus, the most likely reason for the enactment of state legislation is public opposition to human reproductive cloning. Because public opposition is rooted in fallacies, the necessary implication is that state legislatures have acted in response to those fallacies, whether consciously or subconsciously.

State legislative history is often sparse, but California's experience offers some evidence that fallacies undergird anti-cloning legislation. The California State Legislature enacted the nation's first anti-cloning law in 1997, shortly after the birth of Dolly was announced.[52] The initial law, which prohibited reproductive cloning only, had a sunset clause and was due to expire in 2003.[53] However, the law also asked the California Department of Health Services to constitute a committee to provide advice on cloning.[54]

In 2002, the California Advisory Committee on Human Cloning issued a report (California Report) that recited many arguments against reproductive cloning and recommended the Legislature turn the moratorium on reproductive cloning into a permanent ban.[55] Although this recommendation rested primarily on the physical dangers of reproductive cloning, the Report noted that individual members of the Committee also objected to reproductive cloning on various social and political grounds.[56]

The Report did not explain which of these social and political grounds the members found most persuasive. However, many of the reasons it cited in favor of a cloning ban are either based upon scientific fallacies or pander to them. For example, the concern that cloned children may suffer from a loss of individuality is a form of the identity fallacy, as is the worry that cloning can be used to create superior persons as part of eugenic programs.[57]

When it comes to the artifact fallacy, the California Report takes a more subtle position. Fears that parents may treat cloned children as products, or that cloned children may lack an open future,[58] do not speak directly to the ability of cloning to manufacture designer products. However, such concerns do rest on the assumption that society, parents, and even cloned children will believe that cloning can manufacture designer products. In other words, the California Report presents the artifact fallacy as credible and accepts that people will act on it.[59]

The California Report also invokes other fallacies. Its claim that DNA donors may lose self-esteem because they now have copies[60] is a soft version of impostor fallacy, in which humans born through cloning do not steal identities outright, but diminish the individuality of others. Although the California Report understands that cloning is not a means of resurrection, it asserts that parents may clone a dead child in order to replace him.[61] In other words, the Report bows to the power of the resurrection fallacy, representing it as one more reason that cloning is a bad thing.

After it received the California Report, the California State Legislature enacted a bill that repealed the sunset provision and left California with a ban on reproductive cloning.[62] To the extent the Legislature relied upon the Report, California law on human cloning finds its roots in the identity, artifact, impostor, and resurrection fallacies.

D. Essentialism and the Law

To summarize the discussion thus far, public opinion polls, policymaking reports, legislative findings, and statements on the floor of Congress support the conclusion that regulatory actions, bills, and laws against reproductive cloning are based in part on the identity, artifact, impostor, and resurrection fallacies. Even those who reject the fallacies advocate prohibition on the ground that others will believe in the fallacies.

It is tempting to blame these fallacies on science fiction. As Part II discussed, films have been portraying humans born through cloning as copies, artifacts, impostors, and resurrections long before Dolly was born.[63] Certainly, the visual images and storylines contained in these films are powerful. However, the United States is a nation comprised largely of educated persons who should be able to distinguish obvious fantasy from fact. Science fiction portrayals should not have a strong influence upon voters and lawmakers – unless those portrayals speak to something deeper in the human psyche.

Part II made the case that the four fallacies are rooted in psychological essentialism. To briefly recap the analysis, when it comes to cloning, there are various ways in which essentialist intuitions can lead people

ESSENTIALISM AND THE LAW OF REPRODUCTIVE CLONING 189

astray. First, as discussed in Chapter 4, the identity fallacy is consistent with folk biological intuitions. The realization that multiple persons can be cloned from the same nuclear DNA may trigger a living-kind conceptualization in which shared essence causes those persons to share physical, intellectual, and psychological traits. This transformation of the individual to kind is a frightening thing: recall that 22 percent of the respondents in the Time/CNN poll stated that their main reason for opposing human cloning was its potential to interfere with human uniqueness and individuality.

The identity fallacy is also consistent with folk sociological intuitions. The realization that a group of humans born through cloning can have essentially the same nuclear DNA may promote a human-kind conceptualization in which shared essence causes those persons to have the same physical, intellectual, psychological, and even occupational traits. Folk sociological intuitions make humans born through cloning seem possible as occupational kinds, such as the clone armies that 22 percent of the respondents in the Time/CNN poll feared.

Second, as discussed in Chapter 5, the artifact fallacy is likely the result of essentialism (or the design stance for those who prefer that characterization). The realization that scientists could select DNA and use it to conceive babies in laboratories triggers the intuition that those babies are products. As such, they are expected to exhibit the physical, intellectual, and personality traits that their creators intend. This intuition not only frames the babies as more thing than human but also encourages the false belief that it is possible to make a human copy, as per the identity fallacy. In addition, this shift from the human to artifact domain may account for the revulsion many people feel when confronted with the prospect of reproductive cloning.

Third, essentialism may play a role in intuitions not only about living kinds or artifacts, but also human individuals. There is evidence that people believe a unique essence permeates the body of an individual. Moreover, many organ transplant recipients have the intuition that the essence of the donor has been transferred to them along with the organ.

This essence is considered capable of conveying personality traits, acquired tastes, and even memories. Translating this to the context of cloning, the somatic cell could be perceived as carrying the essence of the donor into the egg and eventual cloned organism. If that donor is alive, the transfer of essence may be viewed as a diminishment of individuality, as per subtle versions of the impostor fallacy. If the donor is dead, the transfer of essence can lead to the false belief that he has been restored in a new body, as per the resurrection fallacy.

If the identity, artifact, impostor, and resurrection fallacies are the product of psychological essentialism, and regulatory actions, bills, and laws are based on those fallacies, it follows that the regulatory actions, bills, and laws also find their roots in psychological essentialism.

Some may counter that there are many other reasons that people wish to ban human reproductive cloning, including religious beliefs and safety concerns. However, as explained earlier in this chapter, religious opposition has not been enough to produce legislation against other controversial reproductive technologies, such as IVF. Nor can safety concerns alone account for the outpouring of public and legislative hostility toward reproductive cloning. When asked why they opposed reproductive cloning, only 14 percent of respondents in the 2001 Time/CNN poll cited safety as their primary concern.[64] Similarly, the Congressional Record is replete with statements indicating that conservative and liberal lawmakers oppose reproductive cloning on grounds other than safety[65] and would continue to oppose it even if it was safe.[66]

Without the four fallacies, people would not fear reproductive cloning as much as they do. Public opinion would not be as overwhelmingly negative; scientists would not need to urge FDA regulation as a strategic move to protect their own research against legislation; and politicians would find it much harder to muster a majority to pass anti-cloning legislation.

E. Consequences

When intuitive snap judgments masquerade as reasoned discourse and drive public policy decisions, what are the results? Anti-cloning laws may have stymied some stem cell research, but that topic will be taken up later, in Chapter 9. This chapter addresses the consequences of bans on human reproductive cloning.

FDA regulation and the laws of seventeen states have prevented infertile men and women, gays and lesbians, and single women from conceiving genetic offspring through cloning. However, some might argue the point is moot; no one could have procreated through cloning during the past fifteen years because that is not possible yet, let alone efficient or safe. From this point of view, no prospective parents have been harmed.

However, this argument ignores the role that the law has played in blocking the research necessary to make reproductive cloning possible, efficient, and safe. When the FDA asserted jurisdiction over reproductive cloning, it signaled that it would not grant permission to clone, thereby chilling research.[67] Similarly, the states that ban reproductive cloning have sent a clear message that scientists should not invest time and effort in that field. Such restrictions have discouraged efforts to perfect reproductive cloning, and will continue to slow progress for years to come.

1. Do Cloning Bans Undermine Reproductive Freedom?

Moreover, cloning regulation and legislation are already having an ideological impact. As the FDA, Congress, and state legislatures battle a despised technology, they are unwittingly waging war on important American values.

America cherishes reproductive freedom.[68] Most of us take for granted that we have the right to decide for ourselves whether to have children or not. However, this cultural value does not exist and thrive in a vacuum; it is rooted in a strong constitutional jurisprudence.

Nearly seventy years ago, in the landmark case of *Skinner v. Oklahoma*, the U.S. Supreme Court invalidated on equal protection grounds a eugenics law that provided for the sterilization of some convicted criminals but not others.[69] The key to the decision was the Court's declaration that procreation was a basic liberty; for that reason, the

Court applied a strict form of judicial scrutiny that the law could not withstand.[70]

In the decades since then, the Supreme Court has issued other opinions that protect the individual's right to make reproductive decisions. Married or not, Americans have the right to use birth control.[71] Women have the right to have an abortion before the fetus becomes viable, subject to reasonable government regulation that does not unduly burden that right.[72] Although the Supreme Court has not ruled on the point, a lower federal court has held that infertile women have a constitutional right to use assisted reproductive technologies in an effort to get pregnant.[73]

Cloning is a reproductive technology. If it can be perfected, it may one day benefit infertile men and women, gays and lesbians, single women, and others who find that sexual reproduction is an ineffective or undesirable means of conceiving genetic offspring.[74] In this area, however, regulators and legislators have rejected the cultural norm that the individual should decide whether or not to have children. Cloning bans eliminate cloning as a reproductive option, even for those who will remain childless without it. Thus, the erosion of reproductive freedom has already begun.

The damage has not been limited to cloning. Other reproductive technologies have also been affected. Once the FDA asserted jurisdiction over reproductive cloning, it felt emboldened to assert jurisdiction over novel forms of IVF that involved laboratory manipulation of human eggs prior to their fertilization with human sperm. These technologies, intended to aid older women with aging eggs, are no longer available in the United States thanks to FDA intervention.[75]

The same fate may await standard IVF and related technologies. Having recommended a federal ban on cloning in 2002, the President's Council on Bioethics followed up in 2004 with a report on assisted reproductive technologies.[76] It recommended that the federal government fund a study of how safe IVF and related technologies are for the children conceived through them.[77] Given the critical tone of the report,

ESSENTIALISM AND THE LAW OF REPRODUCTIVE CLONING 193

the Council apparently hoped that such a study would yield results that could serve as the basis for increased regulatory control.[78] Although the Council has since disbanded, its recommendation must be taken seriously, for the lessons of cloning are clear. Federal regulation is an effective means of taking reproductive technologies away from those who need them, particularly when those affected are as private about their medical condition and reluctant to speak out as infertile men and women tend to be.[79]

Could the courts emerge as protectors of reproductive freedom? Thus far, no court has decided whether cloning bans infringe procreative liberty in a constitutional sense. Lawyers and academics have written on the topic, with several arguing that the bans are unconstitutional as applied to infertile men and women and other individuals who have no reasonable reproductive alternatives.[80] Due to the limited case law on point, however, the issue is not a simple or straightforward one. Other academics lean the other way, concluding that the courts would be unlikely to invalidate cloning bans on constitutional grounds.[81]

Moreover, a court challenge to a cloning ban could have unpredictable side effects. Suppose, for example, that the ban in question allows scientists to clone embryos only so long as they destroy them in the course of research. Professor John Charles Kunich has warned that pro-life groups and their lawyers will challenge those laws. Faced with embryos that exist only in a Petri dish, and not inside a woman, judges may write opinions that protect embryonic life against such exploitation and destruction. Such a line of jurisprudence could later be expanded and undermine abortion rights down the road.[82]

In short, cloning bans may be the first step toward a future in which regulators and legislators interfere with reproductive decisions and the courts fail to safeguard individual rights. To be sure, this prospect may not trouble everyone. Conservatives have long opposed IVF, some methods of birth control, abortion, and other technologies that violate their religious values and moral commitment to protect embryonic human life. However, many liberals have advocated the right of fertile heterosexuals to control their own reproductive destiny. Liberals who oppose the use of cloning by the infertile, gays, lesbians, and others may be surprised when their betrayal of a core value comes back to haunt them in the form of legal restrictions upon other technologies and constituencies that they value more highly.

2. Do Cloning Bans Undermine Egalitarianism?

The United States is known for its commitment to egalitarian ideals. Those who advocate anti-cloning laws unwittingly violate those ideals in two ways.

a) Adults who Need Cloning to Procreate

Before cloning was discovered, reproductive freedom was the order of the day for Americans. Fertile heterosexuals could reproduce through sex. If they preferred to live childfree, they could use birth control or abortion. Meanwhile, Americans who were infertile, homosexual, or single had recourse to assisted reproductive technologies, gamete donors, and surrogates. Although biology rendered many of these individuals incapable of producing genetic offspring, the law did not stand in their way. From a legal point of view, all Americans had reproductive freedom.

Then cloning came along. The technology held out the promise of overcoming biological barriers that were previously insurmountable. No sooner was it discovered, however, than regulators and lawmakers began to issue prohibitions and threaten doctors and prospective parents with imprisonment. Such actions had little practical impact on fertile heterosexuals, who could still reproduce sexually (or not), but many severely infertile men and women lost the only hope of procreating they had. Similarly, gays and lesbians and single women lost the option to create a family from their own genetic line without the nuclear DNA of strangers.

Some might counter that biology, rather than law, is what has taken reproductive options away from infertile men and women, gays and

ESSENTIALISM AND THE LAW OF REPRODUCTIVE CLONING 195

lesbians, and single women. That, however, is a cruel half-truth, for we live in a modern society in which technology is used to overcome inborn biological limitations. Whenever the law takes a technology away from individuals who could have used it to achieve parity with other individuals, the law deserves to be recognized as a source of inequality. In this case, regulatory actions and laws have taken a reproductive technology away from individuals who might have used it to conceive genetic offspring in the only manner possible or reasonable for them. The laws disadvantage some Americans and not others, and are antiegalitarian for that reason.[83]

b) Humans Born Through Cloning

Despite anti-cloning efforts, there is a good chance that reproductive cloning will be perfected. Scientific research aimed at creating healthy cloned embryos for stem cell research inevitably creates the knowledge necessary to create healthy cloned embryos for reproductive purposes. Once the embryos are cloned, transferring them to the wombs of prospective mothers is a relatively easy task. Of course, American scientists cannot make such transfers without incurring the wrath of the FDA. Scientists in countries where cloning is not yet prohibited may be the ones to conduct the first clinical trials and verify the viability of cloning as an assisted reproductive technology.

Once cloning is established as a reproductive technology, legislative or regulatory bans cannot entirely prevent the birth of cloned children. Infertile men and women, gays and lesbians, and single women will travel outside the United States to obtain cloning services and come back pregnant. Those with the necessary scientific backgrounds and laboratory access may pursue cloning clandestinely within the United States.[84] As a result, some cloned babies will be born in the United States, grow up here, and live among us. Elsewhere I have described all the challenges these persons will face.[85] Here, I focus more narrowly on one particular threat: the stigma that anti-cloning laws will unjustly impose on them.

Cloning is a reproductive technology. Rationales for banning it include objections to use of the technology itself, such as the argument that human beings should not play God and create human life.[86] A reproductive technology, however, is more than an abstract laboratory exercise. It has an end result – in this case, a baby or child. As explained at length throughout this chapter, the fallacies that motivate regulatory actions, bills, and laws focus on the degenerate traits or negative impacts of humans born through cloning. In other words, these are not just bans on cloning – they are bans on a type of person who is expected to have negative traits or impacts upon others due to his or her inherent traits.[87]

Recall the 2001 public opinion poll from Time/CNN. Twenty-two percent of respondents believed that cloning interfered with human uniqueness and individuality. In other words, they perceived humans born through cloning as lacking in individuality (as per the identity fallacy) or as threats to the individuality of others (as per the impostor fallacy). Another 22 percent of respondents worried cloning could be used to create a master race or clone armies. In other words, they perceived humans born through cloning as copies and a menace to others.

Regulators and legislators who ban reproductive cloning may seek to propitiate those who hold false beliefs about humans born through cloning. Alternatively, they act because they hold such beliefs themselves. For example, many congressmen and congresswomen have also associated cloning with duplication or eugenic programs.[88]

The artifact fallacy has also played a role in efforts to enact anti-cloning legislation. In the Council Report that was written to inform Congress, and on the floor of Congress itself, the claim that cloning treats children as designer products shades into the claim that humans born through cloning are in fact designer products.[89]

Finally, government reports produced to inform and influence lawmakers invoke the resurrection fallacy. For example, the Council Report and the California Report raise concerns about premature aging, as if babies born through cloning could have the same biological age as their donors.[90] Such concerns portray humans born through cloning as unhealthy and decrepit.

ESSENTIALISM AND THE LAW OF REPRODUCTIVE CLONING

In our democratic society, laws are an expression of public beliefs and values. When laws are based upon false beliefs, they validate those beliefs.[91] Cloning bans based on the identity, artifact, impostor, and resurrection fallacies stigmatize humans born through cloning as dangerous copies, products, impersonators, and reincarnations who do not deserve to exist.[92] These stigmatizing laws undermine the fundamental American principle that all men and women are created equal.[93]

Government reports sometimes take a more nuanced stance, perhaps because the experts behind them are informed on the science and understand that certain popular beliefs are false. So, for example, rather than claim outright that humans born through cloning are copies, as per the identity fallacy, the reports suggest parents would hold unreasonable expectations for their children.[94] Rather than claim outright that humans born through cloning are designer products, as per the artifact fallacy, some reports worry that parents might treat the children as if they were designer products.[95] Rather than cast humans born through cloning as impostors, one report argues that donors will suffer diminished individuality when they realize they are no longer unique but have genetic copies.[96] Rather than claim that humans born through cloning are resurrections, the reports suggest that bereaved parents will use the technology to create replacement children.[97]

In short, the reports anticipate that prospective parents and others will believe in the fallacies and act improperly. Given the pervasiveness of essentialist intuitions, the reports are correct to identify these risks. Instead of recommending strategies to dispel the fallacies and forestall misuses of human cloning, however, the reports recommend that legislatures prohibit the existence of all cloned children.

This legislative strategy is inappropriate for several reasons. First, as explained previously, parents who cannot reproduce sexually may be able to reproduce asexually through cloning. There is no reason to ban their use of the technology. Second, cloning bans will fail to halt illegitimate uses. For example, a grieving parent who is determined to raise her child from the dead will defy any law. The only way to stop her is to make it clear that cloning cannot do what she wants it to do. Third, by capitulating to ignorance in this manner, the reports implicitly send the message that it is reasonable for people to believe in the fallacies. In so doing, the reports (and laws based upon them) legitimize the fallacies and further stigmatize cloned children.

F. Summary

In this chapter, I have argued that psychological essentialism is a hidden driver behind the legal response to human reproductive cloning. The heuristic has led liberal lawmakers to betray their longstanding allegiance to reproductive freedom. It has also lured liberals and conservatives into supporting laws that run counter to egalitarianism. In the rush to fend off clone armies and the like, politicians have not taken the time to question various fallacies, let alone ponder what the psychological bases of those fallacies might be.

The next chapter will continue to explore the link between psychological essentialism and the law of human cloning. The focus will shift, however, from reproductive cloning to research on cloned human embryos.

9 Essentialism and the Law of Research Cloning

THIS CHAPTER FOCUSES ON RESEARCH CLONING, that is, the cloning of human embryos for use in research and medical therapies. It begins with a brief discussion of the science of embryonic stem cell research and explains that research cloning is a subset of that broader field.

Next, this chapter describes the legal regime governing embryonic stem cell research in general and research cloning in particular. The discussion will emphasize the impact that opposition to human reproductive cloning has had upon the field of research cloning.

Finally, the chapter discusses how essentialist intuitions have affected the debate over research cloning. Insisting on the sanctity of embryonic human life, conservative lawmakers have employed a slippery slope rhetoric in which all cloning must be banned to prevent the birth of babies imagined to be copies or artifacts. Meanwhile, liberal lawmakers have championed the rights of scientists to engage in research. In the course of so doing, they have not only framed cloned embryos as things to be exploited, but have argued that scientific freedom must be curtailed to prevent the birth of copied or manufactured babies. These political strategies on the right and left are not only self-defeating but produce laws that erode American values of scientific freedom and egalitarianism.

A. Stem Cells: Science and Ethics

Dolly was not the only biological surprise that the late twentieth century had in store for the world. In 1998, scientists at the University of Wisconsin announced that they had taken cells from the inner cell mass of human blastocysts and used them to establish stem cell colonies (lines) that could proliferate indefinitely in the lab.[1] The stem cells were *pluripotent*, meaning they had the ability to develop into every cell type in the adult body.[2]

Many people strongly support embryonic stem cell research. They note that the technology offers fresh opportunities to conduct research and perhaps derive novel medical therapies.[3] However, others note a serious ethical problem: to create a stem cell line, a scientist must disaggregate the embryo, and that process kills the embryo. For this reason, religious leaders and others who cherish human life from its inception strongly oppose embryonic stem cell research. From this perspective, destroying human embryos in the course of research is illicit because no human life should be sacrificed, even for scientific or medical ends.[4]

Scientists engaged in embryonic stem cell research often use leftover IVF embryos that would otherwise be discarded. However, when scientists must create embryos for research, two additional ethical concerns arise. First, the scientists treat these embryos solely as a means to an end. Some critics have protested that such objectification devalues human life.[5] Second, scientists must find women who are willing to take powerful drugs to stimulate the ripening of multiple eggs and undergo surgical retrieval of those eggs. Although the health risks associated with this process are generally few, in rare cases women have been hospitalized or even died because of adverse drug effects or overstimulation of their ovaries.[6] Thus, critics question whether it is ethical to recruit women as egg donors for research purposes. They oppose financial compensation on the ground that it could unfairly induce women into making donations.[7]

1. Stem Cells from Cloned Human Embryos

As Chapter 3 explained in detail, scientists have cloned human embryos for research. They have not yet succeeded in creating a normal stem cell line from a cloned human embryo.[8] However, research continues apace because scientists would like to create DNA-matched stem cell lines for research and therapy.[9]

Like all embryonic stem cell research, research cloning involves the disaggregation and destruction of human embryos. Thus, it invokes the central ethical question of whether it is morally acceptable to kill nascent human life.[10] In addition, because cloning is not yet a reproductive technology in humans, there are no leftover cloned embryos to use. Scientists engaged in research cloning must recruit women to supply eggs and must create their own embryos to serve as research subjects. Like other cases in which embryos are created solely for research, cloning raises concerns about safety and the objectification of human life.[11]

Finally, research cloning presents a unique concern: the slippery slope to reproductive cloning. Once stem cell researchers publish the results of their experiments, mavericks can use their discoveries and methods to clone human embryos for reproductive purposes. Mavericks can also misappropriate embryos created for research purposes and transfer them to women, leading to unsanctioned births.[12] Therefore, research cloning inevitably raises all of the objections to reproductive cloning discussed in previous chapters.

2. Induced Pluripotent Stem Cells

The reader may have heard that recent developments in stem cell science eliminate the need to conduct research on human embryos, including cloned embryos. Before continuing the analysis of research cloning, this chapter will briefly describe those developments.

In 2006, Japanese scientists reported that they had discovered a way to create stem cells without eggs or embryos. They selected four *transcription factors* (that is, genes known to regulate the expression of other genes[13]); added the factors to retroviruses; and transfected fibroblasts from mice with the retroviruses. Amazingly, this method directly reprogrammed the cells; in other words, the cells lost the epigenetic marks that had inactivated most of their DNA, causing them to function like embryonic stem cells. The scientists dubbed the product *induced pluripotent stem cells.*[14]

One year later, in 2007, the Japanese team demonstrated that the same transcription factors and technique were capable of reprogramming human fibroblasts into induced pluripotent stem cells.[15] Since then, scientists around the world have experimented with different combinations of transcription factors and means of ferrying them into cells.[16] Some have gone farther, seeking out methods that bypass the need to transfer the factors into the cells. For example, scientists have reprogrammed human fibroblasts with synthetic messenger ribonucleic acid (mRNA) that mimics the effects of the transcription factors.[17] Others have reprogrammed human fibroblasts with *microRNAs*[18] – that is, molecules of ribonucleic acid that help to regulate the expression of genes.[19]

As exciting as these developments are, induced pluripotent stem cell science is in its infancy and has its drawbacks. For example, transcription-factor methods convert adult cells to induced pluripotent stem cells at a relatively low rate.[20] Also, induced pluripotent stem cells have different patterns of gene expression than embryonic stem cells, and differentiate into specific tissues at a lower rate than embryonic stem cells do.[21]

Further, there are reasons to be concerned about the medical utility of induced pluripotent stem cells. One recent experiment found genetic mutations in human induced pluripotent stem cells.[22] Another showed that murine induced pluripotent stem cells provoked immune responses when implanted into mice with the same genetic profile, thereby challenging the common assumption that the new technology can generate DNA-matched cells for transplant without rejection.[23]

In sum, we are a long way from the day when induced pluripotent stem cells will be reliable and safe enough to eliminate any need for embryonic stem cells. Research on human embryos, including cloned human embryos, is necessary if stem cell science is to advance. It is of paramount importance that the laws affecting such research be grounded in scientific fact, rather than intuition.

B. Federal Laws

Therefore, this chapter now proceeds to describe the federal legal regime that governs embryonic stem cell research in general and research cloning in particular. The reasons for Congressional efforts to ban research cloning will be set forth, so that they can be analyzed in-depth later in the chapter. This section ends with a brief discussion of federal funding of embryonic stem cell research.

1. The Legality of Embryonic Stem Cell Research

In the United States, research on human embryos and embryonic stem cell lines is legal at the federal level and is likely to remain so.[24] In a 2011 Gallup Poll, 62 percent of respondents found medical research on embryonic stem cells to be morally acceptable; only 30 percent disagreed.[25] Given this public sentiment, it is unlikely that Congress would outlaw embryonic stem cell research.[26]

2. The Legality of Research Cloning

Research cloning is a type of embryonic stem cell research; therefore, it is legal in the United States. However, this particular branch of stem cell research is more controversial.

As explained in Chapter 8, the House of Representatives passed bills to ban all human cloning in 2001 and again in 2003. These bills would have criminalized research cloning. Fortunately for scientists, these bills failed in the Senate.[27] However, if Congress and the White House tilt to the right in the next elections, research cloning may yet be banned.

As Chapter 8 also discussed, in 2007 liberal lawmakers introduced a bill to ban only reproductive cloning. The House of Representatives rejected the bill by a close vote. However, if Congress and the White House tilt to the left in the future, such a proposal might be enacted. In that event, research cloning will be legal, but cloned embryos will become the only human embryos in the United States that must be destroyed based on their genetic heritage.

Because a future Congress could enact a law to regulate research cloning, it is worthwhile to review issues raised and arguments made in the recent past. In 2001, the House of Representatives debated a proposal to ban all human cloning. For brevity's sake, the following sections focus on the issues and arguments presented at that time. The endnotes provide additional citations to similar issues and arguments raised when Congress debated cloning bills in 2003 and 2007.

a) Do Cloned Embryos have the same Moral Status as Other Embryos?
During the 2001 debate, conservative lawmakers staked out the position that cloned embryos were worthy of protection against destructive research.[28] The obvious move for liberals would have been to question the moral significance of embryos in general, but few took that position.[29] Instead, several attempted to sidestep the issue by denying that entities created via somatic cell nuclear transfer were embryos at all. For example, Ted Deutsch (D-Florida) stated: "Calling that an embryo does not make it an embryo. It is not an embryo."[30] Similarly, James Greenwood (R-Pennsylvania) characterized a cloned blastocyst as a collection of cells in a Petri dish and deemed it ridiculous to imagine it had a soul.[31]

Such claims provoked a spirited response from Dave Weldon (R-Florida), the sponsor of the proposed total ban: "I further want to dismiss this notion that has been put forward by some of the speakers here in general debate that a cloned human embryo is somehow not alive or it is not human. There is just literally no basis in science to make that sort of claim."[32] Weldon was correct that the entity generated through

ESSENTIALISM AND THE LAW OF RESEARCH CLONING

cloning is alive and carries human genes. However, is it truly the equivalent of a fertilized embryo?

On this point, experts differ. When the President's Council on Bioethics released its report on human cloning in 2002, it decided to describe the entity in question as a cloned human embryo.[33] The Council reasoned that the moral questions before it centered on the developmental potential of the entity. Thus, function mattered more than origin. Because the entity was human and in the first stage of its development, the Council felt the term "embryo" was appropriate, even without proof that development to term was possible.[34]

Other experts have attacked this reasoning in two ways. First, some accept the Council's focus on function but deny that a cloned human embryo has the same developmental potential as other human embryos. For example, in an essay published in 2004, Dr. Rudolf Jaenisch argued that stem cells can be harvested from cloned embryos because they are biologically flawed and have little chance of developing into healthy human beings.[35]

This argument rests on two flawed assumptions. One is that human reproductive cloning is impossible. Given how many other mammalian species have been cloned, that seems unlikely. Another is that all cloned embryos must be developmentally competent in order for any to deserve protection against destructive research. That is not the standard by which fertilized embryos are judged, however. From 45–75 percent of fertilized embryos spontaneously miscarry within a few weeks.[36] Despite that fact, many ethicists take seriously the claim that fertilized embryos are human beings who should not be subjected to destructive research. Reasoning by analogy, if embryos are the moral equivalent of born persons, then no cloned embryos should be destroyed if even a few are developmentally competent.

Second, Dr. Paul McHugh, who was once a member of the Council, published an essay in 2004 claiming that origins matter more than function. According to his view, IVF begets new human beings who should not be exploited. Cloning, however, is more like tissue culture in that it expresses the intrinsic potential somatic cells have for growth and replication outside the body. Dr. McHugh claims it is acceptable to harvest stem cells from what he calls "clonotes."[37]

By focusing on origins, rather than function, Dr. McHugh emphasizes the one aspect of cloned embryos that most distinguishes them from other human embryos. Further, by giving these embryos a special name that sets them apart from other human embryos, Dr. McHugh marks them as fodder for research. Although his rhetoric is clever, I believe the Council gets the better of Dr. McHugh on this issue. If a cloned embryo has the potential to function like other embryos, and produce a human child, it should be characterized as an embryo.

For purposes of this book, however, whether cloning produces embryos is less important than the willingness of scientists and politicians to deny that it does. Part D will analyze the essentialist intuitions that inspire such denials. For now, this chapter continues with a review of other ethical concerns related to research cloning.

b) Is it Ethical to Clone Embryos for Research?

During the 2001 debate on the proposed total ban, conservative lawmakers also questioned the morality of cloning embryos specifically for research.[38] As Dave Weldon (D-Florida) stated: "It is one thing to talk about stem cell research using embryos that are slated for destruction. It is a whole separate issue to say, we are going to now sanction an industry that creates human embryos."[39] In other words, no human being – even one as tiny as an embryo – should be treated as a means, rather than an end.

Weldon's argument did not sway liberal lawmakers, even though many had stated in previous debates that embryos should not be created for research.[40] Once again, the debate reflects a double standard, in which embryos derived through fertilization are thought to be more deserving of protection against exploitation than cloned embryos.

c) Will Research Cloning Lead to Reproductive Cloning?

During the 2001 debate on the proposed total ban, conservatives argued that research cloning would lead to reproductive cloning, as scientists might illegally implant cloned embryos in women.[41] Liberals responded that criminal penalties would render a ban on reproductive cloning effective.[42] Conservatives retorted that such penalties would force scientists to destroy embryonic human life.[43]

This debate reveals much about the psychology of lawmakers on both sides. If conservatives voted to ban research cloning in part because it might lead to reproductive cloning, it follows that their votes must have rested in part on their reasons for opposing reproductive cloning. As explained in Chapter 8, their reasons for opposing reproductive cloning included the identity and artifact fallacies.[44] Thus, false perceptions of humans born through cloning as copies and things were a factor in motivating conservative attempts to ban research cloning along with reproductive cloning.

As for the liberal lawmakers, if they had simply wanted research cloning to remain legal, they could have achieved that goal without enacting any law whatsoever. Instead, they demanded enactment of a partial ban that would have forced scientists to destroy cloned embryos or go to prison. In other words, liberal policy on research cloning was also shaped by opposition to reproductive cloning.

To be sure, some of these liberal lawmakers might have feared that cloned embryos would otherwise lead to the birth of disabled children.[45] Yet, they did not propose the destruction of non-cloned embryos that could lead to the birth of disabled children (such as IVF embryos with abnormal chromosomes). Thus, liberals must have opposed reproductive cloning for reasons that went beyond safety. As revealed in Chapter 8, these reasons included the identity and artifact fallacies.[46] In other words, because they viewed humans born through cloning as copies and things, liberals wanted to mandate their destruction before they could be born.

Finally, on both sides of the aisle, lawmakers knew of the groundswell of public opposition to reproductive cloning. As discussed in Chapter 8, opinion polls from 2001 indicate that this opposition was based on the identity and artifact fallacies, and possibly the impostor and resurrection fallacies also. To the extent lawmakers acted to appease the public, their votes on research cloning were affected by nightmare visions of humans born through cloning as copies, artifacts, impostors, and reincarnations.

To summarize the discussion thus far, three issues have pervaded the debate over research cloning: whether cloned embryos have the same moral status as other human embryos; whether it is ethical to clone embryos for research; and whether research cloning leads down a slippery slope to reproductive cloning. The intuitions lurking behind these issues will be identified and analyzed in Part D of this chapter.

3. Federal Funding of Embryonic Stem Cell Research

This discussion of federal law would not be complete without a brief account of how the government funds embryonic stem cell research. Since 1996, the U.S. Congress has included a rider to every appropriations bill for the Department of Health and Human Services. Known as the Dickey-Wicker Amendment after its original sponsors, this rider prohibits the use of federal funds for research projects that involve the creation or destruction of human embryos.[47]

Shortly after President Barack Obama took power, the National Institutes of Health (NIH – an agency within the Department of Health and Human Services) published guidelines that attempt to work around these restrictions.[48] The NIH guidelines make federal funds available for research on embryonic stem cell lines created from leftover IVF embryos.[49] In other words, when it comes to disaggregating embryos and creating stem cell lines, the federal government cannot fund the work, but once stem cell lines exist, the NIH believes it is free to fund research on them.[50]

However, the NIH guidelines do not make federal funds available for research on stem cell lines derived from embryos created for research purposes – including cloned human embryos.[51] In explaining this omission, the NIH claimed there was a lack of ethical and scientific consensus regarding the propriety of funding such research.[52] Therefore, although research cloning remains legal at the federal level, scientists cannot obtain the funds they need to engage in such investigations. In this regard, the federal government has treated research cloning less favorably than other stem cell research.

C. State Laws

Embryonic stem cell research faces restrictions in some states, particularly those with conservative voters and legislators. For example, in 2010 Arizona enacted a law that prohibits "destructive human embryonic stem cell research,"[53] that is, "any research that involves the disaggregation of any human embryo for the purpose of creating human pluripotent stem cells or human pluripotent stem cell lines."[54] This provision clearly bars disaggregation, but its full import is unclear. Once embryonic stem cell lines are created in another state, is it illegal to use them in Arizona on the reasoning that the research depends upon, and thus involves, the disaggregation of an embryo?[55]

Several other states have laws that are not aimed at embryonic stem cell research per se, but are broad enough to preclude the act of disaggregation that converts an embryo into a stem cell line. For example, Louisiana prohibits farming or culturing IVF embryos for research purposes.[56] Michigan, Minnesota, and South Dakota ban research that is destructive or harmful to embryos.[57] Florida, North Dakota, Maine, Pennsylvania, and Rhode Island have abortion laws that prohibit fetal experimentation[58]; some scholars believe these laws bar experimentation on embryos in vitro.[59]

The majority of states have no relevant laws; in these jurisdictions, embryonic stem cell research is legal by default. However, seven states have not been content to regulate this emerging scientific field through inaction. California, Connecticut, Illinois, Iowa, Massachusetts,

Missouri, and New Jersey have adopted constitutional provisions or laws that explicitly authorize embryonic stem cell research.[60] In general, these research-friendly states are also politically liberal and/or are home to major universities and research institutions.

1. Research Cloning

When it comes to research on cloned human embryos, state laws reflect the same conservative/liberal political divide. Some insights can be gleaned through a comparison of laws on embryo research in general and cloning in particular.

Let us begin with the more conservative states. Arizona, Arkansas, Indiana, Michigan, North Dakota, Oklahoma, and South Dakota have enacted laws specifically to prohibit the cloning of human embryos for any purpose, including research.[61] Four of these states consistently value embryonic life, for they also ban embryo research in general: Arizona, Michigan, North Dakota, and South Dakota. Another three states do not: Arkansas, Indiana, and Oklahoma. If these states permit research that destroys human embryos, why should they ban the cloning of embryos? One likely answer is fear of the slippery slope. If allowed to exist, cloned embryos might lead to the birth of cloned babies.

Turning to the more liberal states, California, Connecticut, Illinois, Iowa, Maryland, Massachusetts, Missouri, Montana, New Jersey, and Virginia permit research cloning but ban reproductive cloning.[62] For the most part, these states are consistent in their policies toward cloned and non-cloned embryos: all are considered appropriate fodder for research. As discussed above, California, Connecticut, Illinois, Iowa, Massachusetts, Missouri, and New Jersey have provisions that authorize embryonic stem cell research.[63] Maryland and Montana take care to mention that their cloning bans do not prohibit embryonic stem cell research.[64]

However, there are two ways in which these liberal states treat cloned embryos less favorably than non-cloned embryos. First, the only

ESSENTIALISM AND THE LAW OF RESEARCH CLONING

permissible destiny for a cloned embryo is death. No one can transfer it to a woman without breaking the law. This grim state of legal affairs is the result of the various fallacies that drive opposition to reproductive cloning, as discussed in Chapter 8.

Second, Massachusetts and Missouri have adopted provisions that permit scientists to create embryos for research via cloning but not via fertilization.[65] In other words, lawmakers in these states consider it wrong to treat fertilized embryos as a means to an end, but do not oppose the objectification of cloned embryos, which occupy a lower moral rung.

D. Essentialism and the Law

Having reviewed federal and state laws, the chapter turns to examine the role that psychological essentialism has played in the political and legal debate over research cloning.[66] To sharpen the focus of the analysis, it must begin by identifying concerns that are specific to cloning, as opposed to general concerns that apply to research involving any type of embryos.[67]

First, whether embryos should be subjected to destructive research is a general concern. Politicians and lawmakers who believe life begins at conception oppose research on all human embryos, whether fertilized or cloned. However, some federal lawmakers have attempted to bypass this issue by questioning whether cloned embryos are indeed embryos – a curious response that is specific to cloning and thus deserving of analysis here.

Second, whenever embryos are created solely for research, scientists treat embryonic human life as a means to an end. Moreover, health risks arise, as women must take drugs to generate the eggs needed to create the embryos. At first glance, these concerns appear to be general ones, because they apply as much to embryos created via fertilization as embryos created via cloning. However, for purposes of this book, the key question is whether politicians and lawmakers have treated both classes of embryo the same. In some cases the answer is yes. For example, the

NIH does not fund work on any embryos created for research. Similarly, congressional conservatives object to the creation of any embryos for research. However, congressional liberals have a more uneven record. Some who disapprove the creation of fertilized embryos for research embrace the cloning of embryos for research. Moreover, in Massachusetts and Missouri, the law prohibits scientists from fertilizing embryos for research but allows them to clone embryos for research. This disparate treatment of cloned embryos will also be analyzed here.

Third, and most importantly, research cloning is different from all other embryonic stem cell research in that it raises the specter of reproductive cloning. Congressional conservatives fear that cloned embryos will lead to the birth of cloned babies; congressional liberals share this concern, but believe law can prevent this outcome by mandating the destruction of cloned embryos. State laws mirror this pattern. Some laws ban all cloning, even if other embryo research is permitted. Other laws permit research cloning but take care to prohibit reproductive cloning. This section will address the ways in which concerns about reproductive cloning have affected laws on research cloning.

1. Why Do Some Politicians Deny that Cloned Embryos Are Embryos and Refuse Them Legal Protection Against Destruction?

Some lawmakers deny that cloned embryos can be embryos. Others oppose the creation of fertilized embryos for research, but accept the creation of cloned embryos for research. From a scientific point of view, these reactions seem strange; fertilized and cloned embryos are both nascent human life.

From the point of view of psychological essentialism, however, these two kinds of embryos are quite different. As explained in Chapter 5, one male and one female uniting through coitus to produce offspring is the paradigmatic method of creating a member of a living kind.[68] When scientists create fertilized human embryos, their actions mimic mating in certain respects. A woman still produces the eggs involved, and a man still contributes the sperm; as a result, the process is sexual and that anchors the embryos within the realm of living kinds. Factors that might tip the embryos into the artifact realm are limited. Scientists do create the embryos in a laboratory, which might seem like a factory to some observers[69]; however, the gametes are capable of uniting to create an embryo without extensive assistance from the scientists.

Contrast that process with the creation of cloned human embryos. As explained in Chapter 5, cloning is asexual reproduction – a fact that intuitively challenges the status of the embryos as members of the human kind. Moreover, factors beyond the laboratory setting make it seem as if the cloned embryos are man-made. Because the scientists select the DNA for the cloning, there is an element of design – albeit a more limited one than most people realize. Also, the scientists do not use eggs in their natural state; they enucleate them. They use technology (electricity or chemicals) to unite the DNA with the eggs. This level of human intervention may trigger the intuition that cloned embryos belong in the artifact domain.

Once the mind classifies the cloned embryos as artifacts, essentialism further teaches that the intention of the creator determines their properties, uses, and type.[70] If the scientists intend these embryos not as ends in themselves, but rather as resources to be utilized and discarded, lawmakers are more likely to believe that the embryos do not deserve legal protection against exploitation.

Interestingly, this same distinction between living kinds and artifacts is reflected in Dr. McHugh's essay on human cloning. He asserts that origins are determinative of ethical status. In his opinion, IVF involves the begetting of embryos who are human beings from the beginning. By contrast, cloning generates clonotes that can be harvested for their cells.[71] Dr. McHugh's rhetoric is clever because it takes advantage of a psychological predisposition to view life as less than human when it is made in the lab through asexual processes.

Finally, as Nick Haslam predicts, once intuition shifts cloned embryos to the artifact domain, people are more likely to view them with indifference.[72] No one reacts with moral outrage when an object is objectified. That may explain why liberal lawmakers do not protest when cloned embryos are created solely for the purpose of research.

2. What Do Slippery Slope Arguments Imply about Political Reactions to Research Cloning?

Chapter 8 analyzed regulatory actions, bills, and laws that ban reproductive cloning. It found that the identity, artifact, impostor, and resurrection fallacies were motivating factors in imposing the bans. Moreover, as explained in Part II, these cloning fallacies are the product of psychological essentialism. Thus, Chapter 8 concluded that regulatory actions, bills, and laws that ban reproductive cloning are the product of psychological essentialism.

This chapter has examined proposed federal legislation and state laws against research cloning. It has shown that research cloning is perceived as a slippery slope to reproductive cloning. Conservative and liberal lawmakers differ in their proposed solutions. Conservatives want to ban all cloning; liberals want to mandate the destruction of cloned embryos. Either way, opposition to reproductive cloning drives a large portion of the political and legal debate over research cloning. In other words, the cloning fallacies – and the essentialist intuitions that undergird them – not only inspire bans on reproductive cloning but also distort political and legal responses to what should be regarded as just another branch of embryonic stem cell research.

E. Consequences

Chapter 8 described the impacts of regulatory actions and laws that ban reproductive cloning. This chapter now considers the impacts of attempts to regulate research cloning.

Thus far, the legal consequences have been limited. Congress has been unable to enact a law on cloning, so research cloning remains legal in the United States, except in the seven states that have enacted total bans. Ten states have laws that explicitly permit research on cloned embryos; these laws reaffirm an existing state of legal affairs.

Yet, there is potential for big change. With conservatives and liberals divided on how to handle research cloning, each side risks a loss in Congress. A federal law could preempt contrary state laws and create a uniform national policy on research cloning – one that would infuriate whichever side lost. Therefore, it is timely to evaluate the essentialist arguments used in this debate – not only to gauge their persuasiveness, but also to judge their consistency with the core values of those who use them. The following analysis considers the issue from the conservative and liberal perspectives.

1. How Conservatives Act Against Their Own Interests

The conservative drive for a law that bans all human cloning is based in part on a desire to protect embryonic life from exploitive research. In aid of this goal, conservative lawmakers have enlisted slippery slope arguments, warning that research cloning will inevitably lead to reproductive cloning. However, slippery slope arguments are persuasive only if there are good reasons to oppose reproductive cloning. To justify their opposition, lawmakers have relied on fallacies grounded in essentialism.[73] As discussed in Chapter 8, lawmakers have portrayed humans born through cloning as copies and artifacts in floor debates and proposed legislative findings.

What these conservative lawmakers don't seem to realize is that the very fallacies that make a strong intuitive case against reproductive cloning undercut their efforts to prevent the exploitation of cloned embryos. As discussed in Chapter 5, people associate certain traits with human nature: emotional responsiveness, warmth, cognitive openness, individuality, and depth. These are the same traits that the identity and artifact fallacies deny to humans born through cloning. When humans born through cloning are falsely characterized as fungible copies, or products condemned to preordained lives, they are dehumanized in a mechanistic fashion.[74] That dehumanization makes it much more difficult to persuade others that these individuals share our humanity and are deserving of respect, even in the earliest stages of life.

Thus, conservative lawmakers face a dilemma. The same slippery slope argument that distinguishes cloning from other stem cell research and reinforces the case for a total ban suggests that no human life is at stake. If no human life is at stake – if cloning is a manufacturing process that generates fungible objects – then the case for protecting cloned embryos crumbles, opening the door to enactment of a federal law that mandates the destruction of cloned embryos.

Further, by making such arguments, conservative lawmakers act inconsistently with their own core values. They have articulated a deeply held and sincere belief that embryonic human life is sacrosanct and deserving of protection. Their fight to protect even cloned embryonic life against deliberate creation and destruction is admirable for it demonstrates the consistency and sincerity of their beliefs. Moreover, conservative opposition to research cloning displays a commitment to egalitarianism that is very American. There is no room in conservative philosophy for a distinction between cloned embryonic life and other embryonic life – all is equally deserving of protection. Similarly, there should be no room in conservative philosophy for a distinction between humans born through cloning and other human beings.

To be sure, many conservative lawmakers and their constituents hold sincere religious beliefs that cloning is against the will of God[75] and cannot accept the technology. Still, conservatives would benefit by abandoning slippery slope arguments that rely upon the identity and artifact fallacies, for two reasons. First, as demonstrated throughout this book, the identity and artifact fallacies stand in direct contradiction to the scientific facts. As evidence continues to mount that cloned animals are unique individuals and ordinary members of their species, those who adhere to the fallacies will appear increasingly foolish. Second, conservatives must prioritize. If protection of embryonic life is their primary goal, they should consistently emphasize the humanity of that life, or their credibility and persuasiveness will fade.

For those who respect embryonic life, but are not ready to accept reproductive cloning, Arizona offers a new model. Its cloning law prohibits the creation of a human embryo through any means other than fertilization of egg by sperm.[76] Because cloning is not fertilization, the provision bars the creation of cloned embryos, which is the first step in reproductive cloning. Cloning an embryo is a class 1 misdemeanor[77] that carries only a six-month sentence.[78] There is no additional penalty for transferring that embryo to a woman so that it has the chance to develop and be born.

By contrast, Arizona makes it a class 6 felony to engage in "destructive human embryonic stem cell research,"[79] that is, research that involves the disaggregation of any human embryo (cloned or not)[80] to create stem cells.[81] The presumptive sentence for a class 6 felony is one year.[82] In other words, Arizona is the only state that treats research cloning as a more serious crime than reproductive cloning.[83]

The Arizona law demonstrates respect for embryonic life, without regard to origin or genotype. By making reproductive cloning only a misdemeanor, the law also takes a first step toward reducing the stigma that humans born through cloning will face on account of having been conceived via a prohibited technology (as discussed at length in Chapter 8). Perhaps one day, after people get to know people born through cloning as human beings, Arizona and other conservative states will move to decriminalize reproductive cloning altogether.

2. How Liberals Act Against Their Own Interests

This chapter now considers the debate over research cloning from the liberal point of view. Research cloning is legal except in the seven states that have banned it. Why, then, have lawmakers pushed hard for a federal law that permits research cloning while banning reproductive cloning?

As explained in Chapter 8, scientists and biotechnology companies that are interested in stem cell research want a stable legal environment in which to do business. No one wants to invest in cloning only to find later on that the state legislature has criminalized their research and destroyed the profitability of their venture.[84] A federal law prohibiting reproductive cloning would eliminate that threat and provide the stability that scientists and businesspeople crave.

In furtherance of this strategy, liberal lawmakers have resorted to arguments based on the identity and artifact fallacies. If humans born through cloning are copies or manufactured products, it is easier to make the case that their existence should be prevented. Besides, as explained in the previous section, such argumentation has a further benefit: by dehumanizing humans born through cloning, it lessens the revulsion people feel when contemplating research that creates embryos in order to disaggregate them.

The essentialist arguments, however, are a double-edged sword for liberal lawmakers. By painting the consequences of reproductive cloning as dire, liberals have invited the slippery slope arguments that conservatives have made so effectively. Laws are broken every day. There simply is no way to be sure that cloned embryos will not be implanted in a womb and born as children nine months later.

Moreover, by joining the clamor for a ban on reproductive cloning, liberals have demonstrated their willingness to sacrifice scientific freedom to popular hysteria. This bad example invites attacks on other technologies that hold scientific promise but offend the sensibilities of some people. Chief among these technologies is research cloning, which might end up prohibited at the federal level because liberal lawmakers did not do enough to defend scientific freedom at the start of the debate.[85]

Some might protest that the U.S. Constitution protects scientific freedom and can be used to invalidate any law that prohibits research cloning. That is not necessarily the case. Although legal academics have opined that the First Amendment protects scientific research,[86] the U.S. Supreme Court has never addressed the question squarely.[87] If Congress enacts a total ban on cloning, and scientists challenge that law, there is no guarantee that the Supreme Court will do what they want. Cloning is very unpopular. The Court may be reluctant to recognize a constitutional right to conduct scientific research, or may define the contours of the right so narrowly that it provides no protection to research cloning and other controversial scientific experiments.[88]

Finally, if Congress does ban human cloning, enforcement will be imperfect; people will be cloned here or abroad and become our family members, neighbors, coworkers, and friends. As Chapter 8 explained, however, the anti-cloning law will mark those individuals as unworthy to exist. Arguably, a law that bans only reproductive cloning would heighten this stigma. Under such a legal regime, all human embryos would have a chance to be implanted and grow, except for cloned embryos, which could only be destroyed. This disparate treatment would reinforce the message that cloned life is less valuable than other human life.[89] Liberals have made significant efforts to secure equality for racial and ethnic minorities, women, gays, and lesbians; it would be ironic if their campaign against human cloning created a new class of outcasts.

Fortunately, there is a simple way for liberal lawmakers to combat these negative consequences: stop attacking human cloning. There is nothing to fear from humans born through cloning. They can never be copies, manufactured products, or any of the other freakish beings that essentialism predicts. If scientists and biotechnology companies are afraid that the public will demand a total ban, the best strategy is to debunk cloning fallacies now, with the aid of fifteen years of experimental evidence. Attacking reproductive cloning does nothing but maintain public hysteria and increase the likelihood of a total ban at the federal level.

F. Summary

This chapter has explained that psychological essentialism has shaped federal and state bills and laws that address research cloning. In making the case that research cloning leads down a slippery slope to reproductive cloning, conservative lawmakers have exploited essentialist fears about humans born through cloning. However, because such arguments undermine the dignity of cloned human life, these conservatives have unwittingly encouraged others to conclude that laws mandating the destruction of cloned human embryos make sense.

Meanwhile, liberal lawmakers have used the same essentialist fears to justify laws that mandate the killing of cloned embryos. They don't seem to realize, however, that their strategy also makes the slippery slope seem all the more dangerous. In the end, Congress may react by banning all human cloning, including cloning for stem cell research.

It is time to cast aside tired old canards. If the quality of the human cloning debate improves, so will public policy and the law. The Conclusion to this book makes recommendations for constructive change.

Conclusion

CHAPTERS 8 AND 9 EXPLAINED HOW REGULATORS and legislators have attacked human cloning in response to public opinion and their own prejudices. Humans born through cloning will not be copies, manufactured products, impostors, or resurrections of the dead. In the political and legal battle over human cloning, however, false intuitions have prevailed over scientific fact, resulting in policies and laws that run counter to basic American values. This Conclusion recommends ways of reversing this unfortunate state of affairs.

A. Lessons from History

Chapter 4 discussed the psychological essentialism of living kinds, such as plant or animal groups. We assume that the members of a living kind share an essence; from there, we draw inferences about the hidden and nonobvious traits that all members of the kind possess. Chapter 4 further explained how we employ essentialism when dealing with human social categories or kinds, such as racial and ethnic groups, occupations, castes, and other classes. The assumption of shared essence prompts us to infer the supposedly innate physical, mental, emotional, behavioral, and other traits of group members. Essentialism provides rough assessments that can be of practical use; but when utilized to characterize entire groups of human beings, it can also promote stereotyping and unjust discrimination.

Fortunately, essentialism is not omnipotent. The United States, with its long and shameful history of enslaving and discriminating against African Americans, offers an example. Civil rights laws, integration, and education have improved the situation to the point where Americans elected Barack Obama, an African-American man, as their president in 2008.

To be sure, African Americans had the laboring oar in achieving this remarkable transformation. Without their demonstrations, strikes, lawsuits, and powerful voices, essentialism would have been much harder to overcome. Yet, despite their relatively privileged position within society, European Americans have also contributed to this societal change. From political leaders to members of the electorate, their willingness to work toward the fair treatment of all demonstrates that it is possible for the conscious mind to overcome essentialist intuitions.

However, there is one obvious difference between racial and ethnic minorities and humans born through cloning: the former number in the millions, but the latter have not yet been born. Once the technology becomes viable, anti-cloning laws will discourage some prospective parents from conceiving children through cloning. Others will defy the laws, but the number of humans born through cloning and living in the United States will be limited.[1] Parents and children are likely to hide their involvement with cloning in order to avoid prosecution, stigma, and discrimination.[2] In other words, they will be too scared to come out of the closet and argue their case. Therefore, when it comes to human cloning, something other than raw political power must be used to combat the pernicious effects of essentialism.

B. Unveiling the Opponent

Psychological essentialism is a shadowy opponent. It operates at an intuitive, subconscious level. Thus, the first step in combatting essentialism is to force it out into the open. Psychologists, anthropologists, sociologists, and biologists have done a superb job of describing essentialism and documenting its effects in multiple domains. Where any one of these domains is present, essentialism should be suspected as an influence.

Human cloning touches upon three of these domains. Because cloning is reproductive, it sparks intuitions about social categories or human kinds. Because cloning is technological, it invokes the artifact domain, thereby encouraging intuitions that human beings are products that can be classified according to the intent of their creators. Finally, because cloning starts with a cell taken from a human being, it prompts intuitions that the unique essence of that person has been stolen or transferred to another. Given that multiple domains are involved, it is not surprising that essentialism has a profound influence upon the conceptualization of humans born through cloning. This book has taken a first step toward unveiling its role in the cloning debate.

C. Changing the Politics and Law of Human Cloning

Fifteen years have passed since Ian Wilmut and Keith Campbell announced the birth of Dolly the sheep. Essentialism has already done much damage in that time. Politicians have banned human cloning on the strength of the identity, artifact, impostor, and resurrection fallacies. This book alone is not enough to undo this damage, particularly when matched up against authoritative government reports that either promote or condone those fallacies.

1. Scientists

There are two groups in society that have the means and a responsibility to change the politics and law of human cloning. The first is comprised of scientists active in the fields of animal or human cloning. These individuals know that humans born through cloning cannot be copies, artifacts, impostors, or resurrections. Because they have full command of the scientific facts, they are uniquely positioned to declare those facts to the public and media and debunk cloning fallacies.

Scientists may feel that keeping silent or joining the attack on human reproductive cloning is the safest way to protect their own reputations and research, but this is a dangerous strategy. When ignorance goes unchallenged, it persists; persistent ignorance about cloning can have serious consequences.

a) Fairness to Children

As Part II explained, government reports have warned that people may pursue human cloning for the wrong reasons. For example, parents may believe they can select DNA from a person with a history of success and manufacture a copy with the same traits. Or they may think cloning can resurrect a dead child or other loved one. False intuitions may lead to human suffering if the children are pressured to exhibit certain traits or behaviors in order to fulfill parental expectations.

Because essentialism is powerful, these warnings have some force. Fortunately, however, there is no need to sacrifice children on the altar of unreasonable parental expectations. Instead, scientists must have the courage and integrity to speak the truth about their own research. Once the true facts of cloning are widely known, those with inappropriate goals will realize the technology is of no use to them.

There may be a legitimate market for human cloning among those for whom sexual reproduction is impossible or impractical, such as infertile men and women, gays, and lesbians. If human cloning is scientifically possible, these persons will pursue it, even if they must travel abroad to obtain cloning services. Thus, cloned children will be born. They may very well encounter others who wrongly view them as copies, artifacts, impostors, or resurrections. However, this is not a reason to advocate against their existence. It is not ethical to surrender to bigotry and discrimination.[3] Rather, as our experience with racism demonstrates, we can and should combat the essentialism that leads to bigotry and discrimination.

Scientists have a moral responsibility to educate the public because they are the ones who create and perfect cloning technology. Without their work, these issues would not arise. They should act now, before public attitudes harden further, and before the first cloned children are born into a society that holds fallacious opinions about them.

b) Promoting Science

Scientists should also consider their own self-interest. Ignorance about cloning fuels hostility toward the work they want to do. Chapter 9 explained how essentialist fallacies have encouraged legislative attacks against research as well as reproductive cloning. Even animal cloning may not be safe from legal prohibitions in the future. In a 2011 Gallup Poll, 84 percent of respondents stated that cloning humans was morally wrong,[4] a level of opposition that has remained relatively stable over the years. More surprising was this finding: 62 percent of respondents considered the cloning of animals to be morally wrong.[5] Although the poll did not reveal the reasons behind this opposition, it seems likely that essentialist fallacies have distorted opinion on animal as well as human cloning. If scientists find the courage to debunk those fallacies, they can defuse public opposition to their work and forestall oppressive legislation that undermines scientific freedom.

2. Politicians

The second group that has the means and responsibility to make a difference is comprised of federal and state politicians. Some of these individuals have the power to appoint experts to blue-ribbon commissions that write advisory reports on controversial technologies, and that is the place to begin.

a) The Need for Updated Reports

All three of the government reports discussed in this book were produced ten or more years ago. The NBAC examined the science and ethics of reproductive cloning in 1997, when the technology was brand new.[6] The President's Council on Bioethics and the California Advisory

Committee on Human Cloning issued comprehensive reports on the science and ethics of research and reproductive cloning in 2002.[7] All of these reports are out of date on the science of cloning. The reports also summarize anti-cloning arguments without acknowledging that many are based on essentialist intuitions. This is a significant omission. The reports seduce readers with fallacies that are intuitively appealing, at the same time denying them information about the psychological roots of those fallacies. Even when these reports do acknowledge that a fallacy exists, they pander to it, recommending bans as the solution.

For example, some reports argue that reproductive cloning is wrong because parents might treat cloned children as designer products.[8] However, cloning bans will not eliminate this risk. Would-be parents who falsely believe that cloning can deliver a specific child will travel abroad or go underground to access cloning services. Meanwhile, those who are infertile or otherwise unable to reproduce sexually will go abroad or underground to reproduce asexually through cloning. As a result, some cloned children will be born despite the bans. The bans will serve only to stigmatize children, as explained in Chapter 8.

These dated and inadequate reports cannot be allowed to stand as the last word on human cloning. Having encouraged lawmakers, academics, and others to rely upon the reports, federal and state governments have an ethical responsibility to correct their errors. New reports could update the science of cloning and use experimental data to refute the identity, artifact, impostor, and resurrection fallacies. New reports could also include sections that discuss the role essentialism has played in shaping the fallacies and cloning bans. To ensure that reports adequately consider the impact of essentialism, future blue-ribbon commissions must include members with expertise in cognitive psychology and essentialism.

Once new reports are generated, the governments involved (whether federal or state) should undertake a public education campaign. People expect cloning to cause various harms; but, for the most part, such expectations are the product of scientific misinformation or essentialist instincts. Accordingly, a public education campaign should do two things: disseminate the scientific facts of cloning; and reveal the intuitions behind the identity, artifact, impostor, and resurrection fallacies.

b) Ideology and Legacy

Even if governments issue no further reports on human cloning, this book is enough to place politicians on notice. Their anti-cloning crusade is as illogical as the science fiction films reviewed in this book. Legislators should immediately abandon all efforts to impose new cloning bans. Because the four fallacies have tainted existing anti-cloning laws, legislators should repeal them.

Some readers may respond that reproductive cloning is not yet safe for human use. However, even if that is a concern, federal and state laws that impose a permanent ban on reproductive cloning are unnecessary. Recall that the FDA has assumed jurisdiction over the field and declared that it will reject applications for permission to clone on safety grounds. Although the agency may not have statutory authority to act in this manner, no serious legal challenge to its authority has been mounted. As a result, the United States already regulates reproductive cloning for safety, and will continue to do so for the foreseeable future.

Other readers may protest that anti-cloning laws will never be repealed for political reasons. Politicians must win elections, and human cloning is unpopular with the public. What incentives do politicians have to abandon cloning bans?

As explained at length in Chapters 8 and 9, essentialism is a double-edged sword. Politicians who exploit cloning fallacies in an effort to gain enactment of legislation will find that their opponents turn the same fallacies against them. In Congress, the stakes are particularly high. Essentialism could lead to a winner-takes-all outcome that will savage the principles and pocketbooks of those on the losing side. Conservatives could be forced to accept research cloning and its destruction of human embryos on a national scale; liberals could stand by and watch as an entire branch of stem cell research becomes a federal crime. Surely it is more prudent to leave human cloning alone and deal with the real problems America faces.

Moreover, politicians should care about the legacies they leave behind. At best, those who legislate based on cloning fallacies rather than facts will be remembered by history as fools. At worst, they will be remembered as hypocrites who acted inconsistently with their own political philosophies, or American values more generally. Liberals will be tarred for their betrayal of reproductive and scientific freedom. Conservatives and liberals alike will be criticized for undermining egalitarian values. Rather than risk these outcomes, politicians should clean up the mess they have made of cloning law now – before the first humans are born through cloning.

3. Legal Alternatives

Even if scientists publicize the true facts of cloning, and even if politicians lift cloning bans, it may take time to root out essentialist fallacies that are lodged deep in the public mind. In the meantime, some would-be parents might believe cloning can work miracles: copy the famous, deliver a designer child, or resurrect the dead. If parents pressure a child to meet unreasonable expectations, the child could suffer.

As Chapter 8 explained, banning cloning will drive such parents to clone offshore or underground. Children born despite the bans will suffer not only from parental expectations but also from the stigma the bans impose on them.

Professor John Robertson, an expert in the field of assisted reproduction and cloning, has suggested a narrower strategy: psychological counseling for parents.[9] In other words, legislators or regulators can allow human cloning but require fertility doctors and clinics to refer participants to counselors who are trained to explain what cloning can and cannot do. This strategy would be beneficial on several levels. First, those who wish to copy someone, design a child, or resurrect a departed loved one will be told in no uncertain terms that their projects are impossible. This information will go a long ways toward deterring improper uses of cloning technology. Second, counseling will help infertile couples and others who reproduce asexually to understand their future children better. Counseling will also arm them with the scientific facts they need to help their children cope with prejudice and discrimination. Third, counseling should not be limited to parents. Advice and information from a neutral professional will help ensure that DNA donors understand the procedure and are participating voluntarily. Counseling can also dispel any concerns that donors may have about cloning compromising their individuality.

Even if no laws or regulations mandate that participants receive counseling from qualified professionals, the common law already requires medical professionals to obtain informed consent before providing services to patients.[10] At this point in history, there is much public confusion about human cloning. To obtain informed consent to cloning services, fertility doctors and clinics must explain to prospective parents what they can realistically expect of a child born through cloning. The explanation should place special emphasis on the individuality, unpredictability, and autonomy of the child.[11] As the California Report suggests, fertility doctors and clinics should provide the same explanation to DNA donors to ensure their informed consent and guard against any possible psychological harm to them.[12]

Whether parents hold unreasonable expectations or not, they are likely to love their cloned children. Society will be less caring. What of the concern that cloned children will face prejudice and discrimination at the hands of people who stubbornly cling to their essentialist intuitions? Professor Elizabeth Price Foley, a legal scholar and expert on human cloning, has suggested that the government sponsor counseling for cloned children to reinforce their sense of identity and autonomy.[13] Moreover, instead of enacting cloning bans, federal and state governments could amend existing civil rights laws so that they prohibit discrimination against humans born through cloning.

Finally, what of those who fear cloned impostors? Public education can help dispel needless fears of impersonation. However, a legitimate concern remains: a person cloned without notice and consent will suffer a violation of her reproductive autonomy. Here, too, the law can offer a solution. Rather than criminalize a technology that may be useful to some people, legislators can criminalize non-consensual cloning. Also, regulators can require fertility doctors and clinics to maintain records documenting that DNA donors have consented to the procedure.

D. Beyond Human Cloning

This book has described how faulty intuitions have spawned bad policies and bad laws on human cloning. If cloning represented an isolated case of policy and legislative malfunction, my work would be done. There is a more disturbing possibility, however, and I would be remiss to conclude this book without remarking upon it.

Some have claimed that the twenty-first century will be known for advances in biology, just as the twentieth century is remembered for advances in physics.[14] Our understanding of genetics, epigenetics, and other aspects of mammalian bodies is just beginning to explode. By the end of this century, we will have learned many new biological truths about animals and ourselves. At least some of these truths will lead to medical treatments and other inventions that will upgrade our inborn capabilities and extend our lives.

The problem is this: psychological essentialism affects how we respond to our world, particularly elements that are biological in nature such as animals and other human beings. Essentialism creates its own "truths," many of which are at odds with biological facts. Unfortunately, science fiction increases the confusion by promoting nightmare visions that are more consistent with essentialism than biological fact. If we are not careful, the battle over human cloning will turn out to be the opening salvo in a war between intuition and science that rages throughout the twenty-first century.

CONCLUSION

The solution is clear: we must learn to control kneejerk responses to scientific discoveries. Intuition can be a friend, but it can also be a foe. It can make us resist uncomfortable truths rather than readjust our expectations. It can make us reject useful inventions rather than improve our lives. It can make us mount irrational attacks upon fellow human beings who appear to be different.

Going forward, academics, policymakers, regulators, and legislators who wish to resolve difficult public policy issues must investigate the role of psychological essentialism before they take action. Otherwise, we shall never reap the full rewards of our scientific discoveries, nor achieve a justice deserving of the name.

Notes

PART I. THE SCIENCE OF CLONING

1. Ian Wilmut & Roger Highfield, *After Dolly: The Uses and Misuses of Human Cloning* 125–27 (2006).
2. I. Wilmut et al., "Viable Offspring Derived from Fetal and Adult Mammalian Cells," 385 *Nature* 810 (1997).
3. At the time the mammary gland cells were harvested, the sheep was six years old. Wilmut & Highfield, *supra* note 1, at 114. Noting the source of the cells, the scientists named their lamb after Dolly Parton, the large-breasted country-western singer. *Id*. at 113.
4. P.C. Winter, G.I. Hickey & H.L. Fletcher, *Genetics* 6 (2d ed. 2002).
5. *See generally* Bruce Alberts et al., *Molecular Biology of the Cell* 1131–32 (5th ed. 2008).
6. The President's Council on Bioethics, "Human Cloning and Human Dignity: An Ethical Inquiry" 62 (2002). As this report explains, genes can be switched on and off through "changes in (1) DNA methylation, (b) the assembly of histone proteins into nucleosomes, and (c) remodeling of chromosome-associated proteins such as linker histones." *Id*. at 231.
7. Wilmut & Highfield, *supra* note 1, at 234–39.
8. The scientists used eggs in a key stage known as the second metaphase (abbreviated MII) of meiosis (the process whereby an egg cell prepares itself for fertilization). In the second metaphase, which immediately precedes fertilization, the nuclear membrane has dissolved and the egg is rich in factors that promote replication of DNA. *Id*. at 94–95, 108–09.
9. *Id*. at 107–13. For simplicity's sake, many writers (including this one) refer to this process as enucleation, that is, removal of the nucleus from the egg. Technically, however, this is inaccurate; because scientists are working with an egg in the second metaphase of meiosis, the nuclear membrane has already dissolved and the free chromosomes inside are what scientists remove. *Id*. at 95.

One advantage of working with MII eggs is that the chromosomes are tightly packed and easier to remove. *Id.* at 109.
10 *Id.* at 115. This resting state is known as G0. Wilmut believes there is something about the organization of the cell nuclei in this stage that facilitates cloning. *Id.*
11 *Id.* at 116–19. Activation involves the release of calcium within the egg, which facilitates embryonic development. Ordinarily a sperm initiates this process, but Wilmut and his team were able to mimic the effect with electricity. *Id.* at 118.
12 Wilmut et al., *supra* note 2, at 811 tbl.1.
13 *Id.* at 812 and fig.2.
14 *Id.*
15 *See* Wilmut & Highfield, *supra* note 1, at 95–98 (discussing the cloning of two lambs from embryo-derived cultured cells that had already begun the process of differentiation).
16 Kerry Lynn Macintosh, *Illegal Beings: Human Clones and the Law* 2 (2005).
17 *Id.* at 48.
18 *Id.* In the publication that announced the birth of Dolly, Wilmut and Campbell also reported the results of their attempts to clone lambs from embryonic and fetal cells. Those attempts did produce many miscarriages and one dead lamb. Wilmut et al., *supra* note 2, at 811. However, even in sexual reproduction, many embryos and fetuses are genetically abnormal and miscarry. It can be hard to know whether attempts to clone from embryonic or fetal cells have failed because cloning is inefficient, or because scientists have inadvertently selected DNA that was intrinsically incapable of supporting the life of any organism. For this and other reasons, failure in embryonic or fetal cell cloning does not necessarily forecast failure in adult cell cloning. Macintosh, *supra* note 16, at 49.
19 Wilmut & Highfield, *supra* note 1, at 23–24.
20 Macintosh, *supra* note 16, at 61. A more detailed discussion of telomeres and their role in cloning can be found in Chapter 2 of this book.
21 Paul G. Shiels et al., "Analysis of Telomere Lengths in Cloned Sheep," 399 *Nature* 316, 317 (1999). More specifically, Dolly's telomeres at age one were 20 percent shorter than those of other sheep her age. Some observers have noted this was within the range of experimental error. Macintosh, *supra* note 16, at 61. Experimental variability was confirmed when another telomere measurement after her death suggested her telomeres were only 13 percent shorter than normal. *See* S. Rhind et al., "Dolly: A Final Report," 16 *Reprod., Fertility & Development* 156 (2004); *see also* Dean H. Betts et al., "Telomere Length Analysis in Goat Clones and Their Offspring," 72 *Molecular Reprod. & Development* 461, 466 (2005) (summarizing the measurements of Dolly's telomeres).

NOTES TO PAGES 3–7

22 Shiels, *supra* note 21, at 317.
23 *Id.*
24 Macintosh, *supra* note 16, at 62.
25 Wilmut & Highfield, *supra* note 1, at 24.
26 Macintosh, *supra* note 16, at 63.
27 Wilmut & Highfield, *supra* note 1, at 114.

CHAPTER 1. ANIMALS BORN THROUGH CLONING ARE ORDINARY MEMBERS OF THEIR SPECIES

1 *See* Kerry Lynn Macintosh, *Illegal Beings: Human Clones and the Law* 2 (2005) (explaining how some scientists believed Dolly had been cloned from a stem or fetal cell circulating in the body of the pregnant donor sheep).
2 Alexander Baguisi et al., "Production of Goats by Somatic Cell Nuclear Transfer," 17 *Nature Biotechnology* 456 (1999); Yoko Kato et al., "Eight Calves Cloned from Somatic Cells of a Single Adult," 282 *Science* 2095 (1998); Irina A. Polejaeva et al., "Cloned Pigs Produced by Nuclear Transfer from Adult Somatic Cells," 407 *Nature* 86 (2000); I. Wilmut et al., "Viable Offspring Derived from Fetal and Adult Mammalian Cells," 385 *Nature* 810 (1997).
3 Patrick Chesne et al., "Cloned Rabbits Produced by Nuclear Transfer From Adult Somatic Cells," 20 *Nature Biotechnology* 366 (2002); T. Wakayama et al., "Full-term Development of Mice from Enucleated Oocytes Injected With Cumulus Cell Nuclei," 394 *Nature* 369 (1998); Qi Zhou, "Generation of Fertile Cloned Rats by Regulating Oocyte Activation," 302 *Science* 1170 (2003).
4 Cesare Galli et al., "A Cloned Horse Born to Its Dam Twin," 424 *Nature* 635 (2003); Byeong Chun Lee et al., "Dogs Cloned from Adult Somatic Cells," 436 *Nature* 641 (2005); Taeyoung Shin et al., "A Cat Cloned By Nuclear Transplantation," 415 *Nature* 859 (2002).
5 Min Kyu Kim et al., "Endangered Wolves Cloned from Adult Somatic Cells," 9 *Cloning Stem Cells* 130 (2007).
6 U.S. Fish & Wildlife Service, *Species Profile for Gray Wolf (Canis Lupus)*, at http://ecos.fws.gov/speciesProfile/profile/speciesProfile.action?spcode=A00D#status (last visited on May 17, 2010).
7 Robert P. Lanza et al., "Cloning of an Endangered Species (Bos Gaurus) Using Interspecies Nuclear Transfer," 2 *Cloning* 79 (2000). The baby ox died of a common infection (dysentery) two days after birth. Researchers believe the infection was unrelated to cloning. Kate Tobin, "First Cloned Endangered Species Dies 2 Days After Birth," *cnn.com*, Jan. 12, 2001, at http://archives.cnn.com/2001/NATURE/01/12/cloned.guar. Similarly, European researchers have cloned a bucardo, an extinct wild goat. Unfortunately, the kid died

shortly after birth. *See* J. Folch et al., "First Birth of an Animal from an Extinct Subspecies by Cloning," 71 *Theriogenology* 1026 (2009).
8. Julian Ryall, "Mammoth Could Be Reborn in Four Years," *The Telegraph*, Jan. 13, 2011, at http://www.telegraph.co.uk/science/science-news/8257223/Mammoth-could-be-reborn-in-four-years.html.
9. Scientists have created rhesus monkeys by this method: using IVF to generate monkey embryos, removing blastomeres (individual cells) from those embryos, and inserting single blastomeres into enucleated monkey eggs. Li Meng et al., "Rhesus Monkeys Produced by Nuclear Transfer," 57 *Biology of Reproduction* 454 (1997).
10. J.A. Byrne et al., "Producing Primate Embryonic Stem Cells By Somatic Cell Nuclear Transfer," 450 *Nature* 497 (2007).
11. Bjorn Oback & David N. Wells, "Cloning Cattle: The Methods in the Madness," *Somatic Cell Nuclear Transfer* 30 (Peter Sutovsky, Ed. 2007).
12. *Id.*
13. *Id.* at 48.
14. Ian Wilmut & Roger Highfield, *After Dolly: The Uses and Misuses of Human Cloning*, 137–47 (2006).
15. Oback & Wells, *supra* note 11, at 49.
16. Wilmut & Highfield, *supra* note 14, at 150–54.
17. Oback & Wells, *supra* note 11, at 31–32.
18. *Id.* at 32.
19. *Id.* at 30.
20. I. Wilmut et al., "Viable Offspring Derived from Fetal and Adult Mammalian Cells," 385 *Nature* 810, 811 tbl.1 (1997).
21. Fiona Macrae, "Dolly Reborn! Four Clones Created of Sheep that Changed Science," Mail Online, Nov. 30, 2010, at http://www.dailymail.co.uk/sciencetech/article-1334201/Dolly-reborn-Four-clones-created-sheep-changed-science.html.
22. This book focuses on cattle and mice in order to avoid overwhelming the reader with technical detail. This endnote presents some additional information on the third most commonly cloned species, swine.

    Thus far, swine have proven harder to clone than cattle. When porcine embryos are created through somatic cell nuclear transfer and transferred to surrogate mothers, only 1–5 percent survive to birth. Shiqiang Ju et al., "Analysis of Apoptosis and Methyltransferase mRNA Expression in Porcine Cloned Embryos Cultured In Vitro," 27 *J. Assist. Reprod. Genet.* 49, 49 (2010) (reporting birthrates of 1–5 percent); C.L. Keefer, "Lessons Learned from Nuclear Transfer (Cloning)," 69 *Theriogenology* 48, 49 tbl.1 (2008) (reporting birthrates of 1–3 percent).

    Explanations for the low birthrates are elusive. Cloned porcine embryos exhibit a higher rate of apoptosis (death of individual cells) than IVF porcine embryos, suggesting that laboratory manipulation during cloning causes cellular damage. Ju et al., *supra* at 56. Alternatively, the low birthrates could be due to abnormal gene expression. Enzymes that play a role in gene silencing are more strongly expressed in cloned porcine embryos than IVF porcine embryos, implying the nuclear DNA used for the cloning is not adequately reprogrammed during the procedure. *Id.* at 57; *see also* X. Cindy Tian et al., "Altered Gene Expression in Cloned Piglets," 21 *Reprod., Fertility & Development* 60, 62 (2009) (summarizing additional data indicating that key genes are abnormally expressed in cloned swine).

23 Oback & Wells, *supra* note 11, at 40.
24 *Id.* at 46; David N. Wells et al., "Production of Cloned Calves Following Nuclear Transfer with Cultured Adult Mural Granulosa Cells," 60 *Biology of Reprod.* 996, 1003 (1999) (reporting that 78 percent of cloned bovine fetuses present at sixty days of gestation failed to survive to term; a typical loss for IVF bovine fetuses at that stage would be 30 percent).
25 *See, e.g.*, Oback & Wells, *supra* note 11, at 41 tbl.3 (reporting birthrates ranging from 12 to 16 percent for various adult cell cloning experiments); Heiner Niemann et al., "Epigenetic Reprogramming in Embryonic and Foetal Development upon Somatic Cell Nuclear Transfer Cloning," 135 *Reprod.* 151, 153 (2008) (stating that birthrates as high as 15–20 percent are possible for cattle); M. Panarace et al., "How Healthy Are Clones and Their Progeny: 5 Years of Field Experience," 67 *Theriogenology* 142 (2007) (summarizing data from three countries and reporting that 9 percent of transferred embryos produced calves); Wells et al., *supra* note 24, at 1001 (reporting 10 percent birthrate).
26 Wells et al., *supra* note 24, at 1001.
27 The National Academies, "Scientific and Medical Aspects of Human Cloning," 48–49 (2002) [hereinafter NAS Report].
28 Roberto Bonasio et al., "Molecular Signals of Epigenetic States," 330 *Science* 612, 612 (2010); Pauline A. Callinan and Andrew P. Feinberg, "The Emerging Science of Epigenomics," 15 *Human Molecular Genetics* R95, R95 (2006).

It has been said that epigenetics includes two major modifications: one is DNA methylation of cytosine; the other is posttranslational modification of histones (the protein-based units around which DNA is wound). The latter category of modification includes methylation, acetylation, phosphorylation, and sumoylation. *Id.* at R95. However, epigenetics is a relatively new field, and other factors might turn out to be equally important for efficient reprogramming. *See, e.g.*, Randal Halfmann & Susan Lindquist, "Epigenetics in the Extreme: Prions and the Inheritance of Environmentally Acquired Traits," 300 *Science* 629 (2010) (discussing the role of prions in epigenetics); Elizabeth Pennisi, "Are Epigeneticists Ready for Big Science?" 319 *Science* 1177 (2008) (opining that there may be epigenetic modifications that have not yet been discovered or characterized).

29 The President's Council on Bioethics, "Human Cloning and Human Dignity: An Ethical Inquiry" 62 (2002).
30 *Id.* at 63; Macintosh, *supra* note 1, at 54–55.
31 Sadie L. Smith et al., "Global Gene Expression Profiles Reveal Significant Nuclear Reprogramming by the Blastocyst Stage After Cloning," 102 *PNAS* 17582, 17584 (2005).
32 *Id.* at 17585.
33 Oback & Wells, *supra* note 11, at 40, 42.
34 Kimiko Inoue et al., "Effects of Donor Cell Type and Genotype on the Efficiency of Mouse Somatic Cell Cloning," 69 *Biology of Reprod.* 1394, 1399 (2003) [hereinafter Inoue et al., "Effects of Donor Cell Type"].
35 Oback & Wells, *supra* note 11, at 44. Removing the *zona pellucida* (outer shell) of bovine eggs does make it easier to aspirate the original nucleus and has helped some researchers double their production of cloned cattle. *See id.* at 33.
36 *Id.* at 45.
37 Nguyen Van Thuan et al., "How to Improve the Success Rate of Mouse Cloning Technology," 56 *J. Reprod. & Development* 20, 25 (2010) (explaining how a particular chemical added to activation medium aided reprogramming).
38 NAS Report, *supra* note 27; Wells, *supra* note 24, at 1002.
39 Oback & Wells, *supra* note 11, at 45.
40 *See, e.g.,* Keefer, *supra* note 22, at 49 tbl.1; Kimiko Inoue et al., "Faithful Expression of Imprinted Genes in Cloned Mice," 295 *Science* 297 (2002) (scientists cloned embryos from fetal and adult mice; of those transferred, 2.8 percent developed to term) [hereinafter Inoue et al., "Faithful Expression"].
41 Thuan et al., *supra* note 37, at 21.
42 *Id.*; Inoue et al., "Faithful Expression," *supra* note 40.
43 Some speculate that cloning introduces chromosomal abnormalities in embryos. If this assertion could be proven, it would provide a genetic explanation for the high rates of failure in cloning, but experimental results are conflicting. Compare Sebastian T. Balbach et al., "Chromosome Stability Differs in Cloned Mouse Embryos and Derivative ES Cells," 308 *Developmental Bio.* 309, 314 (2007) (reporting that mouse embryos derived through intracytoplasmic sperm injection exhibited twice the rate of aneuploidy as cloned mouse embryos at the four-cell stage) with Faical Miyara, "Non-equivalence of Embryonic and Somatic Cell Nuclei Affecting Spindle Composition in Clones," 289 *Developmental Bio.* 206, 214 (2006) (citing three studies that found increased rate of chromosomal abnormalities in cloned mouse, rabbit, and bovine embryos).

Those who blame chromosomal abnormalities for cloning failure have not been able to explain why or how those abnormalities occur. One theory centers on the spindle: a tiny cellular structure that helps partition the proper number of chromosomes into each new daughter cell as a parent cell divides. Bruce Alberts et al., *Molecular Biology of the Cell* 208 Fig. 4–19 (5th ed. 2008). For cloning to occur, the chromosomes and spindle of the egg must be removed. Some scientists believe this process also eliminates proteins that are needed to form a new spindle capable of properly managing the donor chromosomes once they are introduced into the egg. When the reconstructed egg begins to divide, mitotic errors occur and aneuploidy results.

Evidence on this issue is divided, however. For example, in one experiment, a group of researchers found some molecular evidence of spindle malfunction in cloned mouse embryos, but was unable to identify the proteins that were missing. Miyara et al., *supra* at 215. Another group discovered that the initial spindles of cloned mouse embryos were abnormal but improved over time. Morphology of spindles at the first and second mitotic divisions was indistinguishable from that of spindles in mouse embryos created through intracytoplasmic sperm injection. Balbach et al., *supra* at 312–13.

Most recently, a different group of scientists reported that a donor cell nucleus contains enough of a certain protein (nuclear mitotic apparatus) to establish normal spindles in cloned human embryos. The scientists opined that low efficiencies in primate cloning were not due to the removal of this protein during enucleation of the egg. Xiaoming Xu et al., "Dynamic Distribution of NuMA and Microtubules in Human Fetal Fibroblasts, Developing Oocytes and Somatic Cell Nuclear Transferred Embryos," 26 *Human Reproduction* 1052, 1057 (2011).

44 *See* Thuan et al., *supra* note 37, at 20 (describing various cell types used in mouse cloning as of 2010 and finding very low success rates for all of them).
45 Inoue et al., "Effects of Donor Cell Type," *supra* note 34, at 1398–99; Jinsong Li et al., "Mice Cloned from Skin Cells," 104 *PNAS* 2738 (2007).
46 Inoue et al., "Effects of Donor Cell Type," *supra* note 34, at 1396 tbl.2.
47 Oback & Wells, *supra* note 11, at 40.
48 Inoue et al., "Effects of Donor Cell Type," *supra* note 34, at 1398.
49 *Id.* at 1399.
50 *Id.* at 1394.
51 Kimiko Inoue et al., "Sex-Reversed Somatic Cell Cloning in the Mouse," 55 *J. Reprod. & Development* 566, 567 (2009).
52 Li et al., *supra* note 45, at 2738.
53 *Id.* at 2741.
54 Macintosh, *supra* note 1, at 24.
55 Oback & Wells, *supra* note 11, at 44.
56 *See* NAS Report, *supra* note 27, at 49 (reporting experimental results that indicate X chromosome inactivation is successful in cloned mice); Oback &

Wells, *supra* note 11, at 44 (reporting experiments in which the X chromosome was improperly inactivated in cloned mouse embryos and also in placentae of cloned mice).

In their review of cloning literature, Oback and Wells reported one experiment in which deceased female cloned cattle showed improper inactivation of the X chromosome in their internal organs and placentae. However, in their own research, Oback and Wells did not find significant differences in the development of cloned cattle when using age and tissue-matched brother-sister pairs, indicating that random inactivation of the X chromosome must have occurred successfully. *Id*.

57 Kimiko Inoue et al., "Impeding Xist Expression from the Active X Chromosome Improves Mouse Somatic Cell Nuclear Transfer," 330 *Science* 496, 496–97 (2010) [hereinafter Inoue et al., "Impeding Xist Expression"].

58 *Id*. at 497.

59 *Id*. at 498. Specifically, the number of X-linked genes that had been down-regulated in wild-type cloned embryos was reduced by 85 percent in both male and female engineered cloned embryos. The number of down-regulated autosomal genes was decreased by 85 percent for females and 73 percent for males. *Id*.

Despite the elimination of Xist, the researchers found that certain genes on the X chromosome remained down-regulated as the result of histone modifications. Chemical treatments intended to relax the histones and improve reprogramming did not fix the problem. *Id*. at 498. For more on such chemical treatments, *see infra* section B.2.c.

60 Inoue et al., "Impeding Xist Expression," *supra* note 57, at 498.

61 Shogo Matoba et al., "RNAi-mediated Knockdown of Xist Can Rescue the Impaired Postimplantation Development of Cloned Mouse Embryos," 108 *PNAS* 20621 (2011).

62 *Id*. at 20623.

63 *Id*. at 20625.

64 Satoshi Kishigami et al., "Significant Improvement of Mouse Cloning Technique by Treatment with Trichostatin A After Somatic Nuclear Transfer," 340 *Biochemical & Biophysical Research Communications* 183, 187 (2006).

65 A different team of scientists found that TSA treatment of cloned mouse embryos improved remodeling of the donor chromatin and generated a birthrate of 3 percent (ten times higher than the rate for untreated embryos). Walid E. Maalouf et al., "Trichostatin A Treatment of Cloned Mouse Embryos Improves Constitutive Heterochromatin Remodeling as Well as Developmental Potential to Term," 9 *BMC Developmental Biology* 11, 15 (2009). This team speculated that TSA accelerated the development of functional *nucleoli* – structures within cell nuclei that assemble the ribosomes responsible for translating messenger RNA (mRNA) into proteins. *Id*. at 17.

66 Kishigami et al., *supra* note 64, at 187.
67 Thuan et al., *supra* note 37, at 24.
68 In this experiment, when no chemical treatments were utilized, only three calves were born from seventy-seven cloned embryos; of those, only two calves lived for more than sixty days. When donor cells and embryos were treated with TSA and 5-asa-2'-deoxycytidine, seventeen calves were born from eighty-two embryos; eleven of those calves survived beyond sixty days. In other words, only 2.6 percent of the untreated embryos produced calves capable of surviving sixty days, whereas 13.4 percent of treated embryos generated healthy calves still alive at sixty days. Y.S. Wang et al., "Production of Cloned Calves by Combination Treatment of Both Donor Cells and Early Cloned Embryos with 5-aza-2'-deoxycytidine and Trichostatin" A, 75 *Theriogenology* 819 (2011).
69 After the group cultured embryos with scriptaid – a histone deacetylase inhibitor – fourteen healthy piglets were born from eight litters, a birthrate of 1.3 percent. Jiangua Zhao et al., "Significant Improvement in Cloning Efficiency of an Inbred Miniature Pig by Histone Deacetylase Inhibitor Treatment After Somatic Cell Nuclear Transfer," 81 *Biology of Reprod*. 525, 528 (2009).
70 Matoba et al., *supra* note 61, at 20625.
71 Macintosh, *supra* note 1, at 15.
72 Mary Shelley, *Frankenstein; or, The Modern Prometheus* (Washington Square Press 1995) (1818). For a brief synopsis of the plot, *see* Macintosh, *supra* note 1, at 15–16.
73 NAS Report, *supra* note 27, at 41.
74 Robin E. Everts et al., "Aberrant Gene Expression Patterns in Placentomes Are Associated with Phenotypically Normal and Abnormal Cattle Cloned by Somatic Cell Nuclear Transfer," 33 *Physiol. Genomics* 65, 65 (2007).
75 NAS Report, *supra* note 27, at 41; Center for Veterinary Medicine, Department of Health and Human Services, "Animal Cloning: A Risk Assessment," 125, tbl.V-3 (Jan. 8, 2008), available at http://www.fda.gov/AnimalVeterinary/SafetyHealth/AnimalCloning/ucm055489.htm [hereinafter CVM Risk Assessment]; Niemann et al., *supra* note 25, at 153.
76 Everts et al., *supra* note 74, at 65.
77 *See* CVM Risk Assessment, *supra* note 75, at 156 (summarizing data and reporting the average death rates for cloned cattle); Wilmut & Highfield, *supra* note 14, at 229 (stating that cloned lambs are more likely to die after birth than other lambs); Panarace et al., *supra* note 25 (summarizing data from three countries and reporting that on average 42 percent of cloned calves died before they reached 150 days of age).
78 Macintosh, *supra* note 1, at 52; Niemann et al., *supra* note 25, at 159.
79 NAS Report, *supra* note 27, at 41.
80 *Id*. at 41; Niemann et al., *supra* note 25, at 159.

81 For example, humans have twenty-two matching pairs of chromosomes and one pair of sex chromosomes. If the sex chromosomes are both X, the person is female; if there is one X and one Y chromosome, the person is male. Sherman J. Silber, *How to Get Pregnant* 291–92, 305 (Little, Brown & Co. rev. ed. Sept. 2005, paperback ed. Aug. 2007).

82 NAS Report, *supra* note 27, at 44; Niemann et al., *supra* note 25, at 157.

83 Niemann et al., *supra* note 25, at 158.

84 *See, e.g.*, NAS Report, *supra* note 27, at 46.

85 *See* CVM Risk Assessment, *supra* note 75, at 156 (stating that it is likely that developmental abnormalities in juvenile cloned animals result from faulty epigenetic reprogramming); Thuan et al., *supra* note 37, at 21–22 (discussing evidence of epigenetic abnormalities in cloned mice).

86 Niemann et al., *supra* note 25, at 159–60.

87 *See, e.g.*, Oback & Wells, *supra* note 11, at 46; C.J. Fletcher, "Somatic Cell Nuclear Transfer in the Sheep Induces Placental Defects That Likely Precede Fetal Demise," 133 *Reprod.* 243 (2007); Niemann et al., *supra* note 25, at 153. Specifically, placentae are often larger than normal and swollen with fluid. Everts et al., *supra* note 74, at 75. *Placentomes* (structures where maternal and fetal systems connect) may be fewer in number but enlarged; umbilical vessels are also enlarged. *See* Wells, *supra* note 24, at 1003.

88 Everts et al., *supra* note 74, at 75.

89 *Id.* at 73.

90 F. Constant et al., "Large Offspring or Large Placenta Syndrome? Morphometric Analysis of Late Gestation Bovine Placentomes from Somatic Nuclear Transfer Pregnancies Complicated by Hydrallantois," 75 *Bio. of Reprod.* 122 (2006); Everts et al., *supra* note 74, at 75; Fletcher et al., *supra* note 87, at 243, 254.

91 Constant et al., *supra* note 90, at 129.

92 Tian et al., *supra* note 22, at 63.

93 *Id.*

94 *See, e.g.*, Thuan et al., *supra* note 37, at 21–22; Inoue et al., "Faithful Expression," *supra* note 40 (reporting placentae two to three times larger than controls).

95 Inoue et al., "Faithful Expression," *supra* note 40.

96 Jiangwei Lin et al., "Defects in Trophoblast Cell Lineage Account for the Impaired In Vivo Development of Cloned Embryos Generated by Somatic Nuclear Transfer," 8 *Cell Stem Cell* 371, 371–72 (2011).

97 Mika Tanaka et al., "Aggregation Chimeras: Combining ES Cells, Diploid, and Tetraploid Embryos," 530 *Methods Mol. Biol.* 287, 288 (2009). A tetraploid embryo can be made by fusing the cells of a diploid embryo early in development, while it is at the two-celled stage. *Id.*

98 Lin et al., *supra* note 96, at 373.

99 *Id.* at 374.

100 Macintosh, *supra* note 1, at 55–57.
101 *Id.* at 57. When mated, the obese mouse clones produce normal offspring. This observation suggests the obesity has an epigenetic source. Some cloning methods may disrupt expression of obesity-related genes in mouse embryos. Kellie L.K. Tamashiro et al., "Phenotype of Cloned Mice: Development, Behavior, and Physiology," 228 *Exp. Biol. Med.* 1193, 1199 (2003) [hereinafter Tamashiro et al., "Phenotype of Cloned Mice"].

Interestingly, much of the research that produced obese clones involved the agouti strain of mouse. *Id.* at 1198. Agouti mice carry a mutant gene related to obesity; epigenetic events can alter its expression, leading to a variety of mouse phenotypes, including obese. Jennifer E. Cropley et al., "Germ-line Epigenetic Modification of the Murine Avy Allele by Nutritional Supplementation," 103 *PNAS* 17308 (2006).

In some experiments, cloned mice of the B6D2F1 strain (a non-agouti strain containing a normal agouti gene) also have developed obese phenotypes in adulthood, but at a significantly lower rate. Kellie L. K. Tamashiro, "Postnatal Growth and Behavioral Development of Mice Cloned from Adult Cumulus Cells," 63 *Bio. of Reprod.* 328, 332 (2000) (reporting incidence of increased body weight at 77 percent for agouti and 20 percent for non-agouti mice). Not all cloned mice are fat, however. In another experiment involving the B6D2F1 strain, the weight gain of the cloned mice did not differ from controls at one year. Narumi Ogonuki et al., "Early Death of Mice Cloned from Somatic Cells," 30 *Nature Genetics* 253, 253 (2002).
102 Inoue et al., "Faithful Expression," *supra* note 40; *but see* David Humpherys et al., "Abnormal Gene Expression in Cloned Mice Derived from Embryonic Stem Cell and Cumulus Cell Nuclei," 99 *Proc. Nat'l Acad. Sci.* 12889 (2002) (reporting improper expression of imprinted genes in mice cloned from adult cells).
103 *See* Tamashiro et al., "Phenotype of Cloned Mice," *supra* note 101, at 1195 (summarizing this research).
104 Robert P. Lanza et al., "Cloned Cattle Can Be Healthy and Normal," 294 *Sci.* 1893 (2001). This was a loss of 73 percent; cattle spontaneously abort IVF pregnancies at a lower rate of 7–24 percent. *Id.*
105 The sixth calf died from enteric complications approximately five months after it was born. *Id.*
106 This 80 percent survival rate compares favorably with the usual rate for cattle, which ordinarily survive from birth to reproductive age at a rate of 84–87 percent. *Id.*
107 *Id.*
108 *Id.* Apparently these cloned cattle were transgenic, that is, scientists had added, deleted, or modified some genes. CVM Risk Assessment, *supra* note

75, at 44. However, this simply means that the animals were normal and healthy despite two different interventions (cloning and genetic engineering). *Id.* at 45.
109 Jose B. Cibelli et al., "The Health Profile of Cloned Animals," 20 *Nature Biotechnology* 13, 14 tbl. 1 (2002).
110 *Id.* at 13. Again, some of the cloned animals discussed in this paper apparently were transgenic; however, their health tends to show that neither cloning nor genetic engineering impaired their health. CVM Risk Assessment, *supra* note 75, at 44–45.
111 CVM Risk Assessment, *supra* note 75, at i.
112 *Conventional* animals are those that are bred through reproductive means other than somatic cell nuclear transfer, presumably including natural mating, artificial insemination, and IVF. *Id.* at 44. Note that these other means are all forms of sexual reproduction, in contrast to cloning, which is a form of asexual reproduction.
113 U.S. Food and Drug Administration, "FDA Issues Documents on the Safety of Food from Animal Clones," Jan. 15, 2008, at http://www.fda.gov/NewsEvents/Newsroom/PressAnnouncements/2008/ucm116836.htm.
114 U.S. Dept. of Agriculture, "Statement by Bruce Knight, Under Secretary for Marketing and Regulatory Programs on FDA Risk Assessment on Animal Clones," Jan. 15, 2008, at http://www.usda.gov/wps/portal/usda/!ut/p/c5/04_SB8K8xLLM9MSSzPy8xBz9CP0os_gAC9-wMJ8QY0MDpxBDA09nXw9DFxcXQ-cAA_1wkA5kFaGuQBXeASbmnu4uBgbe5hB5AxzA0UDfzyM_N1W_IDs7zdFRUREAZXAypA!!/dl3/d3/L2dJQSEvUUt3QS9ZQnZ3LzZfUDhNVlZMVDMxMEJUMTBJQ01IMURERDFDUDA!/?contentidonly=true&contentid=2008%2f01%2f0012.xml.
115 CVM Risk Assessment, *supra* note 75.
116 The CVM report addresses the status of animals it considered just clones – that is, animals with unaltered genomes. However, much of the available scientific literature concerns cloned animals that are considered transgenic because scientists have added, deleted, or modified some genes. The CVM reasoned that if these transgenic animals were normal, it meant that neither cloning nor the genetic alterations had affected their health. Thus, though it gave the most weight to studies of animals that were only clones, it also accepted studies of transgenic clones as secondary, corroborative information. *Id.* at 44–45.
117 *Id.* at 50.
118 *Id.* at 13, 330.
119 *Id.* at 50.
120 *Id.* at ii.
121 CVM Risk Assessment, *supra* note 75, at 156.

122 *Id.* at 12.
123 *Id.* at 156–57; *see also* Everts et al., *supra* note 74, at 65 (cloned cattle that survive the first year of life are similar to cattle conceived through artificial insemination both in health and milk and meat production).
124 Cyagra measured insulin-like growth factor-1 (IGF-I) and estradiol 17-beta (E2) for the cohort of cloned cattle and comparators aged six to eighteen months. The IGF-I hormone, which aids growth and development, was elevated in the cloned cattle. The CVM judged this to be of no clinical significance, given that the cloned cattle would be chosen for superior genetic traits related to growth and development and would also have controlled diets. CVM Risk Assessment, *supra* note 75, at 497. Values for the E2 hormone, which is related to the reproductive system, were increased in some cloned bulls relative to comparators. The CVM stated the higher E2 values could be related to the genetic merit of the animals, and concluded the values fell within the normal range for bulls. *Id.* at 498.
125 *Id.* at 472–73, 477.
126 *Id.* at 483. The reasons for increasing concordance in values between cloned cattle and comparators are unclear. Cyagra provided the CVM with information that represented the status of animals at given points during their development, rather than a longitudinal study of specific animals over a period of time. *Id.* at 473.

However, Cyagra did collect samples from a small subgroup of seven cloned calves at birth and again one to six months later. For this subgroup, most values that deviated from those of comparators at birth normalized by the time of the second measurement. This deviation could be an artifact of differences in treatment: unlike the comparators, the cloned calves did not receive colostrum (nutrient and antibody-rich first milk from mothers) until after the first blood samples were drawn. *Id.* at 486–89. Alternatively, the improvement in values may suggest that the condition of cloned calves improves and normalizes after birth.

The CVM also acknowledged that some values for the cloned subgroup were elevated relative to comparators at one to six months. However, it deemed these differences to lack clinical significance, or attributed them to age-related causes (because the cloned subgroup included two of the youngest animals in the one to six month range). *Id.* at 487–89.
127 *Id.* at 158–62. One experiment reported birth of a piglet without an anus, which had to be euthanized. Another study reported that twenty-two of thirty-five cloned pigs died in the first week of life, but the CVM discounted these deaths as likely attributable to bacterial diseases common in the swine industry. *Id.* at 161–62.
128 *Id.* at 13, 163–64.

129 *Id.* at 13, 165. Although most of the cloned swine in the Viagen dataset appeared to be normal, three had periodic or chronic diarrhea and one exhibited a lung adhesion when it was slaughtered. *Id.* at 165.

130 *See* CVM Risk Assessment, *supra* note 75, at 572, 574, 584–85. Specifically, 80 percent of hematology values for cloned swine fell within the comparator range when the study began; 88 percent two months later; and 84 percent at the end of the study. Similarly, 63 percent of clinical chemistry values for cloned swine were within the comparator range at the outset; 83 percent two months later; and 98 percent at the end of the study. *Id.* at 584–85.

Since the ViaGen study followed specific animals, this normalizing trend could imply that the condition of the clones improved over time. Alternatively, what appear to be meaningful differences at the outset could be artifacts of study design. The cloned animals started at a disadvantage relative to comparators: they were born via Caesarian section rather than vaginally, ate commercial milk replacement, and received no colostrum (unlike comparators, who suckled their mothers until weaning). *Id.* at 573.

Urine values were similar between cloned swine and comparators. *Id.* at 586. Overall, the cloned swine had lower levels of the hormone IGF-I; however, the CVM found that most still fell within the range exhibited in the comparator group. Two cloned swine had levels of IGF-I that fell below the detectable range at time of slaughter; however, since both had normal body weights, the CVM characterized those results as likely artifacts of sample handling and not biologically important. Similarly, levels of the hormone E2 were only slightly lower in the cloned animals, and the CVM concluded the reduction was not biologically relevant. *Id.* at 587.

131 *Id.* at 165–68.

132 *Id.* at 176–81. In one study, three cloned goats died young from bacterial respiratory infections, but the CVM deemed the link to cloning unclear, as respiratory infections are common among goats. *Id.* at 178–79.

133 *Id.* at 328–29.

134 *See, e.g.*, Oback & Wells, *supra* note 11, at 47 (sheep, cattle, and mice); Bashir Mir et al., "Progeny of Somatic Cell Nuclear Transfer (SCNT) Pig Clones Are Phenotypically Similar to Non-Cloned Pigs," 7 *Cloning & Stem Cells* 119 (2005) (swine); Thuan et al., *supra* note 37, at 22 (mice).

135 CVM Risk Assessment, supra note 75, at 14–15; *accord* Oback & Wells, *supra* note 11, at 47; Thuan et al., *supra* note 37, at 22.

136 *Id.* at 329.

137 Thuan et al., *supra* note 37, at 22.

138 Sho Senda et al., "DNA Methylation Errors in Cloned Mice Disappear with Advancement of Aging," 9 *Cloning & Stem Cells* 293, 298 (2007). Specifically, the scientists found that some of the genomic sites in the cloned mice were

NOTES TO PAGES 24–28

hypermethylated (i.e., bore too much of a gene-silencing chemical mark within a given amount of DNA) whereas other sites were *hypomethylated* (i.e., had too little of the chemical mark within a given amount of DNA) relative to controls. *Id.* at 295–96.
139 *Id.* at 298–99.
140 *Id.* at 299. An alternative possibility is that cloned animals that live to an advanced age are those that have more normal epigenetic marks to begin with. *Id.*
141 Scott F. Gilbert, *Developmental Biology* 349–350 (8th ed. 2006).
142 Keith E. Latham et al., "Somatic Cell Nuclei in Cloning: Strangers Traveling in a Foreign Land," in *Somatic Cell Nuclear Transfer* 14, 23 (Peter Sutovsky Ed. 2007).
143 Panarace et al., *supra* note 25, at 144, 147, 149.
144 Everts et al., *supra* note 74, at 75. Obesity is one condition that can have a metabolic origin. As discussed at greater length in note 101, some cloned mice do become obese upon reaching adulthood. In general, however, livestock are not obese. Oback & Wells, *supra* note 11, at 46. Dolly the sheep was fat because she was a celebrity: her keepers and media visitors fed her too many treats. Wilmut & Highfield, *supra* note 14, at 21–22.

CHAPTER 2. ANIMALS BORN THROUGH CLONING ARE UNIQUE INDIVIDUALS AND HAVE THEIR OWN LIFESPANS

1 I first coined the term "identity fallacy" in the following book: Kerry Lynn Macintosh, *Illegal Beings: Human Clones and the Law* 22 (2005).
2 The idea that cloning can be used to overcome death stems in part from misperceptions of the individuality of animals or people born through cloning; thus, in my earlier book, I used the term identity fallacy to describe it. *Id.* at 22, 27. However, for purposes of this book, the narrower term "resurrection fallacy" will be used in order to facilitate Part II's discussion of psychological factors.
3 *See* P.C. Winter, G.I. Hickey, & H.L. Fletcher, *Genetics* 6 (2d ed. 2002).
4 *See generally* Bruce Alberts et al., *Molecular Biology of the Cell* 125–46 (5th ed. 2008).
5 *See generally id.* at 148–52. For a more technical description of tissue architecture and its role in development, see Celeste M. Nelson & Mina J. Bissell, "Of Extracellular Matrix, Scaffolds, and Signaling: Tissue Architecture Regulates Development, Homeostasis, and Cancer," 22 *Ann. Rev. Cell & Dev. Biology* 287 (2006).
6 Macintosh, *supra* note 1, at 23–24; Linda L. McCabe & Edward R.B. McCabe, *DNA: Promise and Peril* 10–11 (2008).

7 The National Academies, "Scientific and Medical Aspects of Human Cloning" 44 (2002) [hereinafter NAS Report]; Heiner Niemann et al., "Epigenetic Reprogramming in Embryonic and Foetal Development upon Somatic Cell Nuclear Transfer Cloning," 135 *Reprod.* 151, 157 (2008).
8 Niemann et al., *supra* note 7, at 158.
9 McCabe & McCabe, *supra* note 6, at 3, 283.
10 Ian C.G. Weaver et al., "Epigenetic Programming by Maternal Behavior," 8 *Nat. Neuroscience* 847, 847 (2004).
11 *Id.* at 847.
12 *Id.* at 848–50. This experiment was directed at establishing the epigenetic state of the rat pups and its link to their maternal care. How the maternal care altered their epigenetic state was unclear; the researchers deemed this a topic for further study. *See id.* at 852.
13 The chemical in question was trichostatin A (TSA), which is a histone deacetylase (HDAC) inhibitor. The researchers hoped the TSA would increase stress response gene expression by decreasing methylation and increasing histone acetylation. *Id.* at 850.
14 *Id.* at 851–52.
15 *Id.* at 852.
16 Jennifer E. Cropley et al., "Germ-line Epigenetic Modification of the Murine Avy Allele by Nutritional Supplementation," 103 *PNAS* 17308, 17309 fig.1 (2006).
17 *Id.* at 17308. Interestingly, this result was obtained only when the sire, and not the dam, contributed the agouti gene. *Id.* at 17309. The epigenetic state of the viable yellow agouti gene may be more resistant to manipulation in the female germline. *Id.* at 17311.

   Another fascinating fact is that the scientists supplemented the chow at mid-gestation. At that point, the epigenotypes of the baby mice should have been determined. *Id.* at 17310. This result implied that environment could affect epigenetic states throughout the life cycle. *Id.* at 17311.
18 *Id.* at 17309–10.
19 In addition to the mitochondria from the egg, the cloned embryo may incorporate some stray mitochondria from the donor cell that came along for the ride. Experiments have documented that cloned animals have mixed mitochondria in their cells, although the mitochondria from the egg predominate. The impact of heterogeneous mitochondria upon phenotype is unclear. Katrin Hinrichs, "Update on Equine ICSI and Cloning," 64 *Theriogenology* 535, 540 (2005).
20 NAS Report, *supra* note 7, at 26.
21 Sebastian T. Balbach et al., "Chromosome Stability Differs in Cloned Mouse Embryos and Derivative ES Cells," 308 *Developmental Bio.* 309, 315–16 (2007).

22 *Id.* at 318–19.
23 Kimiko Inoue et al., "Sex-Reversed Somatic Cell Cloning in the Mouse," 55 *J. Reprod. & Development* 566, 567 (2009).
24 *Id.*
25 X.J. Yin et al., "Production of Second-Generation Cloned Cats by Somatic Cell Nuclear Transfer," 69 *Theriogenology* 1001, 1003 fig.1, 1004 (2008).
26 *Id.* at 1005.
27 Taeyoung Shin et al., "A Cat Cloned by Nuclear Transplantation," 415 *Nature* 859 (2002).
28 *Id.* at 859 fig.1a and 1b.
29 Macintosh, *supra* note 1, at 24–26.
30 Lana Berkowitz, "First Cloned Cat Turns 10," *Houston Chron.*, May 17, 2011, http://www.chron.com/disp/story.mpl/life/main/7568851.html.
31 David N. Wells et al., "Production of Cloned Calves Following Nuclear Transfer with Cultured Adult Mural Granulosa Cells," 60 *Biology of Reprod.* 996, 997 fig.1c and 1d (1999).
32 *Id.* at 1003; *see also* Shinya Watanabe & Takashi Nagai, "Health Status and Productive Performance of Somatic Cell Cloned Cattle and Their Offspring Produced in Japan," 54 *J. Reprod. & Development* 6 (noting that muzzle print patterns vary between cloned cattle and nuclear donors).
33 *See* CVM, Department of Health and Human Services, "Animal Cloning: A Risk Assessment" 495 (Jan. 8, 2008), available at http://www.fda.gov/AnimalVeterinary/SafetyHealth/AnimalCloning/ucm055489.htm [hereinafter CVM Risk Assessment] (reporting three heifers cloned from the same cell line and of approximately the same age that weighed 197 pounds, 215 pounds, and 282 pounds).
34 Kris Axtman, "Quietly, Animal Cloning Speeds Onward," *The Christian Science Monitor*, Oct. 15, 2001, http://www.csmonitor.com/2001/1015/p3s1-ussc.html.
35 Ian Wilmut & Roger Highfield, *After Dolly: The Uses and Misuses of Human Cloning* 42 (2006). Ian Wilmut cloned the four rams in question from embryonic stem cells rather than adult cells, but the principle is the same: the same genome produced varying phenotypes.
36 Macintosh, *supra* note 1, at 24; McCabe & McCabe, *supra* note 6, at 7.
37 Hinrichs, *supra* note 19, at 540 (noting that identical twin horses differ in size and phenotype, and predicting that cloned embryos gestated in different mares could result in animals of different sizes and proportions).
38 *Cf.* McCabe & McCabe, *supra* note 6, at 7 (commenting that identical twins in the same womb can experience different uterine environments).
39 Macintosh, *supra* note 1, at 26 (citing "Copied Cat Hardly Resembles Original," *cnn.com*, Jan. 21, 2003, which is no longer available online).

40 Axtman, *supra* note 34.
41 Wilmut & Highfield, *supra* note 35, at 42.
42 Axtman, *supra* note 34; Russell Goldman, "Cloned Pets: Looks Can Be Deceiving," *ABC News*, Jan. 30, 2009, http://abcnews.go.com/print?id=6762235.
43 *See* Goldman, *supra* note 42 (reporting that a California company called BioArts had worked with Korean scientists to clone a pet dog); Hyung Jin Kim, "Counting Noses – 5 Cloned Pups," *S.F. Chron.*, Aug. 6, 2008, at A-6 (reporting that a South Korean company had cloned a pet dog).
44 Axtman, *supra* note 34.
45 A company called Genetic Savings and Clone first created the cloned cat Cc before cloning a pet cat for its owner, but the company went out of business in 2006. Not enough orders for cats came in and the company failed in its effort to clone dogs. *See* Peter Fimrite, "Pet-cloning Business Closes – Not 'Commercially Viable'," *S.F. Chron.*, Oct. 11, 2006, at B-7.
46 *See* Chapter 7, *infra*.
47 CVM Risk Assessment, *supra* note 33, at 328–29; Kellie L.K. Tamashiro et al., "Phenotype of Cloned Mice: Development, Behavior, and Physiology," 228 *Exp. Biol. Med.* 1193, 1195 (2003).
48 Macintosh, *supra* note 1, at 61.
49 Basil Alexander et al., "Telomere Length Status of Somatic Cell Sheep Clones and Their Offspring," 74 *Mol. Reprod. Dev.* 1525, 1525 (2007). Every cell line has its own unique replicative lifespan based on its individual properties. *Id.* at 1533.
50 *See id.* at 1528 (reporting that telomeres of naturally conceived sheep decreased gradually with age); H.Y. Jeon et al., "The Analysis of Telomere Length and Telomerase Activity in Cloned Pigs and Cows," 71 *Mol. Reprod. Dev.* 315, 317 (2005) (documenting that telomere length in naturally conceived pigs and cattle shortened as those animals aged); Norikazu Miyashita et al., "Remarkable Differences in Telomere Lengths Among Cloned Cattle Derived from Different Cell Types," 66 *Bio. of Reprod.* 1649, 1650–51 (2002) (finding that telomeres of naturally conceived cattle decreased with age).
51 Dean H. Betts et al., "Telomere Length Analysis in Goat Clones and Their Offspring," 72 *Mol. Reprod. Dev.* 461, 462 (2005).
52 I. Wilmut et al., "Analysis of Telomere Lengths in Cloned Sheep," 399 *Nature* 316, 317 (1999).
53 Macintosh, *supra* note 1, at 62.
54 *Id.* at 63.
55 P.G. Shiels & A.G. Jardine, "Dolly, No Longer the Exception: Telomeres and Implications for Transplantation," 5 *Cloning & Stem Cells* 157, 159–60 (2003).
56 Niemann et al., *supra* note 7, at 157. Scientists have reported elongated telomeres in: cloned cattle, Robert P. Lanza et al., "Extension of Cell Life-Span and

Telomere Length in Animals Cloned form Senescent Somatic Cells," 288 *Sci.* 665, 667 (2000); cloned pigs created from fetal cells, Jeon et al., *supra* note 50, at 319; and cloned mice, Teruhiko Wakayama et al., "Cloning of Mice to Six Generations," 407 *Nature* 318, 319 (2000).
57 Chikara Kubota et al., "Serial Bull Cloning by Somatic Cell Nuclear Transfer," 22 *Nature Biotechnology* 693, 694 (2004).
58 Lanza et al., *supra* note 56, at 665.
59 *Id.* at 666–67.
60 Kubota et al., *supra* note 57, at 693–94.
61 X.J. Yin et al., "Production of Second-Generation Cloned Cats by Somatic Cell Nuclear Transfer," 69 *Theriogenology* 1001 (2008).
62 Mayuko Kurome et al., "Production Efficiency and Telomere Length of the Cloned Pigs Following Serial Somatic Cell Nuclear Transfer," 54 *J. Reprod. & Development* 254, 257 (2008).
63 Wakayama et al., *supra* note 56, at 318.
64 *Id.* at 319. Birth rates dropped in successive generations. *Id.* Given the low success rates of cloning in general, failure of serial cloning could occur at any generation as a matter of chance. Nguyen Van Thuan, "How to Improve the Success Rate of Mouse Cloning Technology," 56 *J. Reprod. & Development* 20, 25 (2010).
65 *See* Thuan, *supra* note 64, at 25 (2010) (reporting creation of fifteen generations of cloned mice by infusing embryo culture media with TSA).
66 *See* Alexander et al., *supra* note 49, at 1531 (finding that three cloned sheep had shortened telomeres, but one did not); Betts et al., *supra* note 51, at 465 (finding that female goats cloned from adult granulosa cells had shortened telomeres, but the telomeres of male goats cloned from fetal fibroblasts did not differ significantly from those of age-matched controls); G. Jang et al., "A Cloned Toy Poodle Produced from Somatic Cells Derived from an Aged Female Dog," 69 *Theriogenology* 556, 562 (2008) (finding that telomere lengths in a cloned dog did not differ significantly from those of its aged DNA donor); Jeon et al., *supra* note 50, at 315 (reporting that cloned pigs had elongated telomeres but cloned calves had shortened telomeres); Miyashita et al., *supra* note 50, at 1652–53 (reporting that telomere lengths in cloned cattle varied along with type of donor cell).
67 *See* Miyashita et al., *supra* note 50, at 1653 (noting that telomere binding proteins that inhibit telomerase activity are expressed differently in different cell types); Shiels & Jardine, *supra* note 55, at 158 (opining that unspecified differences in donor cell type affect the extent to which the process of nuclear transfer extends telomeres).

Other possible explanations for variation in telomere length among cloned animals include: species variation (*e.g.*, sheep might be more prone to short telomeres than mice); tissue variation (*i.e.*, telomeres could be short in certain tissues or organs of an animal but not others); natural variation among individual animals; variations in the efficiency of telomerase; and some as yet unidentified effect of the cloning process. Alexander et al., *supra* note 49, at 1535.

68 CVM Risk Assessment, *supra* note 33, at 105, 227–31 (citing M. Yonai et al., "Growth, Reproduction, and Lactation in Somatic Cell Cloned Cows with Short Telomeres," 88 *J. Dairy Sci.* 4097 (2005)); *accord*, Betts et al., *supra* note 51, at 468 (reporting that cloned goats with shortened telomeres were physically normal, fertile, and healthy for their chronological age).

69 *See also* Peter J. Hornsby, "Telomerase and the Aging Process," 42 *Exp. Gerontol.* 575 (2007) (explaining that mice have long telomeres, and yet have brief lives compared to humans, who have short telomeres); *but see* Shiels & Jardine, *supra* note 55, at 159 (suggesting that telomere shortening may not impact the health of cloned animals because terminal lengths are not reached within the short lifespans of their species).

70 CVM Risk Assessment, *supra* note 33, at 101, 183–84.

71 Kellie L.K. Tamashiro et al., "Phenotype of Cloned Mice: Development, Behavior, and Physiology," 228 *Exp. Biol. Med.* 1193, 1196 (2003) [hereinafter Tamashiro et al., "Phenotype of Cloned Mice"].

72 Narumi Ogonuki, "Early Death of Mice Cloned from Somatic Cells," 30 *Nature Genetics* 253, 254 (2002).

CHAPTER 3. HUMANS BORN THROUGH CLONING WILL BE UNIQUE INDIVIDUALS AND HAVE THEIR OWN LIFESPANS

1 In 1990, the U.S. Department of Energy and the National Institutes of Health initiated the Human Genome Project. In 1998, Craig Venter created a company named Celera Genomics in an effort to complete the sequence faster than the public project. This competition from a private project caused the public project to accelerate its pace. On June 26, 2000, the leaders of the public and private projects joined President Clinton in announcing the completion of a rough draft of the human genome. In February 2001, when the draft sequence was 90 percent complete, the public project published its sequence in the journal *Nature*; the private project published its sequence in the journal *Science*. In April 2003, the completed human genome sequence was announced in conjunction with the fiftieth anniversary of the publication of the double helical structure of DNA. *See generally* Linda L. McCabe & Edward R.B. McCabe, *DNA: Promise and Peril* 13–29 (2008); James D. Watson with Andrew Berry, *DNA: The Secret of Life* 165–193 (2003).

2 Kerry Lynn Macintosh, *Illegal Beings: Human Clones and the Law* 22 (2005).

3 *Id.* at 26–27.
4 *Id.* at 12–14.
5 *Id.* at 17–18.
6 Ryan Lister et al., "Human DNA Methylomes at Base Resolution Show Widespread Epigenomic Differences," 462 *Nature* 315 (2009).
7 Alison Abbot, "Project Set to Map Marks on Genome," 463 *Nature* 597 (2010).
8 *E.g.*, McCabe & McCabe, *supra* note 1; John Cloud, "Why Your DNA Isn't Your Destiny: The New Field of Epigenetics Is Showing How Your Environment and Your Choices Can Influence Your Genetic Code – and That of Your Kids," *Time*, Jan. 18, 2010, at 49.
9 In December 2002, gullible media breathlessly reported that a Dr. Brigitte Boisselier, a member of the Raelian religious sect, had cloned a baby girl named Eve. *E.g.*, Carl T. Hall, "First Human Clone Is Born, Sect Claims," *S.F. Chron.*, Dec. 28, 2002, at A-1. No scientific proof was ever provided. Most observers have long since concluded that the claim was a hoax. Macintosh, *supra* note 2, at 127.
10 The President's Council on Bioethics, "Human Cloning and Human Dignity: An Ethical Inquiry" 131–33 (2002).
11 The discussion in the text focuses on experiments the author believes to be real. Unfortunately, not all claims in this field have been true. In 2004 and 2005, Woo Suk Hwang of South Korea published two articles in which he claimed to have derived stem cell lines from cloned human embryos. This research was later found to be fraudulent, and the journal that published the articles retracted them. In 2009, Hwang was convicted of embezzlement and bioethics violations and given a two-year suspended sentence. His most impressive accomplishment in the cloning field remains the cloning of the first dog. "Hwang Convicted but Dodges Jail; Stem Cell Research Has Moved On," 326 *Science* 650 (2009).
12 Andrew J. French et al., "Development of Human Cloned Blastocysts Following Somatic Cell Nuclear Transfer with Adult Fibroblasts," 26 *Stem Cells* 485 (2008); *see also* Jianyuan Li, "Human Embryos Derived by Somatic Cell Nuclear Transfer Using an Alternative Enucleation Approach," 11 *Cloning and Stem Cells* 39 (2009) (Chinese researchers cloned human embryos from somatic cells; 19 percent became blastocysts).
13 French et al., *supra* note 12, at 492.
14 Cal. Health & Safety Code §§ 24185, 24187 (West 2010).
15 French et al., *supra* note 12, at 492.
16 Scott Noggle et al., "Human Oocytes Reprogram Somatic Cells to a Pluripotent State," 478 *Nature* 70 (2011).
17 *Id.* at 70–71.
18 *Id.* at 72.

19 *Id.*
20 *Id.* at 75.
21 Gretchen Vogel, "Human Cells Cloned – Almost," 334 *Science* 26, 27 (2011). The New York team questioned the Stemagen experiment, speculating that the California team succeeded in generating cloned blastocysts only because it inadvertently failed to remove all genetic material from the eggs. Noggle et al., *supra* note 16, at 74.
22 Vogel, *supra* note 21, at 26.
23 Macintosh, *supra* note 2, at 46.
24 *E.g.*, Mark D. Eibert, "Human Cloning: Myths, Medical Benefits and Constitutional Rights," 53 *Hastings L.J.* 1097, 1101–02 (2002); Elizabeth Price Foley, "The Constitutional Implications of Human Cloning," 42 *Ariz. L. Rev.* 647, 656–57 (2000); John A. Robertson, "Liberty, Identity, and Human Cloning," 76 *Tex. L. Rev.* 1371, 1379–80 (1998).
25 Macintosh, *supra* note 2, at 3.
26 Lee Silver, "Public Policy Crafted in Response to Public Ignorance is Bad Public Policy," 53 *Hastings L.J.* 1037, 1041 (2002).
27 Brian P. McEvoy & Peter M. Visscher, "Genetics of Human Height," 7 *Econ. & Human Bio.* 294 (2009); Desiree White & Montserrat Rabago-Smith, "Genotype-phenotype Associations and Human Eye Color," 56 *J. Human Genetics* 5 (2011).
28 X.J. Yin et al., "Production of Second-Generation Cloned Cats by Somatic Cell Nuclear Transfer," 69 *Theriogenology* 1001, 1004–05 (2008).
29 The President's Council on Bioethics, "Beyond Therapy: Biotechnology and the Pursuit of Perfection" 38–39 (2003); Macintosh, *supra* note 2, at 42.
30 Bruce Alberts et al., *Molecular Biology of the Cell* 258 (5th ed. 2008); Melinda Wenner, "Too Little, Too Much: A New Sense for How Variable Numbers of Gene Cause Disease," 301 *Sci. Am.*, June 2009, at 24.
31 Jennifer Couzin, "Interest Rises in DNA Copy Number Variations – Along With Questions," 322 *Science* 1314 (2008); Wenner, *supra* note 30, at 25.
32 Edwin H. Cook Jr. & Stephen W. Scherer, "Copy-number Variations Associated with Neuropsychiatric Conditions," 455 *Nature* 919, 920–21 (2008).
33 Wenner, *supra* note 30, at 25.
34 Macintosh, *supra* note 2, at 23–24.
35 *E.g.*, Carl E.G. Bruder et al., "Phenotypically Concordant and Discordant Monozygotic Twins Display Different DNA Copy-Number-Variation Profiles," 82 *Am. J. Human Genetics* 763 (2008); Sujit Maiti et al., "Ontogenetic De Novo Copy Number Variations (CNVs) as a Source of Genetic Individuality: Studies on Two Families with MZD Twins for Schizophrenia," 6 *PLoS ONE* e17125 (2011).
36 Maiti et al., *supra* note 35.

37 Bruder et al., *supra* note 35, at 766; Maiti et al., *supra* note 35.
38 *See* Cook & Sherer, *supra* note 32, at 922 (discussing new kinds of microarray that could facilitate screening for copy-number variations, including small ones).
39 *See* Chapter 2, Part A.1.
40 The mitochondria from the egg should predominate even if the donor cell contributes some mitochondria as well. The National Academies, "Scientific and Medical Aspects of Human Cloning" 47 (2002) [hereinafter NAS Report]; Katrin Hinrichs, "Update on Equine ICSI and Cloning," 64 *Theriogenology* 535, 540 (2005).

   Some speculate that a mix of mitochondria from two different sources could lead to disease. However, babies conceived through ooplasm transfer (in which the aging eggs of infertile women are infused with ooplasm from healthy donor eggs) have mixed mitochondria; and thus far there has been no sign this mixed population is harmful to them. Jason A. Barritt et al., "Mitochondria in Human Offspring Derived from Ooplasmic Transplantation," 16 *Human Reproduction* 513, 515 (2001).

   Others speculate that the mitochondrial DNA of the egg may be incompatible with the nuclear DNA of the unrelated donor cell. NAS Report, *supra* at 47–48. This theory is interesting but unproven. If such incompatibilities were common or significant, there would not be so many healthy cloned animals and known mitochondrial disease symptoms would be more prevalent.
41 Macintosh, *supra* note 2, at 24.
42 *Id.* at 26; Taeyoung Shin et al., "A Cat Cloned by Nuclear Transplantation," 415 *Nature* 859 (2002).
43 Macintosh, *supra* note 2, at 24.
44 NAS Report, *supra* note 40, at 49.
45 Macintosh, *supra* note 2, at 25.
46 *See* Nancy L. Segal, *Entwined Lives: Twins and What They Tell Us About Human Behavior* 31–32 (1999) (discussing twin pairs where only one member suffers from conditions such as Fragile X Syndrome, Duchenne muscular dystrophy, and color blindness).
47 Jennifer E. Cropley et al., "Germ-line Epigenetic Modification of the Murine Avy Allele by Nutritional Supplementation," 103 *PNAS* 17308, 17311 (2006).
48 Anita C.F. Ravelli et al., "Obesity at the Age of 50 y in Men and Women Exposed to Famine Prenatally," 70 *Am. J. Clin. Nutr.* 811, 814 (1999). In this particular study, fifty-year-old males exposed to the Hunger Winter while *in utero* did not show a significant increase in body mass index or waist circumference. *Id.* at 815. However, an earlier study of nineteen-year-old male conscripts found that those who were exposed to the Hunger Winter as first or second trimester fetuses had higher rates of obesity. Gian-Paolo Ravelli et al.,

"Obesity in Young Men After Famine Exposure in Utero and Early Infancy," 295 *N.E.J.M.* 349, 353 (1976). For a more complete discussion of the Hunger Winter and its effects, see McCabe & McCabe, *supra* note 1, at 3–6.
49 In this study also, the famine had no impact on the adult weight of males. Yonghong Wang et al., "The Great Chinese Famine Leads to Shorter and Overweight Females in Chongqing Chinese Population After 50 Years," 18 *Obesity* 588 (2010).
50 Segal, *supra* note 46, at 12, 22, 26.
51 Macintosh, *supra* note 2, at 24. The research discussed in the text demonstrated that the mouse chow fed to pregnant mice affected the phenotypes not only of the first generation (children), but also the second generation (grandchildren). This happened because the mouse chow altered the epigenome of the eggs of the first-generation mice while they were *in utero*. Cropley et al., *supra* note 47, at 17309–10.

Multigenerational transmission of epigenetic effects in humans is also being investigated. For example, one recent study showed that young boys had increased body mass index when their fathers had begun smoking during the slow-growth period immediately before puberty – in other words, right before the fathers had begun to produce sperm. Marcus E. Pembrey, "Sex-specific, Male-line Transgenerational Responses in Humans," 14 *European J. Hum. Genetics* 159, 161 (2006).

The same study also consulted historical records of an isolated Swedish community that had experienced good and bad harvest years. It found that when a paternal grandfather experienced good food supply as a prepubertal child, not only his sons but also his grandsons had an increased mortality rate. Similarly, when a paternal grandmother experienced good food supply as a prepubertal child, her daughters and granddaughters had an increased mortality rate; however, the effect was more pronounced if she experienced the food glut as a fetus or infant (when her eggs were being formed). *Id*. at 164–65.

Observing the sex-linked nature of the data for smoking and nutrition, the researchers speculated that environmental factors might place epigenetic marks on the sex chromosomes X and Y. *Id*. at 165. These epigenetic marks might affect the function of genes on the sex chromosomes related to production of eggs and sperm. For a presentation of this complicated data for the lay reader, see Cloud, *supra* note 8, at 49–53.

The hypothetical presented in this chapter is different. The environmental factors that the infertile woman's mother experienced while pregnant may have affected the epigenetic status of her eggs; but the infertile woman did not use her eggs for the cloning procedure. Thus, environmental pressures on the infertile woman's mother may not affect the next generation (the cloned baby), unless the epigenetic effects of that original exposure are carried forward in

somatic as well as germ cells. This author is not aware of any studies considering the epigenetic effects when a mammal reproduces sexually and the first generation offspring reproduces clonally.
52 CVM, Department of Health and Human Services, "Animal Cloning: A Risk Assessment" 495 (January 8, 2008), http://www.fda.gov/AnimalVeterinary/SafetyHealth/AnimalCloning/ucm055489.htm [hereinafter CVM Risk Assessment].
53 More specifically, the scientists studied DNA methylation and histone acetylation across the entire genome and in specific loci. Mario F. Fraga et al., "Epigenetic Differences Arise During the Lifetime of Monozygotic Twins," 102 *PNAS* 10604 (2005).
54 *Id*. at 10606–08.
55 *Id*. at 10609.
56 *Id*.
57 Segal, *supra* note 46, at 49–50.
58 *Id*. at 50.
59 Professor Segal reports typical IQ correlations of .86 for monozygotic twins reared together, .75 for monozygotic twins reared apart, and .60 for dizygotic twins. *Id*.
60 *Id*. at 71.
61 *Id*. at 75–78. Non-shared environments can include different treatment within the family, as experienced by children with different birth orders. *See generally id*. at 77–80.
62 Nestor Micheli Morales, "Psychological Aspects of Human Cloning and Genetic Manipulation: The Identity and Uniqueness of Human Beings," 19 *Reprod. BioMed. Online* 43, 46 (2009).
63 *Cf.* Segal, *supra* note 46, at 77 (discussing belief that monozygotic twins who live together make up differences to help themselves establish separate identities).
64 The California Advisory Committee on Human Cloning, "Cloning Californians?, Report of the California Advisory Committee on Human Cloning" 22 (2002).
65 Joe Lauria, "Cloned in the USA: Attempt to Clone Human Being in Secret West Virginia Lab Revealed," *London Times*, Aug. 12, 2001, http://www.cephasministry.com/health_raising_the_dead_through_cloning_clonaid.html.

PART II. THE COGNITIVE PSYCHOLOGY OF CLONING

1 Attempts to regulate cloning illustrate the point. Efforts to enact a federal ban on cloning have foundered because conservatives want to ban the cloning of embryos and liberals (who support stem cell research) disagree. However,

no faction in Congress supports the cloning of babies and all bills that have been proposed would ban that use of the technology. Kerry Lynn Macintosh, *Illegal Beings: Human Clones and the Law* 76–79 (2005). Similarly, although some states permit the cloning of embryos for research and others do not, all states that have enacted cloning laws ban the use of the technology for the creation of babies. *Id.* at 85–87. These laws are discussed at greater length in Chapters 8 and 9.
2 Robert J. Morris, "Not Thinking Like a Nonlawyer: Implications of 'Recogonization' for Legal Education," 53 *J. Legal Education* 267, 273 (2003).
3 The seminal piece establishing the concept of psychological essentialism appeared more than twenty years ago: Douglas Medin & Andrew Ortony, "Psychological Essentialism," in *Similarity and Analogical Reasoning* 179 (Stella Vosniadou & Andrew Ortony, Eds. 1989).
4 Susan A. Gelman, "Essentialism in Everyday Thought," 19 *Psychological Science Agenda (APA Online)*, Issue 5 (May 2005), http://www.apa.org/science/psa/may05scibrfprt.html. Thus, essentialism involves the non-conscious operation of a cognitive module, and not a logical sequence of conscious thought. Susan A. Gelman, *The Essential Child: Origins of Essentialism in Everyday Thought* 7 (2003).
5 Medin & Ortony, *supra* note 3, at 183.
6 Gelman, *supra* note 4, at 299–300.
7 David M. Buss, *Evolutionary Psychology: The New Science of the Mind* 408–10 (1999).

CHAPTER 4. IDENTITY AND ESSENTIALISM

1 Douglas Medin & Andrew Ortony, "Psychological Essentialism," in *Similarity and Analogical Reasoning* 179, 183–86 (Stella Vosniadou & Andrew Ortony, Eds. 1989).
2 *Id.* at 184.
3 Medin & Ortony, *supra* note 1, at 186.
4 *See* Susan A. Gelman, *The Essentialist Child: Origins of Essentialism in Everyday Thought* at 30 tbl.2.1 (2003) (separating experimental test items between living kinds, such as birds and flowers, and nonliving natural kinds, such as gold).
5 *Id.* at 14–15, 137–38.
6 *See id.* at 27 (giving examples of category-based induction in contrast to deduction).
7 For example, children were shown pictures of a tropical fish, dolphin, and shark. The shark looked more like the dolphin than the fish. Researchers informed the children that fish stayed underwater to breathe, but dolphins came up for

NOTES TO PAGES 70-73

air. They also stated that the shark was a fish. Despite the shark's superficial resemblance with the dolphin, children were more likely to infer that the shark also stayed underwater to breathe. *Id.* at 28-31.

8 *Id.* at 61-67. The classic example, of course, is the metamorphosis of caterpillar to butterfly. In one experiment, by age five, children correctly tracked the continuing identity of such an insect at greater than chance levels. *Id.* at 64-65.
9 *Id.* at 67-73.
10 *Id.* at 74-83.
11 Gelman, *supra* note 4, at 89-95, 105.
12 *Id.* at 109-16.
13 *Id.* at 118-28, 135. For example, in one experiment, preschoolers who observed a person carrying an animal from one point to another insisted the animal itself caused the motion. This did not occur when a person was shown carrying an artifact. *Id.* at 124. In another experiment, adults and children were more likely to assume the presence of animal insides (blood and muscles) when a novel creature without an obvious face, such as a jellyfish or stick insect, exhibited motion. In other words, insides were linked with causation (motion). *Id.* at 125-28.
14 For example, Gelman notes that strict category boundaries, in the sense of an individual being either in or out, do not apply to kinfolk, who are related by degrees. *Id.* at 88. For a discussion of how essentialism figures in thinking about parents and offspring, see *id.* at 90-95.
15 *Id. at* 278-79.
16 *Id.* at 13-16.
17 *Id.* at 294-95.
18 Gelman, *supra* note 4, at 9.
19 *Id.* at 11-12.
20 Francisco J. Gil-White, "Are Ethnic Groups Biological 'Species' to the Human Brain?" 42 *Current Anthropology* 515, 524-25 (2001).
21 Lawrence A. Hirschfeld, *Race in the Making: Cognition, Culture, and the Child's Construction of Human Kinds* 42-58, 85-89, 97-98, 107-09, 115, 189 (paperback ed. 1998); Myron Rothbart & Marjorie Taylor, "Category Labels and Social Reality: Do We View Social Categories as Natural Kinds?" in *Language, Interaction and Social Cognition* 10, 12, 20 (Gun R. Semin & Klaus Fiedler, Eds. 1992); Gil-White, *supra* note 20, at 524-29.
22 Hirschfeld, *supra* note 21, at 53; Rothbart & Taylor, *supra* note 21, at 26, 32.
23 *See* Hirschfeld, *supra* note 21, at 12 (explaining that a cognitive structure is specific to a domain when it is devoted to acquiring, organizing, and using knowledge about a specific content area).
24 Medin & Ortony, *supra* note 1, at 186.
25 H. Clark Barrett, "On the Functional Origins of Essentialism," 3 *Mind & Society* 1, 7-8 (2001).

26 Douglas L. Medin & Scott Atran, "Introduction," in *Folkbiology* 1 (Douglas L. Medin & Scott Atran, Eds. 1999).
27 Scott Atran, "Folk Biology and the Anthropology of Science: Cognitive Universals and Cultural Particulars," 21 *Behavioral and Brain Sciences* 547, 548 (1998). Atran observes that folk-biological ranks vary little across cultures. He identifies the standard anthropological terminology for these ranks as: folk kingdom (*e.g.*, animal or plant); life-form (*e.g.*, mammal, tree); generic or generic species (*e.g.*, cat, lemon tree); folk-specific (*e.g.*, Siamese cat, Meyer lemon tree); and folk-varietal (*e.g.*, lilac-point Siamese cat). *Id.* at 549.
28 *Id.* at 549.
29 *Id.* at 548, 550–51; *but see* Susan A. Gelman & Lawrence A. Hirschfeld, "How Biological Is Essentialism?" in *Folkbiology* 403, 411 (Douglas L. Medin & Scott Atran, Eds. 1999) (arguing that evidence for universal essentialism in folk biology is sparse).
30 John D. Coley et al., "Inductive Reasoning in Folkbiological Thought," in *Folkbiology* 205, 211–12 (Douglas L. Medin & Scott Atran, Eds. 1999).
31 Atran, *supra* note 27, at 548, 555.
32 Hirschfeld, *supra* note 21, at 3–4.
33 Rothbart & Taylor, *supra* note 21, at 21; *but see* Gelman & Hirschfeld, *supra* note 29, at 421 (arguing that humans do not belong to the domain of folk biology).
34 Scott Atran, *Cognitive Foundations of Natural History: Towards an Anthropology of Science* 78 (1990); Scott Atran, "Comments," 42 *Current Anthropology* 537, 538 (2001); *but see* Hirschfeld, *supra* note 21, at 154–57 (discussing research in which children categorize according to race based on verbal but not visual clues).

More ambitiously, Francisco Gil-White has argued that ethnic groups have become an evolved part of the living-kind domain. His theory assumes there was adaptive value to being able to forecast the behavior of other human beings in various interactions. Thus, as clusters of humans with shared cultural norms began to emerge, they identified themselves through distinctive dress and body decoration, married within the group, based membership on descent, and acquired labels that defined them. Humans began to process ethnic groups as species because they had become similar for purposes of essentialism, displaying shared morphology (dress and other distinctive marks), hidden traits (cultural norms), reproductive practices (within-group mating and descent-based membership), and labels. Over time, the adaptive benefits of being able to draw accurate inferences about the norms and behavior of other ethnic groups caused the brain to evolve so that ethnic groups became a proper part of the living-kind domain. Gil-White, *supra* note 20, at 518–19, 531–32. The distinct physical traits of racial groups trick the brain into interpreting them as ethnic groups. *Id.* at 534.

As one might expect, Gil-White's theory has proven controversial. For example, it is questionable that excluding others with different cultural norms provides adaptive advantage, given the benefits of cultural exchange and the high costs of intergroup conflict. Atran, *supra* note 34, at 538; Myron Rothbart & Marjorie Taylor, "Comments," 42 *Current Anthropology* 544, 545 (2001).

35 Hirschfeld, *supra* note 21, at 13, 188.
36 *Id.* at 136–40, 154–57, 191–95. Hirschfeld's experiments indicate that young children are more likely to remember the race of a character in a story that is read aloud to them than in a story told through pictures. *See id.* at 140–54. This does not mean that visual cues – such as skin color – are irrelevant, but does suggest an initial focus on conceptual knowledge (*i.e.*, the idea that a relevant racial category exists) as opposed to perceptual cues. Thus, Hirschfeld disagrees with Atran's theory that morphological distinctions drive humans to think about racial categories by analogy to folk-biological living kinds. *Id.* at 87, 116–18, 154–55.
37 *Id.* at 38, 60–61, 196–98.
38 *Id.* at 72. Hirschfeld rejects that possibility on two grounds: first, race is not a real category within nature; and second, humans did not travel far enough to encounter others with sharply differing phenotypes until relatively recently in the history of our species. *Id.* at 13.

Susan Gelman and Marjorie Rhodes have conducted some interesting experiments that shed further light on this issue. According to their data, young children did not interpret race as a natural kind; rather, they viewed race as a social category that was subjective and a matter of convention. Only at older ages, and only in a rural community composed primarily of Caucasians, did children treat race as a natural kind. Thus, Gelman and Rhodes reject the theory that humans have a universal cognitive bias to treat race as a natural kind – a theory they attribute to Hirschfeld. Marjorie Rhodes & Susan A. Gelman, "A Developmental Examination of the Conceptual Structure of Animal, Artifact, and Human Social Categories Across Two Cultural Contexts," 59 *Cognitive Psychology* 244, 269 (2009). However, as Hirschfeld does not argue there is an evolved cognitive module for race as such, the Gelman/Rhodes experiments do not prove him incorrect. Indeed, the outcomes appear consistent with Hirschfeld's claim that children learn which racial groups are important primarily through verbal and social cues. Older children have more experience with such cues and thus might be expected to demonstrate a greater tendency to essentialize racial groups. Moreover, children living in a white, rural community would have fewer interactions with members of racial minorities and thus would have fewer opportunities to learn that essentialist strategies for inferring individual traits from race are ineffective.
39 Hirschfeld, *supra* note 21, at 13.

40 *Id.* at 26, 107.
41 Hirschfeld created an ingenious experiment to test these principles. He created drawings that depicted adults in terms of three characteristics: race, occupation, and body build. Then he asked his subjects to match the adults to one of two drawings of children that exhibited contrasting sets of characteristics. For example, a subject might be asked to match the adult either to a child with the same occupation and body build but a different race, or to a child with the same race and body build but different occupation. One group of subjects was told the drawings of children represented the adults at an earlier age; this part of the experiment assessed understanding of growth over lifespan. Another group of subjects was informed that the drawings of children represented the offspring of the adults; this part of the experiment assessed understanding of inheritance. Most children selected race over the other characteristics, indicating their view that race was more likely to be stable over time and heritable. *See id.* at 93–99 for a detailed account of the experiment.
42 *Id.* at 98. Gelman and Rhodes claim Hirschfeld's experiment stops short of establishing that young children infer social or behavioral traits from race. Rhodes & Gelman, *supra* note 38, at 269. However, it does demonstrate an early ability to draw biological inferences based on race, and that ability may reflect a cognitive architecture that supports the child as his culture teaches him to infer other traits from race.
43 Hirschfeld, *supra* note 21, at 102–04.
44 In the follow-up experiment, researchers showed subjects a drawing of a child dressed as either a fireman (male) or a waitress (female). The subjects were asked to match the child with a drawing of him or her as a grown-up. For both the fireman and the waitress, two choices were offered: an adult dressed in clothing of the same color but without occupational emblems; or an adult dressed in clothing of a different color but with the same occupational emblems. Overall, the researchers found the subjects showed no preference for occupation over color, but when the researchers split the data out, they discovered the subjects considered occupation more predictive of male identity than female identity. *Id.* at 105–06.
45 *Id.* at 106–07.
46 GELMAN, *supra* note 4, at 312–13, 321; *see also* Susan A. Gelman, Gail D. Heyman & Cristine H. Legare, "Developmental Changes in the Coherence of Essentialist Beliefs About Psychological Characteristics," 78 *Child Development* 757, 771 (2007) (suggesting that it takes time and development for children to weave the various elements of essentialist reasoning into a coherent theory).
47 Gelman, *supra* note 4, at 314–15.
48 *Id.* at 315–16.

49 *Id.* at 316–18.
50 *Id.* at 318–19.
51 *Id.* at 319–21.
52 *Id.* at 7.
53 *Id.* at 181–85.
54 Gelman, *supra* note 4, at 193–212, 235. For Gelman's in-depth discussion of the role that language plays in essentialism, *id.* at 179–238.
55 *Id.* at 15.
56 *See generally* Barrett, *supra* note 25 (explaining that an account of essentialism as an evolved feature of the human brain requires cognitive mechanisms capable of handling certain functions; and specifying the empirical evidence necessary to establish that a particular mode of essentialism is adaptive).
57 *See* Gelman, *supra* note 4, at 281–83 (theorizing that essentialism is a universal cognitive mode that takes culture-specific forms); Hirschfeld, *supra* note 21, at 38, 60–61 (claiming that racial thinking is a product of both cognitive and cultural factors).
58 Lee M. Silver, "What Are Clones? They're Not What You Think They Are," 412 *Nature* 21 (2001).
59 *Webster's New World Dictionary of the American Language* 275 (College ed. 1968).
60 Alvin Toffler, *Future Shock* (1970).
61 Silver, *supra* note 58, at 21.
62 *Id.*
63 "Clone," *Merriam-Webster Dictionary*, http://www.merriam-webster.com/dictionary/clone (last visited on June 4, 2011).
64 Alvin Toffler, *Future Shock* 198 (Bantam ed. 1971). This nightmare vision of Hitler copies predated Ira Levin's novel, *The Boys from Brazil* (1976), by six years.
65 Toffler, *supra* note 64, at 198.
66 I have included in Table 1 films and television episodes in which characters born through cloning have been genetically engineered or are alien (in whole or in part) rather than human. However, I have excluded others involving androids or cyborgs on the reasoning that such films and television episodes stray too far from the cloning topic and are not reliable evidence of the fallacies under analysis. *See, e.g., The Stepford Wives* (Columbia Pictures and Paramount Pictures 1975) (showing how sexist men make compliant androids to replace their wives); *Battlestar Galactica* (Sci-Fi Channel 2004–09) (portraying hybrids that are part human but also part Cylon).
67 *Star Wars II: Attack of the Clones* (20th Century Fox 2002).
68 *Id.*
69 *Id.*

70 *Id.*
71 *Id.*
72 *Id.*
73 Patrick D. Hopkins, "Bad Copies: How Popular Media Represent Cloning as an Ethical Problem," 28 *Hastings Center Rep.* 6, 6 (March–April 1998).
74 *Id.* at 7–9; Giovanni Maio, "Cloning in the Media and Popular Culture," 7 *EMBO Reports* 241, 244–45 (2006).
75 Hopkins, *supra* note 73, at 7–8; Maio, *supra* note 74, at 244–45.
76 Hopkins, *supra* note 73, at 7–8; Maio, *supra* note 74, at 244–45.
77 *See, e.g.*, Lori B. Andrews, *The Clone Age: Adventures in the New World of Reproductive Technology* (1999) (showing eight identical babies); John Harris, *On Cloning* (2004) (depicting numerous identical child manikins leaned up against a wall and each other); Aaron D. Levine, *Cloning: A Beginner's Guide* (2007) (depicting torsos and heads of multiple identical adult manikins); Gregory E. Pence, *Who's Afraid of Human Cloning?* (1998) (showing two identical babies reaching toward each other with the same gesture God uses to create Adam in Michelangelo's painting on the ceiling of the Sistine Chapel); *The Human Cloning Debate* (Glenn McGee, Ed. 1998) (patterning cover with dozens of copies of the head of Michelangelo's *David* statue).
78 *See* Gina Kolata, Clone: *The Road to Dolly and the Path Ahead* (1998) (depicting own title in mirror image); *The Human Cloning Debate* (Glenn McGee & Arthur Caplan, Eds. 4th ed. 2004) (reproducing Picasso's famous painting of *Girl Before a Mirror*).
79 *E.g.*, Harris, *supra* note 77, at 108; Pence, *supra* note 77, at 49–51. An earlier book of my own fits this pattern to some degree; inside, it debunks the identity fallacy, but the cover depicts dozens of identical human silhouettes. *See* Kerry Lynn Macintosh, *Illegal Beings: Human Clones and the Law* 23–26 (2005). One of the silhouettes is colored darker than the rest. I like to think this hints that humans born through cloning can be unique, but am not sure all readers would interpret it that way.
80 Maio, *supra* note 74, at 245.
81 Nancy L. Segal, *Entwined Lives: Twins and What They Tell Us About Human Behavior* 205 (1999). Segal rejects the notion that humans born through cloning are later-born twins, however; they would not be conceived at the same time, gestated in the same uterus, and born together, as twins are. *Id.*
82 *Id.* at 3.
83 Toffler, *supra* note 64, at 197.
84 "Supertwins Statistics," Mothers of Supertwins (MOST), http://www.mostonline.org/facts_outsideresources.htm (last visited on October 1, 2010).
85 *E.g.*, Paul Talbot, *The Films of the Dionne Quintuplets* (2007); *Five of a Kind* (20th Century Fox 1938).

86 *E.g.*, Ellie Tesher, *The Dionnes* (1999); *Million Dollar Babies* (1994).
87 David M. Buss, *Evolutionary Psychology: The New Science of the Mind* 408–10 (1999). Buss's account relies heavily on insights from another noted psychologist, Steven Pinker. *See* Steven Pinker, *How the Mind Works* (1997).
88 Buss, *supra* note 87, at 410.
89 Macintosh, *supra* note 79, at 93.
90 Rudolf Jaenisch and Ian Wilmut, "Don't Clone Humans!" 291 *Science* 2552 (2001).
91 Macintosh, *supra* note 79, at 8.
92 National Bioethics Advisory Commission, "Cloning Human Beings, Report and Recommendations of the National Bioethics Advisory Commission" 108–09 (1997) [hereinafter NBAC Report].
93 Macintosh, *supra* note 79, at 9.
94 The President's Council on Bioethics, "Human Cloning and Human Dignity: An Ethical Inquiry" 114, 200, 206 (2002) [hereinafter Council Report].
95 Macintosh, *supra* note 79, at 8.
96 California Advisory Committee on Human Cloning, "Cloning Californians? Report of the California Advisory Committee on Human Cloning," 37 (2002) [hereinafter California Report].
97 The California Advisory Committee on Human Cloning acknowledged that it had considered recommending a moratorium before settling on a flat ban. The Committee gave little explanation, other than to claim that the burden of changing policy should rest with cloning proponents. *Id.* at 37. This statement is disingenuous. Given the public hysteria over human cloning, infertile men and women and others who cannot reproduce sexually are unlikely to ever persuade the California State Legislature to make this change.
98 Council Report, *supra* note 94, at 102–03; California Report, *supra* note 96, at 24; NBAC Report, *supra* note 92, at 66–68.

The California Report also presented the flip side of the concern about diminished individuality: "The person who is the source of the genetic material (if still alive) may experience a loss of self-worth rooted in the knowledge that he or she is no longer unique, but now has a genetic copy." California Report, *supra* note 96, at 26. The Report acknowledged counseling and informed consent could vitiate this concern. *Id.* at 27.
99 NBAC Report, *supra* note 92, at 69.
100 Council Report, *supra* note 94, at 102.
101 Macintosh, *supra* note 79, at 28.
102 Nancy Segal, "Human Cloning: Insights from Twins and Twin Research," 53 *Hastings L.J.* 1073, 1081 (2002).
103 Council Report, *supra* note 94, at 103–04; Macintosh, *supra* note 79, at 29.
104 Macintosh, *supra* note 79, at 29.

105 Council Report, *supra* note 94, at 104.
106 Elizabeth Price Foley, "The Constitutional Implications of Human Cloning," 42 *Ariz. L. Rev.* 647, 719 (2000).
107 *Id.* at 107–108; California Report, *supra* note 96, at 28; NBAC Report, *supra* note 92, at 74–75.
108 Macintosh, *supra* note 79, at 40. An interesting parallel comes from Germany, where one scholar has reviewed documentaries on cloning and found that the danger most often emphasized was the potential for eugenic use. He noted that the association between cloning and eugenics could reflect existing cultural beliefs, but did not identify those beliefs. Maio, *supra* note 74, at 242. Germans may be particularly sensitive to the threat of eugenics in the wake of their experience with Nazism.
109 Council Report, *supra* note 94, at 108–09.
110 The President's Council on Bioethics, "Reproduction & Responsibility: The Regulation of New Biotechnologies" 110–11 (2004).
111 Macintosh, *supra* note 79, at 42.
112 Pence, *supra* note 77, at 130.
113 California Report, *supra* note 96, at 28.
114 *Id.* at 30.
115 *Id.*
116 *Id.*
117 Macintosh, *supra* note 79, at 39.
118 Council Report, *supra* note 94, at 103; California Report, *supra* note 96, at 25; NBAC Report, *supra* note 92, at 69–70.
119 Macintosh, *supra* note 79, at 30.
120 Council Report, *supra* note 94, at 111. The Council's insinuation that the father might subject his daughter to sexual pressure is inconsistent with what we know about families. It is common for children to resemble one parent or another; but most parents are not attracted to children. Raising a child as a member of the family triggers a taboo on sex with that person. Macintosh, *supra* note 79, at 31.

   A recent movie exploits this cloning-as-incest theme. A woman clones her deceased lover in the hopes of one day reinstating their affair, only to find that the young man she raised from babyhood prefers a younger woman. *See* Ray Bennett, "*Womb* – Film Review," *The Hollywood Reporter*, Aug. 10, 2010, at http://www.hollywoodreporter.com/hr/film-reviews/womb-film-review-1004108483.story.
121 Macintosh, *supra* note 79, at 31.
122 John Robertson, "Liberty, Identity, and Human Cloning," 76 *Tex. L. Rev.* 1371, 1449 (1998). Furthermore, Robertson suggests regulations should allow doctors to refuse to treat patients who are committed to inappropriate goals,

such as the duplication of a famous individual. *Id.* However, if patients sense that doctors are empowered to function as gatekeepers, they may not be honest when speaking to counselors about their goals; if that happens, the best chance of dissuading them from pursuing impossible goals will be lost. *Cf.* California Report, *supra* note 96, at 36 (arguing that if regulators limit cloning to legitimate uses, patients will misrepresent their goals to access the technology). For that reason, this book does not advocate placing doctors in the position of gatekeepers.
123 *See generally* W. Page Keeton, *Prosser and Keeton on Torts* 190–92 (5th ed. 1984) (explaining that medical professionals must obtain informed consent before providing services to patients).
124 Robertson, *supra* note 122, at 1449.
125 California Report, *supra* note 96, at 36.
126 *Id.* at 34.
127 *Id.* (emphasis added).
128 California Report, *supra* note 96, at 28 (emphasis added).
129 NBAC Report, *supra* note 92, at 67 (emphasis added).
130 In writing this section, I do not mean to imply that George Lucas and other purveyors of popular culture are consciously employing principles of psychological essentialism. They may not even believe in their own fantasies. What I explain is that the fantasies sell because essentialism makes the identity fallacy credible to the viewer.
131 Nancy L. Segal, *Entwined Lives: Twins and What They Tell Us About Human Behavior* 77–80 (1999).
132 The movie presents the soldiers as genetically engineered for obedience. *Star Wars II: Attack of the Clones* (20th Century Fox 2002). There is no gene for obedience, and it seems unlikely that such engineering would be successful. Nor would such engineering eliminate the hundreds of other genetic, epigenetic, or environmental variables that could lead the clones to develop individual personalities along other dimensions.
133 Other science fiction stories could be analyzed along the same lines, with the essentialism of living kinds predicting rich clusters of shared traits. *See, e.g., The Boys from Brazil* (Twentieth Century Fox 1978) (depicting four children cloned from Adolf Hitler who not only look identical but also have the same cold and contemptuous personality); *Anna to the Infinite Power* (Scorpion Releasing 1983) (showing children cloned from a dead scientist who share her appearance, intellect, and neuroses); *The Third Twin* (CBS Broadcasting, Inc. 1997) (depicting men cloned to be super-soldiers; all resemble each other, and many have criminal or violent tendencies); *The X-Files*, "Eve" (Fox December 10, 1993) (showing numerous cloned females who not only resemble each other physically, intellectually, and psychologically, but share each other's thoughts).

134 NBAC Report, *supra* note 92, at 69.
135 *See Anna to the Infinite Power* (Scorpion Releasing 1983) (relating how a company makes multiple copies of a deceased scientist in the hopes of completing an important scientific project); *The Boys from Brazil* (Twentieth Century Fox 1978) (explaining how Dr. Mengele clones Adolf Hitler ninety-four times in an attempt to recreate the dictator and his dictatorship); *The Third Twin* (CBS Broadcasting, Inc. 1997) (showing how corporation clones multiple men in an effort to make super-soldiers); *Xchange* (Trimark Pictures 2000) (depicting the creation of cloned bodies for use in performing difficult jobs); *Star Trek: Deep Space Nine*, "Ties of Blood and Water" (Paramount Television April 14, 1997) and "Treachery, Faith, and the Great River" (Paramount Television November 4, 1998) (involving serial alien clones that serve as diplomats for an empire known as the Dominion); *The X-Files*, "Herrenvolk" (Fox October 4, 1996) (showing mute children cloned to work on a farm).
136 Gelman, *supra* note 4, at 7.
137 *Id.* at 181–85.
138 Atran, *supra* note 27, at 547, 549.
139 Council Report, *supra* note 94, at 79; California Report, *supra* note 96, at 20–21.
140 Hirschfeld, *supra* note 21, at 184–85.
141 *Star Wars II: Attack of the Clones* (20th Century Fox 2002).
142 For other films in which a single person created through cloning shares the personality and/or skills of his or her DNA donor, *see 2001: A Space Travesty* (Columbia/TriStar 2000) (depicting a cloned man who has the same personality, mannerisms, and ability to play the saxophone as President Bill Clinton); *Alien: Resurrection* (Twentieth Century Fox 1997) (telling the story of how Ellen Ripley is cloned after her death so she can continue to fight aliens); *The Clones* (Filmmakers International 1973) (relating a government plot to clone scientists who have the skill to make a secret weapon); *The Fifth Element* (Columbia Pictures 1997) (showing how a warrior on a mission to save the world is destroyed, but a person cloned from her and born as an adult carries on the same mission); *Multiplicity* (Columbia Pictures 1996) (relating how the first man cloned from the protagonist shares his skills as a contractor and carries out his work); *The Sixth Day* (Columbia Pictures 2000) (depicting a cloned protagonist who shares the occupation of his DNA donor); *see also Godsend* (Lions Gate Pictures 2004) (relating how a cloned child shares the personality of a sociopath whose DNA was surreptitiously added to that of the primary donor).
143 *See Starman* (Columbia Pictures 1984); *see also Multiplicity* (Columbia Pictures 1996) (explaining that the quality of copying is degraded when one clones from a cloned person, rather than from the original); *Replicant* (Artisan

Entertainment 2001) (showing how a cloned man ultimately turns out to be a better person than his serial-killer DNA donor); *Repli-Kate* (Twentieth Century Fox 2002) (relating a story in which creators instill male tastes and traits in a cloned woman).
144 *See* Chapter 6, Part D, *infra*.
145 NBAC Report, *supra* note 92, at 67.

CHAPTER 5. ARTIFACTS AND ESSENTIALISM

1 Douglas Medin & Andrew Ortony, "Psychological Essentialism," in *Similarity and Analogical Reasoning* 179, 183–86 (Stella Vosniadou & Andrew Ortony, Eds. 1989).
2 Paul Bloom, *Descartes' Baby: How the Science of Child Development Explains What Makes Us Human* 55 (paperback ed. 2005).
3 Deborah Kelemen & Susan Carey, "The Essence of Artifacts: Developing the Design Stance," *in Creations of the Mind* 212, 214 (Eric Margolis & Stephen Laurence, Eds. 2007). Kelemen and Carey acknowledge borrowing the term "design stance" from Daniel C. Dennett, but distinguish their theory as one that accepts intention as real and not a mere stance. *Id.*, citing Daniel C. Dennett, *The Intentional Stance* (1987); Daniel C. Dennett, "The Interpretation of Texts, People and Other Artifacts," 50 *Philosophy and Phenomenological Research* 177 (1990).
4 Kelemen & Carey, *supra* note 3, at 214; *but see* Barbara C. Malt & Steven A. Sloman, "Artifact Categorization: The Good, the Bad, and the Ugly," in *Creations of the Mind* 85, 89–93, 114 (Eric Margolis & Stephen Laurence, Eds. 2007) (challenging this conclusion and arguing that intended use is only one of several factors that people consider when classifying artifacts).
5 Adee Matan & Susan Carey, "Developmental Changes Within the Core of Artifacts Concepts," 78 *Cognition* 1, 23–24 App. A (2001).
6 Eighty percent of adult judgments were based on original intended function; thus, adults did sometimes prefer current over intended use. *Id.* at 7. However, the subjects gave justifications indicating feasibility affected their decisions. For example, one question addressed whether an item designed to serve as a plate could be a Frisbee if used for throwing. One can eat off a Frisbee but a plate might break if thrown. Therefore, a subject might have concluded the object had to be a Frisbee. *Id.* at 8–9.
7 *See id.* at 11 (reporting that 86 percent of six-year-old judgments preferred intended function over current use). However, on balance, the judgments of four-year-old children did not favor intended function over current use, and the children were influenced by which use was mentioned first in the scenario told to them. *Id.* at 16–17. This finding is discussed below in note 22.

8 Kelemen & Carey, *supra* note 3, at 214.
9 Susan A. Gelman, *The Essentialist Child: Origins of Essentialism in Everyday Thought* 49, 314 (2003).
10 For a summary of elements of essentialism in various domains, *see id.* at 138, tbl.6.1.
11 *Id.* at 49–53, 138–39.
12 *See, e.g.*, Myron Rothbart & Marjorie Taylor, "Category Labels and Social Reality: Do We View Social Categories as Natural Kinds?" in *Language, Interaction and Social Cognition*, 10, 12–14, 16–18 (Gun. R. Semin & Klaus Fiedler, Eds. 1992); H. Clark Barrett, "On the Functional Origins of Essentialism, 3 *Mind & Society* 18–19 (2001).
13 Gelman, *supra* note 9, at 121–25, 139.
14 *See id.* at 67–69 (citing as examples cuckoo clocks that look like birdhouses and belts that serve as hidden wallets).
15 *Id.* at 61–67, 139, 246. In support of this point, Gelman cites Frank C. Keil, *Concepts, Kinds, and Cognitive Development* (1989). The book discusses experiments in which artifacts with an original function were rebuilt or modified to serve a new function. Child research subjects identified the artifacts consistently with their new function. Keil, *supra* at 183–94. However, other psychologists have questioned whether these experiments really show that artifacts don't have essences. The modifications were extensive enough to create new artifacts with new essences determined by the intention of the new creator. In other words, the experiments proved the point that a creator's intended use is the essence of artifact kinds. Fei Xu & Mijke Rhemtulla, "In Defense of Psychological Essentialism," in *Proceedings of the 27th Annual Conference of the Cognitive Science Society* 2377, 2378–79 (B.G. Bara, L. Barsalou & M. Bucciarelli, Eds. 2005).
16 Gelman, *supra* note 9, at 315; *accord* Barrett, *supra* note 12, at 18–19.
17 *See, e.g.*, Scott Atran, "Folk Biology and the Anthropology of Science: Cognitive Universals and Cultural Particulars," 21 *Behavioral and Brain Sciences* 547, 548, 555 (1998).
18 Barrett, *supra* note 12, at 20; *but see* Kelemen & Carey, *supra* note 3, at 228 (speculating that a child's appreciation of the importance of parental origins in determining living kinds might inform her understanding of the importance of design origin in determining artifact kind).
19 Pascal Boyer & H. Clark Barrett, "Domain Specificity and Intuitive Ontology," in *The Handbook of Evolutionary Psychology* 96, 103–04 (David M. Buss, Ed. 2005).
20 Barrett, *supra* note 12, at 19–20.
21 Boyer & Barrett, *supra* note 19, at 104.

22 Kelemen & Carey, *supra* note 3, at 221. This age range apparently is a compromise between the coauthors, who cite their own prior research in this book chapter. For example, the chapter summarizes Carey's prior experiment in which six year olds preferred intended use over current use in determining the proper category for an artifact, but four year olds did not. *Id.* at 221, *citing* Adee Matan & Susan Carey, "Developmental Changes Within the Core of Artifacts Concepts," 78 *Cognition* 1 (2001). However, the chapter also presents Kelemen's prior experiment in which four and five year olds judged artifacts as being for their intended function rather than alternative use. Kelemen & Carey, *supra* at 223, *citing* Deborah Kelemen, "The Scope of Teleological Thinking in Preschool Children," 70 *Cognition* 241 (1999).
23 Kelemen & Carey, *supra* note 3, at 218–19, 226–27.
24 *Id.* at 227; *see also* Gelman, *supra* note 9, at 181–85, 193–212 (discussing the contribution of common nouns and generic phrases to the development of psychological essentialism).
25 Kelemen & Carey, *supra* note 3, at 227.
26 *Id.* at 224.
27 Gelman, *supra* note 9, at 312–13, 321.
28 *Id.* at 314–15.
29 *Id.* at 318–19.
30 Some academics question the dominance of original intended use in judgments about artifact kinds. They claim multiple factors affect such judgments (including form, relatedness of features, original intended use, intended category, and current use), and that research subjects attempt to rationalize all factors presented to them. Malt & Sloman, *supra* note 4, at 89–93, 114 (citing the Matan and Carey experiment, in which subjects weighed the feasibility of eating off a Frisbee versus throwing a plate for sport). More fundamentally, these academics also question the coherence of categorization as a field. As they interpret the experimental data, the mind does not assign artifacts to stable and bounded categories (although language does so in order to facilitate communication). In other words, psychologically there is no such thing as artifact kinds. *Id.* at 120–21. Still, even these critics concede the presence of a layperson's intuition that artifacts come in kinds, without explaining the source of that intuition. *Id.* at 121.

In the view of this author, the reference to intuition is telling. Cognitive heuristics do not generate nuanced decisions based upon all possible relevant factors; they offer quick, intuitive judgments that serve as good approximations. If the goal is to identify heuristics that laypeople apply to artifacts, then experiments that ask them to categorize on the basis of a single dominant factor could be very informative, even if other factors are relevant, and even if artifact categories are not stable or bounded. Further analysis will proceed on the assumption that it is worthwhile considering how intuitions about artifact kinds apply to humans born through cloning.

31 Gelman, *supra* note 9, at 90–95 (discussing experiments in which young children expect plants, animals, and people to share the species and characteristics of birth parents); Barrett, *supra* note 12, at 9 (noting that reproductive origin is key to the identification of a thing as a member of a kind).

32 Nick Haslam et al., "Essentialist Beliefs About Personality and Their Implications," 30 *Personality and Social Psychology Bulletin*, 1661, 1665 tbl.1, 1667 (2004).

33 Nick Haslam et al., "More Human than You: Attributing Humanness to Self and Others," 89 *J. Personality & Social Psychology* 937, 938 (2005).

34 *Id.* at 939.

35 A fourth element of essentialism – immutability – was not associated with human nature traits. *Id.* at 941.

36 *Id.* Another key finding from this group of experiments was that individual subjects attributed human nature more to themselves than others. *Id.* at 943. The researchers theorized that this effect stemmed from a tendency to reserve essence-like traits for oneself while granting others less ontological depth. *Id.* at 946.

37 Nick Haslam, "Dehumanization: An Integrative Review," 10 *Personality and Social Psychology Review* 252, 256–58 (2006).

38 *Id.*

39 *Id.* at 261. Haslam tentatively classifies animalistic dehumanization as group related and mechanistic dehumanization as a process that could be applied to either individuals or groups. *Id.* at 259.

40 *Star Wars II: Attack of the Clones* (20th Century Fox 2002); *see also* Table 1 in Chapter 4 (citing numerous other examples of films and episodes that portray cloned humans or humanoid aliens as multiple copies).

41 I have included in Table 2 films and television episodes in which characters born through cloning have been genetically engineered or are alien rather than human. However, I have excluded others involving androids and cyborgs on the reasoning that such films and television episodes involve actual machines. Including such stories would confuse the topic here, which is the treatment of living creatures as artifacts. *See, e.g., The Stepford Wives* (Columbia Pictures and Paramount Pictures 1975) (showing how sexist men make compliant androids to replace their wives).

42 *Id.*; *2001: A Space Travesty* (Columbia/TriStar 2000); *Alien: Resurrection* (Twentieth Century Fox 1997); *The Clones* (Filmmakers International 1973); *The Clones of Bruce Lee* (Newport Releasing 1977); *Creator* (Universal Pictures 1985); *Fifth Element* (Columbia Pictures 1997); *The Island* (DreamWorks/

Warner Brothers 2005); *Judge Dredd* (Hollywood Pictures 1995); *Multiplicity* (Columbia Pictures 1996); *Replicant* (Artisan Entertainment 2001); *Replikator* (Aurora Motion Pictures 1994); *Repli-Kate* (Twentieth Century Fox 2002); *The Sixth Day* (Columbia Pictures 2000); *The Resurrection of Zachary Wheeler* (Gold Key Entertainment Film Ventures 1971); *Star Wars II: Attack of the Clones* (20th Century Fox 2002); *Star Trek: Deep Space Nine*, "A Man Alone" (Paramount Television Jan. 17, 1993); *Star Trek Next Generation*, "Up the Long Ladder" (Paramount Television May 22, 1989).

43 *The Sixth Day* (Columbia Pictures 2000); *see also The Resurrection of Zachary Wheeler* (Gold Key Entertainment Film Ventures 1971) (showing cloned bodies with no minds created to serve as organ donors); *Xchange* (Trimark Pictures 2000) (depicting cloned bodies that have been engineered to serve as temporary vessels for the minds of others).

44 *Star Trek III: The Search for Spock* (Paramount Pictures 1984).

45 *Id.*

46 *Star Wars II: Attack of the Clones* (20th Century Fox 2002); *see also Shadow Fury* (Pathfinder Pictures 2001) (depicting cloned ninjas genetically engineered for obedience); *The X-Files*, "Herrenvolk" (Fox October 4, 1996) (showing passive cloned children created as mutes to serve as farmworkers).

47 *The Island* (DreamWorks/Warner Brothers 2005).

48 *Id.*; *see also Alien: Resurrection* (Twentieth Century Fox 1997) (describing woman cloned from Ellen Ripley as a construct); *Star Wars II: Attack of the Clones* (20th Century Fox 2002) (showing Kaminoans describing clone soldiers as units).

49 Patrick D. Hopkins, "Bad Copies: How Popular Media Represent Cloning as an Ethical Problem," 28 *Hastings Center Rep.* 6, 7–9 (March–April 1998); Giovanni Maio, "Cloning in the Media and Popular Culture," 7 *EMBO Reports* 241, 244–45 (2006).

50 *Id.* at 7.

51 *See id.* (noting a *Newsweek* story that included a picture of an Andy Warhol painting of multiple Marilyn Monroes); Maio, *supra* note 49, at 245 (citing images of dolls, wax figures, and marionettes). This visual association of humans born through cloning with artifacts also occurs on the covers of academic books on cloning. *See* John Harris, *On Cloning* (2004) (depicting numerous identical child manikins leaned up against a wall and each other); Aaron D. Levine, *Cloning: A Beginner's Guide* (2007) (depicting torsos and heads of multiple identical adult manikins); *The Human Cloning Debate* (Glenn McGee, Ed. 1998) (patterning cover with dozens of copies of the head of Michelangelo's *David* statue).

52 National Bioethics Advisory Commission, "Cloning Human Beings, Report and Recommendations of the National Bioethics Advisory Commission" (1997) [hereinafter NBAC Report].

53 The President's Council on Bioethics, "Human Cloning and Human Dignity: An Ethical Inquiry" (2002) [hereinafter Council Report].
54 California Advisory Committee on Human Cloning, "Cloning Californians? Report of the California Advisory Committee on Human Cloning" (2002) [hereinafter California Report].
55 *Id.* at 31. In support of this statement, the California Report reasons that women can supply all that is required for cloning: eggs, cell nuclei, and uteri. *Id.*
56 George J. Annas et al., "Protecting the Endangered Human: Toward an International Treaty Prohibiting Cloning and Inheritable Alterations," 28 *Am. J.L. & Med.* 151, 159–60 (2002).
57 Council Report, *supra* note 53, at 110; California Report, *supra* note 54, at 27–28; NBAC Report, *supra* note 52, at 70.
58 Council Report, *supra* note 53, at 110–11.
59 Kerry Lynn Macintosh, *Illegal Beings: Human Clones and the Law* 14 (2005) (*citing Webster's New World Dictionary of the American Language* 1594 (college ed. 1968)).
60 Council Report, *supra* note 53, at 104.
61 Alternative modes of conception have been available at least since 1785, when a Scottish doctor used a syringe to inseminate a patient with the semen of her husband. Judith F. Daar, *Reproductive Technologies and the Law* 27 (2006).
62 *See also* Christof Tannert, "Thou Shalt Not Clone: An Ethical Argument Against the Reproductive Cloning of Humans," 7 *EMBO Reports* 238, 239 (2006) (arguing that a cloned human is an artifact because it results from deliberate human action: the imposition of genetic identity).
63 This is consistent with the Council's earlier decision to classify the product of cloning as a cloned human embryo rather than artifact. Council Report, *supra* note 53, at 50–53.
64 *Id.* at 105–06 (emphasis added).
65 *Id.* at 107.
66 NBAC Report, *supra* note 52, at 72–73.
67 California Report, *supra* note 54, at 25.
68 Macintosh, *supra* note 59, at 19–20.
69 Council Report, *supra* note 53, at 103–04; California Report, *supra* note 54, at 25; NBAC Report, *supra* note 52, at 67–68.
70 Council Report, *supra* note 53, at 103–04; California Report, *supra* note 54, at 25; NBAC Report, *supra* note 52, at 67–68.
71 *Cf.* NBAC Report, *supra* note 52, at 67–68 (characterizing the argument that a cloned human lacks an open future as a form of genetic determinism).
72 Jussi Niemela, "What Puts the 'Yuck' in the Yuck Factor?," 25 *Bioethics* 267, 273, 275 (2011).

73 *Id.* at 278.
74 *Id.* at 276–77.
75 *See id.* at 276 (arguing that technological interventions that are akin to building invoke the artifact domain).
76 *The Boys from Brazil* (Twentieth Century Fox 1978).
77 *Id.*
78 *See* Part C.3.c of this chapter, *supra.*
79 *The Boys from Brazil* (Twentieth Century Fox 1978).
80 *Id.*
81 *Anna to the Infinite Power* (Scorpion Releasing 1983).
82 *Id.*
83 Haslam, *supra* note 37, at 261.
84 *Id.* at 257–58.
85 *Id.* at 258.
86 Niemela, *supra* note 72, at 277.
87 Leon Kass, "The Wisdom of Repugnance," in *The Human Cloning Debate* 137, 147 (Glenn McGee & Arthur Caplan Eds., 4th ed. 2004).
88 *Id.* at 276.

CHAPTER 6. IMPOSTORS AND ESSENTIALISM

1 Susan A. Gelman, *The Essentialist Child: Origins of Essentialism in Everyday Thought* (2003).
2 Douglas Medin & Andrew Ortony, "Psychological Essentialism," in *Similarity and Analogical Reasoning* 179, 184 (Stella Vosniadou & Andrew Ortony, Eds. 1989).
3 Gelman, *supra* note 1, at 151.
4 *Id.* In a later section of her book, Gelman mentions an experiment in which both adults and three-year-old children associated a proper name ("daxy") with a particular doll, even after experimenters moved the doll and gave its green cloak and original location to an identical doll. *Id.* at 319, *citing* Cristina M. Sorrentino, "Children and Adults Represent Proper Names as Referring to Unique Individuals," 4 *Developmental Science* 399 (2001). The experimenters took these results to mean that not only adults but also children view proper names as referring to unique individuals (rather than kinds). The results implied that the adults and children had the ability to track the doll despite changes in its appearance and location. Sorrentino, *supra*, at 405–06. From these results, Gelman infers that historical path is central to individual identity (as reflected in the name). Gelman, *supra* note 1, at 319.
5 Gelman, *supra* note 1, at 151, *citing* Robert J. Sternberg, Marek C. Chawarski & David W. Allbritton, "If You Changed Your Name and Appearance to Those

of Elvis Presley, Who Would You Be? Historical Features in Categorization," 111 *Am. J. Psych.* 327 (1998).
6 *See* Sternberg et al., *supra* note 5, at 339 (discussing results of experiment) and at 348 (reproducing the test questions involving John F. Kennedy).
7 Student research subjects were also reluctant to match named individuals to descriptions that were inaccurate in phenotype but accurate in history. For example, they were asked to decide if a man could be John F. Kennedy if he was tall and balding with white hair, clumsy and accident-prone, and served as president of the United States for three years until he was assassinated in 1963. Students matched names to this sort of pairing only 16.8 percent of the time. *Id.* Although more subjects matched identity to these pairings than to the accurate phenotype but inaccurate history pairings (3.5 percent), the vast majority refused.

Some have taken the Sternberg experimental outcomes as contradictory: sometimes history prevails over appearance and behavior in determining individual identity, but other times the opposite is true. Grant Gutheil et al., "Preschoolers' Use of Spatiotemporal History, Appearance, and Proper Name in Determining Individual Identity," 107 *Cognition* 366, 368 (2008). However, I do not interpret the Sternberg experiments that way. Rather, I see a flaw in experimental design.

Pairings in which phenotype is inaccurate but history is accurate are tricky to design. When genuine (and not faked), appearance and behavior are often the product of personal history. Thus, if appearance and behavior are anomalous, these pairings can implicitly pit incorrect against correct history. The JFK question mentioned above illustrates the point. Baldness and white hair are associated with advanced age, and most people know JFK as the youngest President ever elected (at age forty-three). So right away, the question offers not just a physical discrepancy, but also an implied historical discrepancy. Moreover, the behavioral trait of being clumsy and accident-prone is so strongly associated with former President Gerald Ford that it summons to mind an entirely different President with his own historical path. In other words, the research subjects were asked to weigh not appearance and behavior versus history, but one person's history versus another's. It is not surprising that most refused to identify the man as JFK.
8 Gutheil et al., *supra* note 7, at 371–73. These results appear to conflict with those of a different experiment conducted by other psychologists. Briefly, adult research subjects were told that a lion named Fred was placed in a machine. The machine recorded information about Fred's particles, but the recording process destroyed the original particles. A computer within the machine then copied each particle and the machine reassembled those particles into a creature. However, in each trial, the reassembly process also incorporated a

specified percentage of particles (ranging from 0–100 percent) from another lion named Calvin or a tiger named Joe. Lance J. Rips et al., "Tracing the Identity of Objects," 113 *Psychological Review* 1, 11 (2006).

The psychologists asked their research subjects whether the copy made through this process "was" Fred. The subjects often answered yes, particularly when the percentage of particles copied from the original lion was high (in the range of 75 to 100 percent). *Id*. This experiment and others led the psychologists to conclude that spatiotemporal continuity was not necessary to identity, but causal continuity was. *Id*. at 27.

The researchers that conducted the experiment with the Winnie-the-Pooh stuffed toys struggled to reconcile their results with the lion experiment. In the end, they speculated that children started with a spatiotemporal approach but developed more complex theories of identity as they matured. Gutheil et al., *supra* note 7, at 378–79. However, before reaching this tentative conclusion, the researchers made an interesting observation: subjects in the lion experiment might have inferred that the copy possessed all the memories and behavior of the original Fred. Thus, the bizarre scenario approximated a real-life scenario in which a single lion occupied different points on a spatiotemporal path. *Id*. at 378.

This insight suggests an alternative explanation for the results in the lion experiment. Essentialism is a heuristic, that is, a quick and intuitive means of assessing situations. The similarity between the lion experiment and the more common situation in which a single animal follows a single spatiotemporal path might have prompted the subjects to apply a heuristic familiar to them since childhood – one in which historical path serves as essence – leading to the judgment that the copy was indeed Fred. However, the more particles the machine borrowed from another creature, the less the experimental scenario resembled real-life spatiotemporal continuity, and the less likely the subjects were to apply the heuristic and judge the copy to be Fred.

9 Gutheil et al., *supra* note 7, at 370 (citing as examples *The Frog Prince*, *The Bourne Identity*, and *The Fugitive*).
10 Gelman, *supra* note 1, at 60–61, *discussing* Claire Sylvia & William Novak, *A Change of Heart* (1997).
11 Sylvia & Novak, *supra* note 10, at 88, 92, 107.
12 *Id*. at 89, 104.
13 *Id*. at 124–27.
14 *Id*. at 107, 125, 194–95.
15 *Id*. at 183–85.
16 *See id*. at 128 (discussing how the steroid prednisone caused her to grow a lot of facial hair) and 210 (noting that doctors and nurses involved in organ transplantation attribute personal changes to antirejection medications).

17 Sylvia & Novak, *supra* note 10, at 160, 169, 197.
18 *Id*. at 133–47, 213–16.
19 *Id*. at 140, 217–18.
20 Gelman, *supra* note 1, at 60–61; *see also* Bruce M. Hood, *Supersense: Why We Believe in the Unbelievable* 182 (2009) (concluding that transplant recipients who believe they have taken on donor traits are influenced by essentialism).
21 Hood, *supra* note 20, at 180 (2009), *citing* Y. Inspector et al., "Another Person's Heart: Magical and Rational Thinking in the Psychological Adaptation to Heart Transplantation," 41 *Israel J. Psychiatry & Related Sciences* 161 (2004).
22 Inspector et al., *supra* note 21, at 169.
23 *Id*. at 170. Heart recipients are not the only ones to believe that a transplant can transfer donor traits. As the Israeli researchers noted, the same phenomenon has been observed following kidney transplant, skin graft, and blood transfusion. *Id*. at 162; *see also* Hood, *supra* note 20, at 179–80 (telling the tale of a man who acquired the hobbies, tastes, and dreams of his wife after he received a kidney from her).
24 Gelman, *supra* note 1, at 312–13, 321.
25 *Id*. at 318. For example, psychologists have found that not only adults, but also children as young as four or five years old identify animals by their behavioral traits, despite changes in their names and physical appearances (*e.g.*, having fur shaved off or dyed). Grant Gutheil & Karl S. Rosengren, "A Rose by Any Other Name: Preschoolers' Understanding of Individual Identity Across Name and Appearance Changes," 14 *British J. Developmental Psychology* 477, 495–96 (1996), cited in Gelman, *supra* note 1, at 319.
26 Gelman, *supra* note 1, at 318. Experiments have shown that infants track the identity of an object as it moves through space and time. See Elizabeth S. Spelke et al., "Spatiotemporal Continuity, Smoothness of Motion and Object Identity in Infancy," 13 *British J. of Developmental Psychology* 113 (1995) (discussing an experiment wherein four-month-old infants associated continuous motion through space and time with a single object and discontinuous motion with two objects); Fei Xu & Susan Carey, "Infants' Metaphysics: The Case of Numerical Identity," 30 *Cognitive Psychology* 111 (1996) (discussing an experiment in which ten-month-old infants linked discontinuous motion through space and time with two objects).
27 Gelman, *supra* note 1, at 318–19.
28 *2001: A Space Travesty* (Columbia/TriStar 2000); *The Clones* (Filmmakers International 1973); *Invasion of the Body Snatchers* (United Artists 1978); *The Island* (DreamWorks/Warner Brothers 2005); *Multiplicity* (Columbia Pictures 1996); *Replikator* (Aurora Motion Pictures 1994); *Repli-Kate* (Twentieth Century Fox 2002); *Eureka*, "Many Happy Returns" (The Sci Fi Channel July 25, 2006); *Star Trek Deep Space Nine*, "A Man Alone" (Paramount Television January 17,

1993); *Star Trek Next Generation*, "Rightful Heir" (Paramount Television May 17, 1993); *X-Files*, "Colony" (Fox February 10, 1995); *X-Files*, "End Game" (Fox February 17, 1995); *see also The Sixth Day* (Columbia Pictures 2000) (showing how a cloned man slowly realizes that an impostor who appears to have taken over his life is actually the DNA donor enjoying his own life).
29 *The Third Twin* (CBS Broadcasting, Inc. 1997).
30 Table 3 includes films and television episodes in which characters born through cloning are alien (in whole or in part) rather than human. Films or television episodes featuring android, bioengineered, or cyborg impostors are not included on the ground that such stories extend beyond the realm of cloning and do not substantiate the impostor fallacy as defined here. *See, e.g., The Human Duplicators* (Woolner Brothers Pictures Inc. 1965) (relating a tale of aliens who make android impostors in an effort to take over the world); *Impostor* (Dimension Films 2002) (telling story of aliens who create bioengineered impostors with bombs as hearts); *The Stepford Wives* (Columbia Pictures and Paramount Pictures 1975) (showing how sexist men make compliant androids to replace their wives).
31 *E.g., 2001: A Space Travesty* (Columbia/TriStar 2000); *Multiplicity* (Columbia Pictures 1996); *see also The Island* (DreamWorks/Warner Brothers 2005) (depicting a synaptic scan that shows a cloned man spontaneously developing thirty years of memories in three years).
32 *The Clones* (Filmmakers International 1973); *The Sixth Day* (Columbia Pictures 2000); *Star Trek Next Generation*, "Rightful Heir" (Paramount Television May 17, 1993).
33 For lighthearted examples, see *Multiplicity* (Columbia Pictures 1996) (showing how three cloned men have different personalities than their DNA donor); *Repli-Kate* (Twentieth Century Fox 2002) (showing how a cloned woman is trained to have masculine habits and interests).
34 *See, e.g., Invasion of the Body Snatchers* (United Artists 1978) (showing how aliens use pods to replicate humans and take over their lives); *Replikator* (Aurora Motion Pictures 1994) (recounting the story of an evil cloned man who tries to take over the work of his DNA donor); *The Third Twin* (CBS Broadcasting, Inc. 1997) (showing how a good cloned man struggles to defeat the schemes of an evil cloned man who shares his DNA); *see also* Giovanni Maio, "Cloning in the Media and Popular Culture," 7 *EMBO Reports* 241, 242 (2006) (noting that films often portray the donor as good and the cloned person as evil); *but see Moon* (Sony Pictures Classics 2009) (showing how one newly cloned astronaut unwittingly takes the place of another who has fled to Earth in an effort to expose company misconduct).
35 *See The Clones* (Filmmakers International 1973) (telling the story of a research scientist who loses his wallet and car to a cloned impostor); *The Island*

(DreamWorks/Warner Brothers 2005) (showing how a cloned man takes over the apartment and speed boat of his DNA donor).
36 *See 2001: A Space Travesty* (Columbia/TriStar 2000) (depicting a plot to replace President Bill Clinton with a cloned impostor in the White House); *The Clones* (Filmmakers International 1973) (showing how the government clones a research scientist and creates an impostor to take over his work and create a doomsday weapon); *Replikator* (Aurora Motion Pictures 1994) (recounting the story of an evil cloned man who tries to take over the work of his DNA donor).
37 *See The Clones* (Filmmakers International 1973) (showing how a cloned impostor impersonates a research scientist when dealing with the scientist's girlfriend); *Multiplicity* (Columbia Pictures 1996) (telling the tale of a man who clones himself three times and lives to regret it when all three impostors sleep with his wife); *Repli-Kate* (Twentieth Century Fox 2002) (relating how a cloned woman competes with her DNA donor for the attentions of a man); *The Third Twin* (CBS Broadcasting, Inc. 1997) (showing how an evil cloned man attempts to seduce the girlfriend of a good cloned man); *Eureka*, "Many Happy Returns" (The Sci Fi Channel July 25, 2006) (telling the story of a woman who is upset to discover that her former boyfriend cloned her and married the impostor); *see also The Sixth Day* (Columbia Pictures 2000) (showing how a cloned man wrongly believes the DNA donor has stolen his wife and family).
38 *Multiplicity* (Columbia Pictures 1996).
39 *The Clones* (Filmmakers International 1973).
40 *See Invasion of the Body Snatchers* (United Artists 1978) (showing how alien pods replicate emotionless bodies and destroy the original human beings).
41 *The Island* (DreamWorks/Warner Brothers 2005).
42 The only differences are that Tom Lincoln wears glasses. He also has a Scottish accent. *Id.*
43 *Id.*
44 *Id.*
45 Chapter 4, Part C.2.
46 *Repli-Kate* (Twentieth Century Fox 2002).
47 *The Island* (DreamWorks/Warner Brothers 2005).
48 *See* Hood, *supra* note 20, at 146 (describing research showing that adults and older children believe that essence is spread throughout the body of an animal).
49 *2001: A Space Travesty* (Columbia/TriStar 2000); *see also The Clones* (Filmmakers International 1973) (showing how a woman realizes a cloned man is not her boyfriend because he must think about who he is).
50 *The Parent Trap* (Walt Disney Pictures 1998).
51 *Id.*

52 *Big Business* (Touchstone Pictures 1988).
53 *Id.*
54 *Id.*
55 *Id.*
56 Adams Wai-Kin Kong et al., "A Study of Identical Twins' Palmprints for Personal Verification," 39 *Pattern Recognition* 2149, 2150 Fig.1 (2006).
57 Zhenan Sun et al., "A Study of Multibiometric Traits of Identical Twins," 7667 *Proc. of SPIE* 76670T-1, 76670T-5 (2010). This study found that monozygotic multiples posed a challenge for face-recognition systems. The error rate for general impostors was 3.79 percent, but for identical twins impersonating each other was 13.67 percent. *Id.* at 76670T-9, 76670T-10 Tbl.1. However, many of the participating multiples were children, and the average age was only sixteen. *Id.* at 76670T-6. The researchers also decided which twins were monozygotic based on the similarity of facial images (rather than DNA testing); monozygotic twins with varying appearances may have been excluded, thereby skewing the study results. *Id.*
58 *See id.* at 76670T-8 through 76670T-10 and Tbl.1 (explaining that authentication systems based on irises or fingerprints are very good at detecting twin impostors, particularly when readings from two irises or four fingerprints are used); Kong et al., *supra* note 56, at 2151–56 (discussing a biometric system that can distinguish monozygotic twins based on palm prints).
59 *See* Sun et al., *supra* note 57, at 76670T-4, 76670T-5 (noting that fingerprints are formed based on the flow of amniotic fluids, and that iris texture is result of uterine environment); Kong et al., *supra* note 56, at 2150 (explaining that not only genes but other factors affect the formation of fingerprints, irises, and retinas).
60 Chapter 1, Part C.3.
61 Chapter 3, Part B.
62 Chapter 2, Part B, and Chapter 3, Part B.
63 Patrick D. Hopkins, "Bad Copies: How Popular Media Represent Cloning as an Ethical Problem," 28 *Hastings Center Rep.* 6, 8–9 (March–April 1998).
64 California Advisory Committee on Human Cloning, "Cloning Californians? Report of the California Advisory Committee on Human Cloning" 26 (2002) [hereinafter California Report].
65 Chapter 4, Part C.3.
66 California Report, *supra* note 64, at 27.
67 *See, e.g., 2001: A Space Travesty* (Columbia/TriStar 2000) (recounting an alien plot to clone President Bill Clinton without his knowledge); *The Clones* (Filmmakers International 1973) (showing the travails of a research scientist cloned without his knowledge); *Invasion of the Body Snatchers* (United Artists 1978) (showing how alien pods wait until human victims fall asleep and then

replicate them); *Eureka*, "Many Happy Returns" (The Sci Fi Channel July 25, 2006) (telling the story of a woman who finds that her former boyfriend cloned her without her knowledge or consent and then married the cloned impostor).
68 California Report, *supra* note 64, at 27, 33.

CHAPTER 7. RESURRECTION AND ESSENTIALISM

1 Table 4 includes films and television episodes in which characters born through cloning are genetically altered or alien, in whole or in part. However, it excludes films and episodes involving androids or cyborgs. Thus, for example, the television series *Caprica* (in which a man transfers his dead daughter's artificial intelligence avatar into a mechanical body) is not studied here. *Caprica* (Syfy Channel January 22, 2010 to present).

Table 4 does not include the film *Jurassic Park* for two reasons. First, it deals with the cloning of dinosaurs rather than humans. Second, the film presents the cloned dinosaurs as the reanimation of extinct species, but not as resurrections of individual dinosaur donors. *Jurassic Park* (Universal Pictures 1993). This makes sense, given that our knowledge of the dinosaurs is limited to facts about species. We have no archeological evidence documenting individual dinosaurs with distinct personalities.

2 *See The Boys from Brazil* (Twentieth Century Fox 1978) (depicting an attempt to clone Adolf Hitler); *Sleeper* (United Artists 1973) (showing how a dictatorship attempts to clone a dictator from his nose); *Star Trek Next Generation*, "Rightful Heir" (Paramount Television, May 17, 1993) (telling how Klingon religious leaders clone the Klingon messiah, Kahless, in an effort to increase their own power).

3 *The Boys from Brazil* (Twentieth Century Fox 1978).

4 *Id*.

5 *Anna to the Infinite Power* (Scorpion Releasing 1983).

6 *Alien: Resurrection* (Twentieth Century Fox 1997); *see also The Sixth Day* (Columbia Pictures 1997) (showing how a biotechnology company creates adult replicates to step in for staff members who have died).

7 *See Cloned* (NBC 1997) (showing how a company offers a bereaved mother the chance to clone her dead son, but she refuses); *The Creator* (Universal Pictures 1985) (telling the story of a man who gives up on a project to clone his dead wife after he finds a new lover); *Eleventh Hour: Resurrection* (Granada Television Jan. 19, 2006) (showing how a science advisor thwarts a plot to clone the deceased son of a rich man); *Godsend* (Lions Gate Films 2004); *Morella* (Taurus Films 1997) (relating how a man clones his lover with disastrous results).

8 *Godsend* (Lions Gate Films 2004).

NOTES TO PAGES 150–152

9 *The Boys from Brazil* (Twentieth Century Fox 1978)
10 *Id.*; *see also Anna to the Infinite Power* (Scorpion Releasing 1983); *Cloned* (NBC 1997); *Morella* (Taurus Films 1997) (depicting cloning as a process that creates babies who mature at the normal rate).
11 *Alien: Resurrection* (Twentieth Century Fox 1997); *Fifth Element* (Columbia Pictures 1997); *The Sixth Day* (Columbia Pictures (2000); *see also Star Trek III: The Search for Spock* (Paramount Pictures 1984) (depicting a person cloned from Mr. Spock who matures from childhood to adulthood at an accelerated pace).
12 *See Alien: Resurrection* (Twentieth Century Fox 1997) (showing how a person cloned from Ellen Ripley has some of her memories); *Anna to the Infinite Power* (Scorpion Releasing 1983) (depicting a young girl who has the memories of her DNA donor); *Fifth Element* (Columbia Pictures 1997) (showing a cloned person with partial memories of a prior life); *Morella* (Taurus Films 1997) (recounting the story of a cloned woman who has the memories of her donor).
13 *Anna to the Infinite Power* (Scorpion Releasing 1983).
14 *Id.* For a variation on this theme, consider the film *Godsend*. Parents clone their deceased son. The child is normal until he reaches the precise age at which his DNA donor died. Suddenly, he becomes disruptive at home and school. He draws pictures of a fire. He kills a schoolmate and tries to kill his mother several times. Too late, the parents discover that the doctor who performed the cloning mixed in some DNA from his own sociopathic son, who killed his mother and died in a fire he set. In other words, the DNA of the doctor's son somehow causes the cloned boy to have the same matricidal tendencies and memories. *Godsend* (Lions Gate Films 2004).
15 *The Sixth Day* (Columbia Pictures 2000).
16 *Star Trek Next Generation*, "Rightful Heir" (Paramount Television, May 17, 1993).
17 *Star Trek III: The Search for Spock* (Paramount Pictures 1984). Mr. Spock died in an earlier movie as the result of exposure to nuclear radiation. Before he died, he used a Vulcan mind-meld to transfer his katra (soul) into Dr. Leonard McCoy. *Star Trek II: The Wrath of Khan* (Paramount Pictures 1982).
18 *The Resurrection of Zachary Wheeler*, (Gold Key Entertainment Film Ventures 1971).
19 *The Island* (DreamWorks/Warner Brothers 2005); *see also Parts: The Clonus Horror* (Group 1 International Distribution Organization Ltd. 1979) (depicting the creation and maintenance of cloned persons to be harvested for body parts and organs).
20 *Never Let Me Go* (Fox Searchlight Pictures/Twentieth Century Fox 2010).

21 Compare *The Island* (DreamWorks/Warner Brothers 2005), in which the cloned protagonist spontaneously develops the memories of his genetic predecessor, with *The Resurrection of Zachary Wheeler*, (Gold Key Entertainment Film Ventures 1971), in which the cloned bodies are portrayed as mentally vacant.
22 National Bioethics Advisory Commission, "Cloning Human Beings, Report and Recommendations of the National Bioethics Advisory Commission" 30 (1997) [hereinafter NBAC Report].
23 John Charles Kunich, *The Naked Clone: How Cloning Bans Threaten Our Personal Rights* 20, 127 (2003).
24 *See* Nicole Hebert, "Creating a Life to Save a Life: An Issue Inadequately Addressed by the Current Legal Framework Under Which Minors Are Permitted to Donate Tissue and Organs," 17 *S. Cal. Interdisciplinary. L.J.* 337, 338–39 (2008) (presenting data on organ donations from minors to siblings).
25 The President's Council on Bioethics, Reproduction & Responsibility: "The Regulation of New Biotechnologies" 96 (2004); Yury Verlinsky et al., "Preimplantation Diagnosis for Fanconi Anemia Combined with HLA Matching," 285 *JAMA* 3130 (2001).
26 *See* Hebert, *supra* note 24, at 355–66 (discussing various standards under which courts approve or disapprove tissue and organ donation from minors).
27 *See generally id.* (proposing legislative restrictions upon tissue and organ donation by minors).
28 Jeffrey Kluger, "Will We Follow the Sheep?" 149 *Time*, March 10, 1997, at 67, 71.
29 Wray Herbert et al., "A Clone Would Have a Soul," in *Cloning: For and Against* 16, 19 (M.L. Rantala & Arthur J. Milgram, Eds. 1999).
30 *Id.* at 22.
31 *See* Kris Axtman, "Quietly, Animal Cloning Speeds Onward," *The Christian Science Monitor*, Oct. 15, 2001, http://www.csmonitor.com/2001/1015/p3s1-ussc.html; *see also* Hyung Jin Kim, "Counting Noses – 5 Cloned Pups," *S.F. Chron.*, Aug. 6, 2008, at A-6 (reporting that the owner of five newly cloned puppies joyfully told the canines that they already knew her); Jason Thompson, "Cloning/Waiting for Tundra Too/Here, Kitty, Kitty, Kitty, Kitty, Kitty!," http://articles.sfgate.com/2002-02-24/opinion/17530029_1_pet-dog-missy-genetic-savings-clone-missyplicity-project (last visited on October 19, 2010) (reporting a woman's intuition that her pet cat will be reborn through cloning).
32 *See* Russell Goldman, "Cloned Pets: Looks Can Be Deceiving," *ABC News*, Jan. 30, 2009, *at* http://abcnews.go.com/print?id=6762235.
33 More specifically, in one article a woman concedes that a cloning company warned her that her new dog might have a different personality than the old one. Her goal, however, was to get her old dog back, and the rest of her comments reveal that she has high hopes for that outcome. For example, she states that the

cloned pet has the same appearance as the dead pet and has taken over his leadership role in a household with nine other canines (despite being a puppy). *Id.*

34 *See* Joe Lauria, "Cloned in the USA: Attempt to Clone Human Being in Secret West Virginia Lab Revealed," *London Times*, Aug. 12, 2001, at http://www.cephasministry.com/health_raising_the_dead_through_cloning_clonaid.html.
35 Chapter 2, Part C, *supra*.
36 NBAC Report, *supra* note 22, at 80.
37 The President's Council on Bioethics, "Human Cloning and Human Dignity: An Ethical Inquiry" 79–80 (2002) [hereinafter Council Report].
38 California Advisory Committee on Human Cloning, "Cloning Californians? Report of the California Advisory Committee on Human Cloning" 22 (2002) [hereinafter California Report].
39 *Id.*
40 *See id.* at 34–37 (rejecting counseling and other regulatory approaches in favor of a permanent cloning ban).
41 NBAC Report, *supra* note 22, at 24.
42 Council Report, *supra* note 37, at 90.
43 California Report, *supra* note 38, at 10, 23.
44 Council Report, *supra* note 37, at 132–33; California Report, *supra* note 38, at 40; NBAC Report, *supra* note 22, at 30.
45 Chapter Six, Part A.2.
46 *Star Trek III: The Search for Spock* (Paramount Pictures 1984).
47 A company called Genetic Savings and Clone first created the cloned cat Cc before cloning a pet cat for its owner. The company went out of business in 2006. Not enough orders for cats came in and the company failed in its effort to clone dogs. *See* Peter Fimrite, "Pet-cloning Business Closes – Not 'Commercially Viable'," *S.F. Chron.*, Oct. 11, 2006, at B-7.
48 *The Island* (DreamWorks/Warner Brothers 2005).
49 *Id.*
50 *Never Let Me Go* (Fox Searchlight Pictures/Twentieth Century Fox 2010).
51 *Id.*
52 James A. Thomson et al., "Embryonic Stem Cell Lines Derived from Human Blastocysts," 282 *Science* 1145 (1998).
53 For more information on the state of cloning for research and stem cells, see Chapter Three, Part A.
54 Council Report, *supra* note 37, at 132–33; NBAC Report, *supra* note 22, at 30.
55 Kerry Lynn Macintosh, "'Island' Peers Into Inevitable Controversy of Human Cloning: Fiction Touches Truth of Stem Cell Debate," *S.J. Mercury News*, Aug. 3, 2005, at 23A.
56 *Never Let Me Go* (Fox Searchlight Pictures/Twentieth Century Fox 2010).

CHAPTER 8. ESSENTIALISM AND THE LAW OF REPRODUCTIVE CLONING

1. "Cloning," *Gallup*, http://www.gallup.com/poll/6028/cloning.aspx (last visited June 2, 2011).
2. Eleanor Singer et al., "The Polls – Trends: Genetic Testing, Engineering, and Therapy, Awareness and Attitudes," 62 *Public Opinion Quarterly* 633, 662 (1998). The organizations conducting the three polls were: (1) The Gallup Poll, Cable News Network, and *USA Today* (February 1997) [hereinafter the Gallup Poll]; (2) *Time*, Cable News Network, and surveys by Yankelovich Partners, Inc. (February 1997) [hereinafter the Time poll]; and (3) Hart and Teeter Research Companies, National Broadcasting Company News, and Wall Street Journal Poll (March 1997). *Id.* at 640, 662.
3. *Id.* at 662, notes b and c.
4. The Gallup and Time polls also asked whether human cloning (as so defined) was morally wrong. Unsurprisingly, 88–89 percent of respondents agreed with this vague but leading question. The Time poll also asked whether cloning was against God's will, prompting 74 percent of respondents to agree. *Id.* at 662.
5. Patrick D. Hopkins, "Bad Copies: How Popular Media Represent Cloning as an Ethical Problem," 28 *Hastings Center Rep.* 6, 7–9 (March–April 1998).
6. *Id.* at 6.
7. "America: Animal and Human Cloning," *Time/CNN, Center for Genetics and Society* (February 7, 2001), http://www.geneticsandsociety.org/article.php?id=4831.
8. *Id.*
9. *Id.*
10. *See* Chapter 5, *supra*, in Part C.4.b.
11. "America: Animal and Human Cloning," *supra* note 7.
12. *Id.*
13. Kerry Lynn Macintosh, *Illegal Beings: Human Clones and the Law* 82 (2005). For an excellent history of the politics leading up to the FDA's assertion of authority over reproductive cloning, see Elizabeth C. Price, "Does the FDA Have Authority to Regulate Human Cloning?" 11 *Harv. J.L. & Tech.* 619, 622–25 (1998).
14. Macintosh, *supra* note 13, at 82–83.
15. Elizabeth C. Price, "Does the FDA Have Authority to Regulate Human Cloning?" 11 *Harv. J. L. & Tech.* 619, 623–25 (1998).
16. Macintosh, *supra* note 13, at 85.
17. *See id.* (discussing how an FDA regulator appeared before Congress in 2001 and testified that the agency had no authority to halt human reproductive cloning if it was safe for child and mother).
18. *See* S. 1599, 105th Cong. (1998).

19 *See* S. 1602, 105th Cong. (1998).
20 *See* Price, *supra* note 13, at 625–27 (detailing the history of early legislative efforts and explaining the rationales behind bills).
21 H.R. 2505, 107th Cong. (2001); 147 Cong. Rec. H. 4945 (2001).
22 *See* 147 Cong. Rec. H. 4919 (2001) (recording the words of Lamar Smith, D-Texas, who cited the poll for the proposition that 90 percent of Americans oppose human cloning).
23 Macintosh, *supra* note 13, at 76.
24 H.R. 534, 108th Cong. (2003); 149 Cong. Rec. H. 1438 (2003); Macintosh, *supra* note 13, at 76–77.
25 *See, e.g.*, H.R. 1050, 111th Cong. (2009); H.R. 2564, 110th Cong. (2007); S. 658, 109th Cong. (2005).
26 See H.R. 1050, 111th Cong. (2009).
27 *Id.* § 2.
28 *Id.* §§ 2(1) and (2).
29 *Id.* § 2(3).
30 *Id.* § 2(4).
31 In 2003, Representative Donald A. Manzullo, R-Illinois, made a comment that is virtually the same as the third finding: "Efforts to create human beings by cloning shift human reproduction into a manufacturing process in which children are made in laboratories to preordained specifications and in multiple copies." 149 Cong. Rec. H. 1416 (2003). Many other conservatives have made comments that framed humans born through cloning as copies or designer products. *See, e.g., id.* at 1403 (stating the opinion of Lee Terry, R-Nebraska, that "children could be manufactured with specific genetic traits"); *id.* at 1411 (citing claim of J. Randy Forbes, R-Virginia, that ban is needed to affirm the uniqueness of human beings); *id.* at 1413 (quoting John Sullivan, R-Oklahoma, to the effect that cloning turns "the natural procreation process into the simple manufacturing of human beings"); 147 Cong. Rec. H. 4912 (2001) (recording statement of Michael Ferguson, R-New Jersey, that cloning only "mimics the creation of life" and treats life as an object); *id.* at 4918 (reporting view of Henry Hyde, R-Illinois, that cloning will lead to a world of manufactured men and women); *id.* at 4921 (citing view of Brian Kerns, R-Indiana, that most Americans oppose "re-creation" of human being); *id.* at 4927 (recording opinion of Todd Tiahrt, R-Kansas, that cloning could be used to create a slave or superior species); *id.* at 4928 (reporting view of Bob Barr, R-Georgia, that cloning produces exact genetic replica of a human being); *id.* at 4929 (citing Jim DeMint, R-South Carolina, to effect that there has never been an exact replica of another human before).
32 The President's Council on Bioethics, "Human Cloning and Human Dignity: An Ethical Inquiry" 104–07, 110–11 (2002) [hereinafter Council Report].

33 *Id.* at § 2(5).
34 147 Cong. Rec. H. 4941 (2001); *see also* 149 Cong. Rec. H. 1424 (2003) (reporting later comments in which Greenwood characterized humans born through cloning as duplicates); *id.* at 1432 (noting that Ron Kind, D-Wisconsin, opposed reproductive cloning because it created a genetic "identical copy").
35 147 Cong. Rec. H. 4935 (2001).
36 *Id.* at 4942–43.
37 149 Cong. Rec. H. 1436 (2003).
38 *See* H.R. 2560, 110th Cong. (2007).
39 153 Cong. Rec. H. 6077–78 (2007); Jim Abrams, "House Dems Lose on Cloning Bill – Stem Cell Vote Next," *S.F. Chron.*, June 7, 2007, at A17. The bill came to a vote through an unusual procedure. Representative Diana DeGette (D-Colorado) moved to suspend House rules (which would ordinarily allow debate and amendment) and pass the bill by a two-thirds majority. She did not succeed: the vote was 213 to 204 against the bill. *Id.*
40 153 Cong. Rec. H. 6041 (2007).
41 *Id.* at 6038, 6041, 6042.
42 *Id.* at 6042.
43 153 Cong. Rec. E. 1248 (2007).
44 153 Cong. Rec. H. 6040 (2007).
45 *Id.* at 6039.
46 Ariz. Rev. Stat. Ann. §§ 36–2311, 36–2312 (West, Westlaw through legislation effective March 21, 2012 of Second Reg. Sess. of 50th Legislature (2012)); Ark. Code Ann. §§ 20–16–1001 to -1004 (Michie, Westlaw through 2011 Reg. Sess.); Ind. Code Ann. §§ 16–18–2–56.6, 35–46–5–2 (West, Westlaw through 2011 First Reg. Sess.); Mich. Comp. Laws Ann. §§ 333.16274-.16275, 333.20197, 750.430a (West, Westlaw through P.A. 2012, No. 63 of 2012 Reg. Sess., 96th Legislature) N.D. Cent. Code § 12.1–39–02 (Westlaw through 2011 Reg. and Special Sess.); Okla. Stat. Ann. tit. 63, § 1–727 (West, Westlaw through Chap. 385 of First Reg. Sess. Of 53rd Legislature (2011)); S.D. Codified Laws §§ 34–14–26 to -28 (Michie, Westlaw through 2011 Special Sess., Exec. Order 11–1 and Supreme Court Rule 11–17).
47 Cal. Bus & Prof. Code § 2260.5, 16004, 16105 (West, Westlaw through Ch. 8 of 2012 Reg. Sess.), Cal. Health & Safety Code §§ 24185, 24187 (West, Westlaw through Ch. 8 of 2012 Reg. Sess.); Conn. Gen. Stat. Ann. § 19a-32d (West, Westlaw through 2012 supp. to Conn. Gen. Stat.); 410 Ill. Comp. Stat. Ann. 110/40 (West, Westlaw through P.A. 97–679 of 2011 Reg. Sess.); Iowa Code Ann. §§ 707C.1-.4 (West, Westlaw through legislation signed as of March 28, 2012 from 2012 Reg. Sess.); Md. Code Ann., Econ. Dev., §§ 10–429 to -430, -440 (West, Westlaw through Ch. 1 and 2 of 2012 Reg. Sess. of General Assembly); Mass. Gen. Laws Ann. Ch. 111L, §§ 1–3, 8 (West, Westlaw through

Ch. 42 of 2012 Second Annual Sess.); Mo. Ann. Stat., Const. of 1945, art. III, § 38(d) (West, Westlaw through 2011 First Extraordinary Sess. of 96th Assembly); Mont. Code Ann. §§ 50–11–101 to -103 (West, Westlaw through 2011 laws, Code Commissioner changes, and 2012 ballot measures); N.J. Stat. Ann. § 2C:11A-1 (West, Westlaw through laws effective through L. 2012, c. 1); Va. Code Ann. §§ 32.1–162.21-.22 (West, Westlaw through 2011 Reg. Sess. and 2011 Sp. S.I. and part of 2012 Reg. Sess.).

48 Congregation for the Doctrine of the Faith, "Instruction Dignitas Personae: Bioethical Questions and the Dignity of the Person," 38 *Origins* 437, para. 28 (2008).
49 *Id.* para. 14–16.
50 Macintosh, *supra* note 13, at 160.
51 Price, *supra* note 13, at 625.
52 Cal. Bus. & Prof. Code sections 2260.5, 16004, 16105 (West 1998) and Cal. Health & Safety Code sections 24185, 24187, 24189 (West 1998).
53 Cal. Health & Safety Code §§ 24189 (West 1998).
54 *Id.* § 24186; *see* Macintosh, *supra* note 13, at 8.
55 California Advisory Committee on Human Cloning, "Cloning Californians? Report of the California Advisory Committee on Human Cloning" 37 (2002) [hereinafter California Report].
56 *Id.*
57 *Id.* at 24, 28.
58 *Id.* at 25. Although the California Report briefly notes that education could combat such false beliefs, it devotes more time defending the position that genes could drive expectations. For example, it speculates that parents who clone would usually do so in order to have a child with a specific genetic makeup (as opposed to overcoming infertility), and argues that insurers and employers would use genetic information on progenitors against cloned children. *Id.* at 26.
59 Moreover, the California Report argues that asexual reproduction is unnatural and holds the potential to confound family relations. *Id.* at 27–28, 31. As discussed in Chapter 5, these arguments imply humans born through cloning are unnatural, rather than normal members of their species – an idea that is related to the artifact fallacy. *See* Chapter 5, *supra*, Part C.3.a.
60 California Report, *supra* note 55, at 26.
61 *Id.* at 22.
62 Macintosh, *supra* note 13, at 86.
63 For lists of films that support the fallacies, including films that predate 1997, see Table 1 in Chapter Four (identity fallacy); Table 2 in Chapter Five (artifact fallacy); Table 3 in Chapter Six (impostor fallacy); and Tables 4 and 5 in Chapter Seven (resurrection fallacy).

64 "America: Animal and Human Cloning," supra note 7.
65 *See, e.g.*, 153 Cong. Rec. H. 6042 (2007) (recording the argument of Zachary Space, D-Ohio, that cloning replaces the chance and wonder of a child's birth with a cold and sterile process); 149 Cong. Rec. H. 1424 (2003) (citing the argument of James Greenwood, R-Pennsylvania, that cloning is cruel because it creates a child who is a duplicate of another); *id.* at 1400 (printing the argument of Marilyn Musgrave, R-Colorado, that cloning makes human life a commodity and could render some people more desirable than others); *id.* at 1403 (reporting the claim of Lee Terry, R-Nebraska, that cloning would lead to the manufacture of children with specific genetic traits); *see also* Macintosh, *supra* note 13, at 92–96 (reporting statements against reproductive cloning from various Congressmen).
66 *See* 147 Cong. Rec. H. 4910 (2001) (recording Billy Tauzin, R-Louisiana, as he claims a statutory ban is needed because the FDA can only regulate cloning for safety); *Id.* at 4917–18 (quoting F. James Sensenbrenner, R-Wisconsin, that FDA can only regulate reproductive cloning, not stop it).
67 *See* Macintosh, *supra* note 13, at 82–83.
68 Diane B. Paul, *Controlling Human Heredity, 1865 to the Present* 71 (1995).
69 316 U.S. 535 (1942).
70 For the interested reader, here is the complete passage from the opinion:

We are dealing here with legislation which involves one of the basic civil rights of man. Marriage and procreation are fundamental to the very existence and survival of the race. The power to sterilize, if exercised, may have subtle, farreaching and devastating effects. In evil or reckless hands it can cause races or types which are inimical to the dominant group to wither and disappear. There is no redemption for the individual whom the law touches. Any experiment which the State conducts is to his irreparable injury. He is forever deprived of a basic liberty. We mention these matters not to reexamine the scope of the police power of the States. We advert to them merely in emphasis of our view that strict scrutiny of the classification which a State makes in a sterilization law is essential, lest unwittingly or otherwise invidious discriminations are made against groups or types of individuals in violation of the constitutional guaranty of just and equal laws.

Id. at 541.
71 *See, e.g.*, Griswold v. Connecticut, 381 U.S. 479 (1965) (recognizing a right to privacy that protects the right of married persons to use contraception); Eisenstadt v. Baird, 405 U.S. 438 (1972) (holding that law prohibiting contraceptives to single but not married persons violated equal protection guarantee).
72 Planned Parenthood of Southeastern Pennsylvania v. Casey, 505 U.S. 833 (1992).
73 Lifchez v. Hartigan, 735 F. Supp. 1361, 1376–77 (N.D. Ill. 1990), *aff'd*, 914 F.2d 260 (1990) (unpublished opinion).

74 *See* Chapter 3, Part A, *supra*.
75 Ooplasm transfer is a technique in which the aging egg of an infertile woman is infused with ooplasm taken from the egg of a younger donor prior to fertilization with sperm. Thirty babies were born through this technique worldwide before the FDA blocked its use in the United States in 2001. Nuclear transfer is an experimental treatment in which doctors take the nuclear DNA of an infertile egg and transfer it into an enucleated donor egg prior to fertilization with sperm. Nuclear transfer was in clinical trials in the United States before the FDA halted its use in 1998. For a more extensive discussion of these events, see Kerry Lynn Macintosh, "Brave New Eugenics: Regulating Assisted Reproduction in the Name of Better Babies," 2010 *J.L. Tech & Policy* 257, 269–72.
76 President's Council on Bioethics, "Reproduction and Responsibility: The Regulation of New Biotechnologies" (2004).
77 *Id*. at 208–09.
78 Macintosh, *supra* note 75, at 277. Unfortunately, the Council's report did not adequately explore the possibility that parental traits associated with long-term infertility may cause the negative health effects observed in some of the children conceived through assisted reproductive technologies. For an extensive discussion of the link between parental traits and health effects in children, *see generally id*.
79 *Id*. at 305.
80 *E.g.*, Mark D. Eibert, "Human Cloning: Myths, Medical Benefits, and Constitutional Rights," 53 *Hastings L.J.* 1097 (2002); Elizabeth Price Foley, "The Constitutional Implications of Human Cloning," 42 *Ariz. L. Rev.* 647 (2000); John Robertson, "Liberty, Identity, and Human Cloning," 76 *Tex. L. Rev.* 1371 (1998).
81 *E.g.*, Cass R. Sunstein, "Is There a Constitutional Right to Clone?" 53 *Hastings L.J.* 987 (2002).
82 John Charles Kunich, *The Naked Clone* 135–38 (2003).
83 Macintosh, *supra* note 13, at 114–15.
84 *Id*. at 117–18.
85 *Id*. at 118–30.
86 *Id*. at 10–12.
87 *Id*. at 121. This distinguishes anti-cloning laws from laws that criminalize forcible rape. The law prohibits John from raping Mary because sexual and reproductive coercion is wrong, not because the law objects to the traits of a child that might be conceived. If the same two people engaged in consensual sexual intercourse and conceived a child with the same traits, the law would not object. The same holds true for laws that criminalize statutory rape. If John is forty and Mary is sixteen years old, the law prohibits sex between them because

the older partner might exploit the vulnerability of the younger, not because the pair might conceive a child with nefarious traits. Once Mary turns eighteen years old, the same sexual relationship would be legal, no matter what kind of child might be conceived.

By contrast, under anti-cloning laws, all reproductive cloning is simply banned. It doesn't matter whether the doctors and patients act voluntarily and with informed consent. It doesn't matter whether all of them are adults capable of formulating a considered decision. Cloning remains illegal because the four fallacies teach that humans born through cloning have negative traits and impacts.

88 In addition to the material presented earlier in this chapter, see *id.* at 93–94.
89 In addition to the material presented earlier in this chapter, see *id.* at 92–93 and Council Report, *supra* note 32, at 104–07.
90 Council Report, *supra* note 32, at 90; California Report, *supra* note 55, at 10, 23.
91 Macintosh, *supra* note 13, at 120.
92 For specification of stereotypes related to these fallacies, see *id.* at 121–22.
93 The Declaration of Independence para. 2 (U.S. 1776).
94 Council Report, *supra* note 32, at 103; California Report, *supra* note 55, at 25; National Bioethics Advisory Commission, "Cloning Human Beings, Report and Recommendations of the National Bioethics Advisory Commission" 69–70 (1997) [hereinafter NBAC Report].
95 California Report, *supra* note 55, at 22; NBAC Report, *supra* note 94, at 72–73.
96 California Report, *supra* note 55, at 26.
97 Council Report, *supra* note 32, at 79–80; California Report, *supra* note 55 at 22; NBAC Report, *supra* note 94, at 80.

CHAPTER 9. ESSENTIALISM AND THE LAW OF RESEARCH CLONING

1 *See* James A. Thomson et al., "Embryonic Stem Cell Lines Derived from Human Blastocysts," 282 *Science* 1145 (1998).
2 *Id.* at 1146; *see also* Joseph Panno, *Stem Cell Research: Medical Applications and Ethical Controversy* 5 (2005) (explaining that embryonic stem cells can develop into cells from all three embryonic germ layers but cannot create an entire organism).
3 *See* Thomson, *supra* note 1, at 1146–47 (explaining that once embryonic stem cells are differentiated into specific cell types, they could be used for drug testing or transplantation).
4 *See, e.g.*, Congregation for the Doctrine of the Faith, "Instruction Dignitas Personae: Bioethical Questions and the Dignity of the Person," 38 *Origins* 437, para. 30 & 32 (2008).

5 1 The National Bioethics Advisory Commission, "Ethical Issues in Human Stem Cell Research" 55–56 (1999).
6 President's Council on Bioethics, "Reproduction and Responsibility: The Regulation of New Biotechnologies" 42–43 (2004).
7 The President's Council on Bioethics, "Human Cloning and Human Dignity: An Ethical Inquiry" 164–65 (2002) [hereinafter Council Report]. In response to such concerns, the National Academies have issued guidelines providing that women who donate eggs for stem cell research should be compensated only for direct expenses associated with the donation procedure, including medical care, health insurance, travel, lost wages, and child care. National Academies, "Final Report of the National Academies' Human Embryonic Stem Cell Research Advisory Committee and 2010 Amendments to the National Academies' Guidelines for Human Embryonic Stem Cell Research" app. C, § 3.4(b) at 27 (2010). Moreover, some states have enacted laws that restrict payments to egg donors. For example, Massachusetts provides that no person shall sell or purchase human embryos or gametes for research purposes. Mass. Gen. Laws. Ann. Ch. 111L, § 8(c) (West, Westlaw through Ch. 42 of 2012 Second Annual Sess.). Similarly, California bars researchers from compensating egg donors for anything more than direct expenses incurred as a result of the donation procedure. Cal. Health & Safety Code § 125355 (West, Westlaw through Ch. 8 of 2012 Reg. Sess.).

Reasoning that such restrictive rules have discouraged donation and impeded stem cell research, New York has adopted a more lenient approach. Researchers may pay egg donors for their expenses, time, burden, and discomfort. Public funds not only can be used to support research on stem cell lines derived using such eggs, but even can be used to reimburse researchers for their payments to donors. "Statement of the Empire State Stem Cell Board on the Compensation of Oocyte Donors," *New York State Stem Cell Science*, http://stemcell.ny.gov/docs/ESSCB_Statement_on_Compensation_of_Oocyte_Donors.pdf (last visited on May 11, 2011).
8 *See* Chapter 3, Part A (discussing the state of research).
9 Council Report, *supra* note 7, at 131–33.
10 *See generally id.* at 152–59 (discussing the moral standing of the human embryo).
11 *Id.* at 161, 164–65.
12 *Id.* at 165; Kerry Lynn Macintosh, "Human Clones and International Human Rights," 4 *Santa Clara J. Int'l L.* 134, 146 (2006).
13 P.C. Winter, G.I. Hickey, & H.L. Fletcher, *Genetics* 58 (2d ed. 2002).
14 Kazutoshi Takahashi and Shinya Yamanaka, "Induction of Pluripotent Stem Cells from Mouse Embryonic and Adult Fibroblast Cultures by Defined Factors," 126 *Cell* 663 (2006). The four transcription factors used in this initial report were Oct3/4, Sox2, c-Myc, and Klf4. *Id.*

15 Kazutoshi Takahashi et al., "Induction of Pluripotent Stem Cells from Adult Human Fibroblasts by Defined Factors," 131 *Cell* 861 (2007).
16 *See, e.g.*, Matthias Stadtfeld et al., "Induced Pluripotent Stem Cells Generated Without Viral Integration," 322 *Science* 945 (2008) (creating murine induced pluripotent stem cells from fibroblasts and liver cells with the aid of adenoviruses that do not integrate themselves into the genome); Junying Yu et al., "Human Induced Pluripotent Stem Cells Free of Vector and Transgene Sequences," 324 *Science* 797 (2009) (creating induced pluripotent stem cells from human fibroblasts with the aid of episomal vectors that can be removed afterwards); Junying Yu et al., "Induced Pluripotent Stem Cell Lines Derived from Human Somatic Cells," 318 *Science* 1917 (2007) (demonstrating that Oct 4, Sox2, Nanog, and Lin28 reprogram human fibroblasts to pluripotency).
17 Luigi Warren et al., "Highly Efficient Reprogramming to Pluripotency and Directed Differentiation of Human Cells with Synthetic Modified mRNA," 7 *Cell Stem Cell* 618 (2010). Some basic biology may help clarify how this alternative reprogramming method works. Ordinarily, gene expression begins with the transcription of a DNA sequence into a molecule known as messenger RNA (mRNA). The mRNA migrates into the cytoplasm of the cell; there, ribosomes translate it into an amino acid sequence that makes up a protein. P.C. Winter et al., *supra* note 13, at 10–11, 25, 30–31.

Thus, in the initial experiments involving induced pluripotent stem cells, scientists introduced a transcription factor into a cell and let the above process run its course. The expression of the factor triggered the reprogramming of the DNA of the cell. Later, scientists realized it wasn't necessary to introduce the factor (and its foreign DNA) into the cell. All they had to do was add the same mRNA molecules that the factor would have generated, had it been there. The scientists also modified the mRNA to bypass antiviral responses. Warren et al., *supra* at 619–21.
18 Frederick Anokye-Danso et al., "Highly Efficient miRNA-Mediated Reprogramming of Mouse and Human Somatic Cells to Pluripotency," 8 *Cell Stem Cell* 376 (2011). The scientists used a lentiviral vector to transfer the miR302/367 cluster, which comprised five miRNAs, into the cells. *Id.* at 379–81.
19 Bruce Alberts et al., *Molecular Biology of the Cell* 493–95 (5th ed. 2008).
20 *See* Shinya Yamanaka & Helen M. Blau, "Nuclear Reprogramming to a Pluripotent State by Three Approaches," 465 *Nature* 704, 710 (discussing efforts to improve efficiency of conversion) and fig.5 (reporting conversion rates of 0.01–0.1 percent for methods involving transcription factors) (2010). However, scientists who have reprogrammed fibroblasts without transcription factors have reported higher conversion rates. *See* Warren et al., *supra* note 17, at 623 (showing that the mRNA reprogramming method can achieve conversion rate

as high as 4 percent); Anokye-Danso et al., *supra* note 18, at 383 (reporting conversion rate of nearly 10 percent achieved through microRNA reprogramming method).
21. Gretchen Vogel, "Reprogrammed Cells Come Up Short, for Now," 327 *Science* 1191 (2010); *see generally* Yamanaka & Blau, *supra* note 20, at 710 fig. 5 (comparing advantages of cloned embryonic stem cells and induced pluripotent stem cells).
22. Athurva Gore et al., "Somatic Coding Mutations in Human Induced Pluripotent Stem Cells," 471 *Nature* 63 (2011). The scientists studied cell lines created from human fibroblasts via five different reprogramming methods: three that integrated transcription factors into the DNA of the cell; one that ferried transcription factors into the cell via a nonintegrating episomal vector; and one that utilized messenger RNAs rather than transcription factors. They found not only mutations that had been present in the original donor cell, but also mutations acquired during and after the conversion process. Many of the genes found to be mutated in this experiment are also mutated in some cancers, while others play a role in heritable genetic disorders. *Id.*
23. Tongbiao Zhao et al., "Immunogenicity of Induced Pluripotent Stem Cells," 474 *Nature* 212 (2011). Overexpression of certain genes in the induced pluripotent stem cells contributed to the immune responses.
24. Judith F. Daar, *Reproductive Technologies and the Law* 767 (2006).
25. Lydia Saad, "Doctor-Assisted Suicide Is Moral Issue Dividing Americans Most," *Gallup* (May 31, 2011), http://www.gallup.com/poll/147842/Doctor-Assisted-Suicide-Moral-Issue-Dividing-Americans.aspx.
26. To be sure, congressional conservatives regularly introduce bills that would establish a constitutional right to life in embryos and fetuses. *See, e.g.*, H.R. 212, 112th Cong. (2011); H.R. 374, 112th Cong. (2011); H.R. 227, 111th Cong. (2009); S. 346, 111th Cong. (2009); H.R. 4157, 110th Cong. (2007). However, because legal abortion has much public and political support, such bills have repeatedly failed in the past.
27. Kerry Lynn Macintosh, *Illegal Beings: Human Clones and the Law* 76–77 (2005).
28. *See, e.g.*, 147 Cong. Rec. H. 4906 (2001) (reporting opinion of Sue Myrick, R-North Carolina, that it is wrong to clone human embryos for experimentation and destruction); *id.* at 4907 (citing Dave Weldon, R-Florida, to effect that cloning creates a human embryo); *id.* at 4910 (reporting opinion of Billy Tauzin, R-Louisiana, that cloned embryos are human beings); *id.* at 4914 (stating view of Lee Terry, R-Nebraska, that destructive research threatens sanctity of human life); *id.* at 4922 (recording view of Tom DeLay, R-Texas, that cloning treats human embryos as raw material and violates sanctity of human life); *see also* 149 Cong. Rec. H. 1397, 1416, 1420 (2003), 153 Cong. Rec. H. 6042 (2007),

and 153 Cong. Rec. S. 4173 (2007) (reporting similar comments in subsequent debates).
29 *See* 147 Cong. Rec. H. 4920 (2001) (reporting the view of Jerrold Nadler, D-New York, that a blastocyst is a clump of cells and not a person).
30 *Id.* at 4909.
31 *Id.* at 4910. For more views of this kind, see *id.* at 4933 (reporting view of Steve Horn, R-California, that cloned embryos are mere cells dividing in a petri dish and not worthy of better protection than leftover IVF embryos); *id.* at 4934–35 (noting view of Henry Waxman, D-California, that cloning is "genetic cell replication" and the resulting cells do not need the same rights and protection as a person); *id.* at 4938 (stating opinion of Anna Eshoo, D-California, that the debate was not about embryos); *see also* 153 Cong. Rec. S. 2907 (2007) (recording argument of Dianne Feinstein, D-California, that research cloning involves no sperm and only unfertilized blastocysts).
32 147 Cong. Rec. H. 4924 (2001); *see also id.* at 4935 (recording sentiment of Jim Sensenbrenner, R-Wisconsin, that it is ridiculous to argue that cloned embryos are not really embryos).
33 Council Report, *supra* note 7, at 53. The Council rejected the argument that a man-made cloned embryo was an artifact rather than an embryo. *Id.* at 50. However, as discussed in Chapter 5, other passages in its report frame persons born through cloning as artifacts. Chapter 5, Part C.3.b, *supra*.
34 Council Report, *supra* note 7, at 51. The Council acknowledged that there was no proof that a cloned embryo could produce a baby. However, its entire report was based on the assumption that cloning human beings was possible. *Id.*
35 Rudolf Jaenisch, "Human Cloning – The Science and Ethics of Nuclear Transplantation," 351 *N. Engl. J. Med.* 2787, 2791 (2004).
36 Tony Ord, "The Scourge: Moral Implications of Natural Embryo Loss," 8 *Am. J. Bioethics* 12, 16 (2008).
37 Paul R. McHugh, "Zygote and 'Clonote' – The Ethical Use of Embryonic Stem Cells," 351 *N. Engl. J. Med.* 209, 210 (2004).
38 *See, e.g.*, 147 Cong. Rec. H. 4911 (2001) (reporting the objections of Greg Ganske, R-Iowa, to the creation of cloned embryos for research); *id.* at 4914 (recording the opposition of Mike Pence, R-Indiana, to the creation of human life for experimentation and destruction); *id.* at 4927 (citing Todd Tiahrt, R-Kansas, to effect that life should not be created in order to be destroyed); *id.* at 4938 (stating the view of Christopher Smith, R-New Jersey, that human beings should not be created "for the purpose of exploitation, abuse, and destructive experimentation"); *see also* 149 Cong. Rec. H. 1309, 1310, 1399 1400, 1404, 1409, 1410, 1418, 1421, 1426, 1432 (2003), 153 Cong. Rec. H. 6040, 6041 (2007), and 153 Cong. Rec. S. 4173 (2007) (printing similar comments from later debates).

39 147 Cong. Rec. H. 4937 (2001).
40 *See id.* (recording Dave Weldon, D-Florida, as he quoted from the remarks of liberal colleagues in a previous debate on the funding of stem cell research).
41 *See, e.g., id.* at 4925 (citing Christopher Smith, R-New Jersey, to effect that law won't stop implantation of cloned embryos); *id.* at 4929 (stating opinion of Bob Barr, R-Georgia, that human cloning will occur); *id.* at 4939 (reporting opinion of Michael Bilirakis, R-Florida, that once research cloning is allowed, illegal implantation will occur); *see also* 149 Cong. Rec. H. 1309, 1311, 1397, 1406, 1408, 1409, 1412, 1413, 1422, 1425, 1426, 1428, 1429, 1432 (2003) (printing similar comments from subsequent debates).
42 *See, e.g.*, 147 Cong. Rec. H. 4921 (2001) (stating opinion of Jerrold Nadler, D-New York, that research cloning is harder to stop than reproductive cloning); *id.* at 4935 (citing Henry Waxman, D-California, that felony penalties will deter reproductive cloning); *id.* at 4943 (recording view of Zoe Lofgren, D-California, that people will not violate a law against reproductive cloning); *see also* 149 Cong. Rec. H. 1409 (2003) (recording similar comment in later debate).
43 *See, e.g.*, 147 Cong. Rec. H. 4925 (2001) (recording opposition of Christopher Smith, R-New Jersey, to bill criminalizing failure to kill embryos); *id.* at 4932 (stating view of Jim Sensenbrenner, R-Wisconsin, that ban on reproductive cloning would require researchers to destroy embryos); *id.* at 4935 (reporting opposition of Joe Pitts, R-Pennsylvania, to bill that would require killing of cloned embryos); *see also* 149 Cong. Rec. H. 1425, 1428 (2003) and 153 Cong. Rec. H. 6038, 6039, 6041 (2007) (reporting similar statements from later debates).
44 Chapter 8, Part B.2, *supra*.
45 *See* 147 Cong. Rec. H. 4909, 4941 (2001) (reporting remarks of James Greenwood, R-Pennsylvania, that is not safe to clone a human being); *see also* 149 Cong. Rec. H. 1417, 1424 (2003), 153 Cong. Rec. H. 6041 (2007), and 153 Cong. Rec. S. 2907 (2007) (recording similar comments in later debates).
46 Chapter 8, Part B.3, *supra*.
47 Sherley v. Sebelius, 644 F.3d 388, 389–90 (D.C. Cir. 2011). In a recent incarnation, the Dickey-Wicker Amendment read as follows:
    (a) None of the funds made available in this Act may be used for –
        (1) the creation of a human embryo or embryos for research purposes; or
        (2) research in which a human embryo or embryos are destroyed, discarded, or knowingly subjected to risk of injury or death greater than that allowed for research on fetuses in utero under 45 CFR 46.204(b) and section 498(b) of the Public Health Service Act (42 U.S.C. 289g(b))
    (b) For purposes of this section, the term "human embryo or embryos" includes any organism, not protected as a human subject under 45 CFR 46

as of the date of the enactment of this Act, that is derived by fertilization, parthenogenesis, cloning, or any other means from one or more human gametes or human diploid cells.

Consolidated Appropriations Act, 2010, Pub. L. No. 111-117, § 509, 123 Stat. 3034, 3280-81 (2009).

48 National Institutes of Health Guidelines for Human Stem Cell Research, 74 Fed. Reg. 32170 (June 30, 2009) [hereinafter NIH Guidelines].
49 *Id.* at 32174.
50 There is an ongoing legal battle as to whether the NIH guidelines conform to the restrictions imposed under the Dickey-Wicker Amendment. In 2009, a lawsuit was brought to enjoin the Secretary of Health and Human Services from implementing and applying the guidelines. The plaintiffs included the Christian Medical Association, Nightlight Christian Adoptions, some prospective adoptive parents of embryos, leftover embryos that might be destroyed through stem cell research, and two adult stem cell researchers who would compete for NIH funding with those who pursue embryonic stem cell research. The District Court for the District of Columbia dismissed the lawsuit on the ground that none of the plaintiffs had standing to sue. Sherley v. Sebelius, 686 F. Supp. 2d. 1 (D.D.C. 2009). However, the U.S. Court of Appeals ruled the two adult stem cell researchers had competitor standing. As to them, it reversed the order of dismissal and sent the case back to the District Court. Sherley v. Sebelius, 610 F.3d 69 (D.C. Cir. 2010).

Next, the District Court granted plaintiffs' motion for a preliminary injunction halting the funding of embryonic stem cell research pursuant to the NIH guidelines. Sherley v. Sebelius, 704 F. Supp. 2d 63 (D.D.C. 2010). The court's conclusion that plaintiffs were likely to succeed on the merits was key to its decision. It reasoned that the Dickey-Wicker Amendment unambiguously prohibited all research in which an embryo was destroyed. Because embryonic stem cell research necessarily begins with the destruction of an embryo, the court concluded that the Dickey-Wicker Amendment precluded the funding of such research. *Id.* at 70-72.

The U.S. Court of Appeals disagreed and vacated the preliminary injunction. Claiming that the language of the Dickey-Wicker Amendment was ambiguous, the Court of Appeals concluded that the NIH interpretation allowing funding of research on stem cell lines after their creation was reasonable and entitled to deference. Sherley v. Sebelius, 644 F.3d 388, 393-96 (D.C. Cir. 2011). The Court of Appeals also reasoned that the balance of equities weighed against the granting of a preliminary injunction. Many scientists had already started embryonic stem cell research projects in reliance on NIH grants and would lose their work if funding was withdrawn. *Id.* at 398-99.

The case was sent back to the District Court. Bowing to the will of the Court of Appeals, the District Court ruled on summary judgment that the NIH guidelines do not violate the Dickey-Wicker Amendment. Sherley v. Sebelius, 776 F. Supp. 2d 1 (D.D.C. 2011). Plaintiffs appealed again, and the case is pending before the Court of Appeals. No matter how this latest appeal is resolved, the U.S. Supreme Court may have the final say on the proper interpretation of the Dickey-Wicker Amendment and the validity of the NIH guidelines.

51 NIH Guidelines, *supra* note 48, 74 Fed. Reg. at 32175.
52 *Id*. at 32171. The NIH identified only one specific concern: women would have to take powerful drugs to induce ovulation of the eggs necessary to create such embryos. *Id*. Presumably it had other concerns, but these were not highlighted in the guidelines.
53 Ariz. Rev. Stat. Ann. § 36–2313 (West, Westlaw through legislation effective March 21, 2012 of the Second Reg. Sess. of the 50th Legislature (2012)).
54 *Id*. § 36–2311.1.
55 *Cf.* Sherley v. Sebelius, 704 F. Supp. 2d 63 (D.D.C. 2010) (reasoning that Dickey-Wicker Amendment prohibition on funding of research in which a human embryo is destroyed encompasses research conducted after the stem cell line is created).
56 La. Rev. Stat. Ann. § 9:122 (West, Westlaw through 2011 First Extraordinary and Reg. Sess.).
57 Mich. Comp. Laws Ann. § 333.2685 (West, Westlaw through P.A. 2012, No. 70, of the 2012 Reg. Sess., 96th Legislature.); Minn. Stat Ann. §§ 145.421-.422 (West, Westlaw through 2012 Reg. Sess. through Ch. 131); S.D. Codified Laws §§ 34–14–16 to -20 (Michie, Westlaw through 2011 Special Sess., Executive Order 11–1, and Supreme Court Rule 11–17).
58 Fla. Stat. Ann. § 390.0111(6) (West, Westlaw through chapters in effect from the 2012 Second Reg. Sess. Of the 22nd Legislature through March 29, 2012); Me. Rev. Stat. tit. 22, § 1593 (West, Westlaw through Ch. 540 of the 2011 Second Reg. Sess. of the 125th Legislature); N.D. Cent. Code Ann. § 14–02.2–01 (West, Westlaw through 2011 Reg. and Special Sess.); 18 Pa. Cons. Stat. Ann. § 3216(a) (West, Westlaw through 2011 Reg. Sess.); R.I. Gen. Laws Ann. § 11–54–1 (West, Westlaw through Ch. 409 of the 2011 Reg. Sess.).
59 *See, e.g.*, Daar, *supra* note 24, at 372.
60 Cal. Const. art. 35, § 5 (West, Westlaw through Ch. 8 of 2012 Reg. Sess.); Conn. Gen. Stat. Ann. § 19a-32d(d) (West, Westlaw through 2012 supp. to Conn. Gen. Stat.); 410 Ill. Comp. Stat. Ann. 110/5(1) (West, Westlaw through P.A. 97–679 of the 2011 Reg. Sess.); Iowa Code Ann. §§ 707C.2 (West, Westlaw through legislation signed as of March 28, 2012 from 2012 Reg. Sess.); Mass. Gen. Laws Ann. Ch. 111L, § 3 (West, Westlaw through Ch. 42 of 2012 Second

Annual Sess.); Mo. Ann. Stat., Const. of 1945, art. III, § 38(d).2 (West, Westlaw through 2011 First Extraordinary Sess. of 96th Assembly); N.J. Stat. Ann. § 26:2Z-2(a)(1) (West, Westlaw through laws effective through L. 2012, c.1).

61 Ariz. Rev. Stat. Ann. §§ 36–2311, 36–2312 (West, Westlaw through legislation effective March 21, 2012 of Second Reg. Sess. of 50th Legislature (2012)); Ark. Code Ann. §§ 20–16–1001 to -1004 (Michie, Westlaw through 2011 Reg. Sess.); Ind. Code Ann. §§ 16–18–2–56.6, 35–46–5–2 (West, Westlaw through 2011 First Reg. Sess.); Mich. Comp. Laws Ann. §§ 333.16274-.16275, 333.20197, 750.430a (West, Westlaw through P.A. 2012, No. 63 of 2012 Reg. Sess., 96th Legislature); N.D. Cent. Code § 12.1–39–02 (Westlaw through 2011 Reg. and Special Sess.); Okla. Stat. Ann. tit. 63, § 1–727 (West, Westlaw through Chap. 385 of First Reg. Sess. Of 53rd Legislature (2011)); S.D. Codified Laws §§ 34–14–26 to -28 (Michie, Westlaw through 2011 Special Sess., Exec. Order 11–1 and Supreme Court Rule 11–17).

62 Cal. Bus & Prof. Code § 2260.5, 16004, 16105 (West, Westlaw through Ch. 8 of 2012 Reg. Sess.), Cal. Health & Safety Code §§ 24185, 24187 (West, Westlaw through Ch. 8 of 2012 Reg. Sess.); Conn. Gen. Stat. Ann. § 19a-32d (West, Westlaw through 2012 supp. to Conn. Gen. Stat.); 410 Ill. Comp. Stat. Ann. 110/40 (West, Westlaw through P.A. 97–679 of 2011 Reg. Sess.); Iowa Code Ann. §§ 707C.1-.4 (West, Westlaw through legislation signed as of March 28, 2012 from 2012 Reg. Sess.); Md. Code Ann., Econ. Dev., §§ 10–429 to -430, -440 (West, Westlaw through Ch. 1 and 2 of 2012 Reg. Sess. of General Assembly); Mass. Gen. Laws Ann. Ch. 111L, §§ 1–3, 8 (West, Westlaw through Ch. 42 of 2012 Second Annual Sess.); Mo. Ann. Stat., Const. of 1945, art. III, § 38(d) (West, Westlaw through 2011 First Extraordinary Sess. of 96th Assembly); Mont. Code Ann. §§ 50–11–101 to -103 (West, Westlaw through 2011 laws, Code Commissioner changes, and 2012 ballot measures); N.J. Stat. Ann. § 2C:11A-1 (West, Westlaw through laws effective through L. 2012, c. 1); Va. Code Ann. §§ 32.1-162.21-.22 (West, Westlaw through 2011 Reg. Sess. and 2011 Sp. S.I. and part of 2012 Reg. Sess.).

63 *See* text accompanying note 60, *supra*.

64 Md. Code Ann., Econ. Dev., § 10–430 (West, Westlaw through Ch. 1 and 2 of 2012 Reg. Sess. of General Assembly); Mont. Code Ann. § 50–11–103(3) (West, Westlaw through 2011 laws, Code Commissioner changes, and 2012 ballot measures).

65 Mass. Gen. Laws Ann. Ch. 111L, § 8(b) (West, Westlaw through Ch. 42 of 2012 Second Annual Sess.); Mo. Ann. Stat., Const. of 1945, art. III, § 38(d).2(2) (West, Westlaw through 2011 First Extraordinary Sess. of 96th Assembly).

66 This chapter does not examine the possibility that psychological essentialism lies at the root of the belief that human embryos have the same moral worth as human persons who have been born. That topic is outside the scope of this book.

67 Psychological essentialism may explain political and legal responses to embryonic stem cell research in general. However, because this is a book about cloning, I will reserve examination of the ways in which essentialism affects the regulation of embryonic stem cell research for a future research project.
68 Chapter 5, Part C.4.a, *supra*.
69 Chapter 5, Part C.4.b, *supra*.
70 *Id.*
71 McHugh, *supra* note 37, at 210; *see also* Council Report, *supra* note 7, at 50 (acknowledging arguments that a cloned embryo is an artifact rather than embryo because it is made rather than begotten).
72 Chapter 5, Part C.4.b, *supra*.
73 As Jussi Niemela has noted, it matters little whether these politicians are articulating their own deep intuitions or exploiting essentialism for its rhetorical power. In either case, essentialism lies at the root of their claims. Jussi Niemela, "What Puts the 'Yuck' in the Yuck Factor?," 25 *Bioethics* 267, 276 (2011).
74 Chapter 5, Part B, *supra*.
75 *See* Macintosh, *supra* note 27, at 10–11 (discussing religious attitudes toward human cloning). Whether religious opposition to human cloning is itself based upon the identity, artifact, or other fallacies is too broad a topic to analyze here.
76 Ariz. Rev. Stat. Ann. § 36–2312 (West, Westlaw through legislation effective March 21, 2012 of Second Reg. Sess. of 50th Legislature (2012)).
77 *Id.*
78 *Id.* § 13–707.A.1
79 *Id.* § 36–2313.
80 *See id.* § 36–2311.3 (defining human embryo as "a living organism of the species homo sapiens through the first fifty-six days of its development").
81 *Id.* § 36–2311.1.
82 *Id.* § 13.702.A, D. A judge in Arizona has discretion to reduce a class 6 felony to a class 1 misdemeanor when the offense is not dangerous and the judge believes it would be unduly harsh to sentence the defendant for a felony. *Id.* § 13.604. Whether judges will apply this provision to benefit scientists convicted of destructive stem cell research is unknown.
83 Interestingly, Arizona's law appears to be consistent with Roman Catholic doctrine. The leadership of the Church has released an instruction that strongly opposes reproductive cloning, but condemns research cloning as the greater moral wrong because it involves the destruction of a human life. Congregation for the Doctrine of the Faith, "Instruction Dignitas Personae: Bioethical Questions and the Dignity of the Person," 38 *Origins* 437, para. 28, 29, 30 (2008).
84 *See* Chapter 8, Part C, *supra*.

85 *See* Lee Silver, "Public Policy Crafted in Response to Public Ignorance is Bad Public Policy," 53 *Hastings L.J.* 1037, 1046 (2002) (arguing that scientists who attack reproductive cloning to demonstrate solidarity with public may be rewarded with a ban on their own research).
86 *See, e.g.*, John Robertson, "The Scientist's Right to Research: A Constitutional Analysis," 51 *S. Cal. L. Rev.* 1203 (1977).
87 John Charles Kunich, *The Naked Clone* 94 (2003).
88 Macintosh, *supra* note 27, at 116.
89 *Id.* at 122.

CONCLUSION

1 Kerry Lynn Macintosh, *Illegal Beings: Human Clones and the Law* 165 (2005).
2 *Id.* at 125–29.
3 Gregory E. Pence, *Who's Afraid of Human Cloning?* 46 (1998).
4 Lydia Saad, "Doctor-Assisted Suicide Is Moral Issue Dividing Americans Most," *Gallup* (May 31, 2011), http://www.gallup.com/poll/147842/Doctor-Assisted-Suicide-Moral-Issue-Dividing-Americans.aspx.
5 *Id.*
6 National Bioethics Advisory Commission, "Cloning Human Beings, Report and Recommendations of the National Bioethics Advisory Commission" (1997) [hereinafter NBAC Report].
7 The President's Council on Bioethics, "Human Cloning and Human Dignity: An Ethical Inquiry" (2002); California Advisory Committee on Human Cloning, "Cloning Californians? Report of the California Advisory Committee on Human Cloning" (2002) [hereinafter California Report].
8 *See, e.g.*, California Report, *supra* note 7, at 25 (expressing the concern that parents may treat cloned children as if they were designer objects); NBAC Report, *supra* note 6, at 72–73 (same).
9 John Robertson, "Liberty, Identity, and Human Cloning," 76 *Tex. L. Rev.* 1371, 1449 (1998).
10 *See* W. Page Keeton, *Prosser and Keeton on Torts* 190–92 (5th ed. 1984) (discussing basics of informed consent doctrine).
11 *See* Robertson, *supra* note 9, at 1449 (arguing that doctors should inform couples of the social and psychological challenges that cloning poses).
12 California Report, *supra* note 7, at 27.
13 Elizabeth Price Foley, "The Constitutional Implications of Human Cloning," 42 *Ariz. L. Rev.* 647, 719 (2000).
14 *See* Craig Venter & Daniel Cohen, "The Century of Biology," 21 *New Perspectives Q.* 73 (2004).

Index

2001: A Space Travesty, 135
Advanced Cell Technology, Inc. (ACT), 19
Alien: Resurrection, 148
Andrews, Lori, 112
animal cloning
   cell type, 11, 12–13
   chemical activators, 11
   culture media, 11
   genotype, 12–13
   gestation, role of, 35–36
   placenta, 11, 12, 17–18, 24–25, 61
   reconstruction of eggs, methods of, 11
   trichostatin A (TSA), 15
Animal Cloning: A Risk Assessment, 20–23
animals born through cloning
   aging, 38–41, 155, 159–60
   birth and development, 19, 21, 22, 38, 57, 58, 62, 108, 138, 147, 155, 157
   cats, 7, 34, 35, 36, 39, 48, 54, 156
   cattle, 7, 8, 9–12, 15, 16, 17, 19, 20, 21, 24, 35, 36–37, 39, 40, 53, 54, 61, 154
   death, 19, 20, 21, 24
   goats, 7, 20, 22
   individuality, 33–37, 61, 88, 92, 145, 147, 162, 171
   lifespan, 40–41, 57, 62, 147, 155, 157, 171
   mice, 7, 8, 12–15, 18, 19, 20, 24, 34, 39–40, 41, 57, 61, 62
   normalcy, 18–20, 21–24, 58, 61, 108, 114, 118, 171
   offspring, 20, 21, 22, 23, 35
   sheep, 7, 9, 16, 17, 20, 36, 54, 61
   species cloned, 7–8
   swine, 7, 8, 15, 17, 20, 21, 22, 35, 36, 39
   telomeres, 38–40, 57, 62, 155, 157
   transgenic, 8
Anna to the Infinite Power, 121, 148, 150–51
Annas, George, 112
artifact fallacy, 16, 25, 44, 61, 62, 63, 64, 66, 103, 108, 109, 111, 112, 114, 115, 116, 117, 118, 122, 123, 165, 166, 171, 172, 175, 178, 182, 183, 184, 185, 187, 188, 189, 190, 196, 197, 207, 208, 214, 215, 216, 218, 223, 226, 227
   defined, 16, 103
asexual reproduction, cloning as, 3, 25, 46, 47, 58, 112–14, 118–19, 166, 182, 197, 213
assisted reproductive technologies, 192, 194
Atran, Scott, 73, 74, 95, 108

Barrett, H. Clark, 105
Big Bertha, 35, 36
Big Business, 136–37
biometrics, 137, 139
Biotechnology Industry Organization, 179
Bloom, Paul, 104
Boys from Brazil, The, 120–21, 148, 150, 153
Bush, George W., 85, 112
Buss, David, 84

California Advisory Committee on Human Cloning, 85, 112, 139, 156, 187, 226

303

California Report, 85, 86, 91–92, 93, 112, 115, 139, 140, 141, 142, 156, 157, 187–88, 196, 229
California State Legislature, 85, 112, 139, 187, 188
Campbell, Keith, 1, 3, 7, 9, 19, 43, 223
Carey, Susan, 104, 105, 106
Cc, 35, 36, 54, 156
Center for Veterinary Medicine (CVM), 20–23
civil rights legislation, 88, 117, 123, 222, 229
Clinton, Bill, 84, 85, 112
clone, meaning of term, 77–78, 97–98
Clones, The, 131
Council Report, 85, 86, 87, 112, 113, 114–15, 156, 157, 182, 196
Cumulina, 41
Cyagra, Inc., 21

DeGette, Diana, 184
design stance, 104, 105, 106, 119, 189
Deutsch, Ted, 204
Dolly, 1–4, 7, 9, 27, 81, 85, 155, 159, 223
　arthritis, 4, 155
　death, 4, 39, 155, 159
　lung disease, 4, 39
　offspring, 3
　telomeres, 3–4, 38–39, 155
Dutch Hunger Winter, 52

egalitarianism, 172, 175, 194–98, 199, 216, 228
embryo, cloned human
　clonote, as alternative term, 205–6, 213
　moral status of, 204–6, 211, 216
embryonic stem cell research, 161, 200–1
　Dickey-Wicker Amendment, 208
　egg donors, 200, 211
　federal funding of, 208–9, 212
　morality of, 162, 200, 211
　National Institutes of Health guidelines, 208
　objectification of human life, 200, 211
environmental influences, 32–33, 36–37, 54–55
epigenetic factors, defined, 10

eugenics, 86, 89–90, 93, 187, 191, 196

families and cloning, 85, 86, 90–92, 113, 182
Feinstein, Dianne, 180
Foley, Elizabeth Price, 88, 229
folk biology, 73–74, 94–96, 97, 99, 108, 118, 122, 168, 189
folk sociology, 74–75, 96–97, 99, 168, 189
Food and Drug Administration (FDA)
　approval of food products, 20
　ban on human reproductive cloning, 56, 179–80, 191, 227
　regulation of IVF, 192
Frankenstein, 16
Future Shock, 78, 82, 101

Gelman, Susan, 70, 71, 76, 104, 106, 126, 168
genes
　copy number variations, 48–49
　defined, 2, 28
　epigenetic modifications of, 29–31, 35–36, 50–53
　imprinted, 16–17, 29
　mutations, 10, 33–34, 48
　reprogramming of, 2, 10–11, 12, 13, 15, 17, 23, 24
genetic diversity, 86, 90
genetic engineering, 89
Godsend, 149
Great Chinese Famine, 52
Greenwood, James, 183, 204

Haslam, Nick, 107, 108, 121, 122, 213
Hirschfeld, Lawrence, 74, 75, 96
Hopkins, Patrick D., 82, 139, 177
Human Genome Project, 43
human reproductive cloning
　defined, 46, 63, 171, 175
　fertility treatment, as alternative, 46, 177, 191, 192–95, 224, 226
　gestation, role of, 51–53
human research cloning
　defined, 44, 171, 199
　egg donors, 201, 211
　experiments, 45–46, 62, 180, 201
　lack of federal funding, 209

INDEX

morality of, 162, 185, 201, 204–6, 211
objectification of human life, 201, 206, 211–12, 213, 214
slippery slope, as, 199, 201, 207–8, 210, 212, 214, 215, 216, 218, 220
therapies based on, 44–45, 158, 161
humans born through cloning
aging, 157, 196
birth and development, 57, 62, 92, 138, 147, 167
dehumanization of, 121–22, 172, 216, 218
human beings, as, 57–59, 62, 108, 114, 122, 152, 171
individuality, 47–56, 62, 88, 91, 92, 93, 115, 138–39, 140, 144, 147, 150, 151, 162, 166, 167, 171
lifespan, 57, 62, 171
normalcy, 57–58, 62
open future, 116, 120, 121, 122, 140, 187
organ donors, as, 151–53, 160–61, 178
parental expectations, 90–91, 92, 101, 115–16, 156, 157, 197, 224, 228
psychological damage to, 85, 86, 101
replacements for loved ones, as, 149, 154–57, 159, 160, 163, 188, 197, 224
stigma, 92, 116, 197, 198, 217, 219, 222, 226, 228
telomeres, 157
threat to individuality of donor, as, 125, 139–40, 141–42, 144, 167, 188, 190, 197, 229
Hunt, Mark, 56, 154, 159

identity fallacy, 27, 43, 61, 62, 63, 64, 66, 69, 77, 78, 81, 84, 86, 88, 90, 91, 92, 93, 94, 98, 100, 103, 109, 120, 123, 126, 142, 143, 145, 147, 165, 166, 167, 171, 172, 175, 176, 177, 178, 179, 182, 183, 184, 187, 188, 189, 190, 196, 197, 207, 208, 214, 215, 216, 218, 223, 226, 227
defined, 27, 69, 77
impostor fallacy, 64, 66, 125, 126, 131, 133, 139, 140, 144, 145, 148, 165, 166, 171, 172, 175, 178, 183, 184, 188, 190, 196, 197, 208, 214, 223, 226, 227
defined, 64

in vitro fertilization (IVF), 45, 153, 186, 190, 192, 193, 206, 213
induced pluripotent stem cells (iPSC), 201–3
informed consent, 91, 115, 123, 140, 142, 144, 145, 156, 163, 173, 229
International Human Epigenome Consortium, 44
Invasion of the Body Snatchers, The, 132
Island, The, 111, 132–33, 152, 161, 162

Jackson-Lee, Sheila, 184
Jaenisch, Rudolf, 18, 85, 205

Kass, Leon, 122
Kelemen, Deborah, 104, 105, 106
Kennedy, Teddy, 180
Kunich, John Charles, 193

large offspring syndrome (LOS), 16–18, 61
defined, 16
law of cloning
federal, 179–85, 203–9, 211–12, 214
state, 185–88, 210–11, 212, 214, 215, 217
law of embryonic stem cell research
federal, 203–9
state, 209–11
Lohan, Lindsay, 136, 137
Lott, Trent, 180
Lucas, George, 78, 84

McHugh, Paul, 205, 206, 213
Medin, Douglas, 69, 70, 73, 77
Midler, Bette, 136, 137
mitochondria, 28, 50
mitochondrial DNA
cloning, role in, 33, 50
defined, 28
influence on phenotype, 28
monozygotic multiples
triplets and higher order, 83–84, 93, 119, 166
twins, 49, 51, 52, 53, 54–55, 83, 87, 93, 119, 135–38, 165
Multiplicity, 131

National Bioethics Advisory Commission (NBAC), 85, 94, 95, 112, 155, 225

NBAC Report, 85, 86, 94, 97, 100, 112, 115, 156, 157
Never Let Me Go, 152, 161, 162
Niemela, Jussi, 118, 122, 123
non-consensual cloning, 125, 141–42, 144, 183, 230
  prohibition of, 142, 145, 230
nuclear DNA
  cloning, role in, 1–3, 33
  defined, 1, 28

Obama, Barack, 208, 222
Ortony, Andrew, 69, 70, 73, 77

Parent Trap, The, 136, 137
pets, cloning of, 36–37, 147, 154, 159, 160, 163
President's Council on Bioethics, 85, 89, 91, 112, 122, 155, 182, 192, 193, 205, 206, 225
Price, David, 183
psychological counseling
  for children, 88, 116, 123, 144, 173, 229
  for donors, 140, 145, 173, 229
  for parents, 91–92, 101, 115, 123, 144, 145, 156, 163, 168, 173, 228, 229
psychological essentialism
  artifacts, 66, 103–6, 119, 120, 121, 122, 123, 166, 168, 189, 213, 223
  clone kind, 95, 97, 142, 143, 166
  defined, 64, 69, 104
  elements of, 70–71
  evolutionary origin of, 73–77, 105–6, 130–31
  historical path, 126–27, 129, 130, 133–35, 136, 138, 144, 159, 166
  human kinds, 70, 74, 75, 94, 96, 98, 189, 213, 221, 223
  individuals, 66, 100, 126–31, 143, 148, 158–59, 166, 168, 189, 223
  living kinds, 65, 70, 71, 73, 74, 76, 94, 95, 97, 98, 103, 104, 105, 106, 109, 118, 119, 122, 123, 166, 189, 212, 213, 221
  natural kinds, 70, 74, 104
  occupational kinds, 65, 75, 96, 97, 189, 221
  organ transplants, 127–30, 134, 158, 166, 189

philosophical essentialism, distinguished from, 64–65
racial and ethnic groups, 65, 71, 73, 74–75, 94, 96, 108, 221
  stereotyping, 73
public education, 88, 101, 117, 123, 142, 144, 145, 156, 163, 168, 173, 226, 230
public opinion polls, 175–79, 190, 196, 203, 225

Repli-Kate, 134
reproductive freedom, 113, 172, 175, 191–94, 198, 228
resurrection fallacy, 27, 37–38, 43, 57, 62, 63, 64, 66, 147–48, 153, 155, 156, 158, 159, 163, 165, 167, 171, 172, 175, 178, 183, 184, 188, 190, 197, 208, 214, 223, 226, 227
  defined, 27, 147
Resurrection of Zachary Wheeler, The, 152
Robertson, John, 91, 228

scientific freedom, 172, 199, 218, 225, 228
Second Chance, 36–37, 54, 154
Seed, Richard, 179
Segal, Nancy, 83, 87, 95
Silver, Lee, 77, 78
Sixth Day, The, 109, 151
Skinner v. Oklahoma, 191
Sleeper, 153
Smith, Christopher, 185
somatic cell nuclear transfer, defined, 3
Space, Zachary, 184
Star Trek III: The Search for Spock, 109, 151, 160
Star Trek Next Generation, 151
  Rightful Heir, 151
Star Wars II: Attack of the Clones, 78–81, 94–97, 98, 99, 109, 111
Starman, 100
Stemagen, 45
Sylvia, Claire, 127–29

telomeres, defined, 3, 38
Tiny Tina, 36
Toffler, Alvin, 78, 82, 83, 84
Tomlin, Lily, 136, 137

INDEX

United States Congress, 18, 56, 85, 177, 179, 180–85, 196, 203–9, 227
United States Constitution, 191–92, 193, 218–19
United States Department of Agriculture (USDA), 20, 23
United States Supreme Court, 191, 192, 218, 219

Viagen, Inc., 22

Weldon, Dave, 185, 204, 205, 206
Wilmut, Ian, 1, 2, 3, 4, 7, 8, 36, 38, 43, 54, 81, 85, 223

X chromosome inactivation, 13–14, 35, 50–51

See series list continued after page iii

Marcus Radetzki, Marian Radetzki, Niklas Juth
Genes and Insurance: Ethical, Legal and Economic Issues

Ruth Macklin
Double Standards in Medical Research in Developing Countries

Donna Dickenson
Property in the Body: Feminist Perspectives

Matti Häyry, Ruth Chadwick, Vilhjálmur Árnason, Gardar Árnason
The Ethics and Governance of Human Genetic Databases: European Perspectives

Ken Mason
The Troubled Pregnancy: Legal Wrongs and Rights in Reproduction

Daniel Sperling
Posthumous Interests: Legal and Ethical Perspectives

Keith Syrett
Law, Legitimacy and the Rationing of Health Care

Alastair Maclean
Autonomy, Informed Consent and the Law: A Relational Change

Heather Widdows, Caroline Mullen
The Governance of Genetic Information: Who Decides?

David Price
Human Tissue in Transplantation and Research

Matti Häyry
Rationality and the Genetic Challenge: Making People Better?

Mary Donnelly
Healthcare Decision-Making and the Law: Autonomy, Capacity and the Limits of Liberalism

Anne-Maree Farrell, David Price and Muireann Quigley
Organ Shortage: Ethics, Law and Pragmatism

Sara Fovargue
Xenotransplantation and Risk: Regulating a Developing Biotechnology

John Coggon
What Makes Health Public?: A Critical Evaluation of Moral, Legal, and Political Claims in Public Health

Mark Taylor
Genetic Data and the Law: A Critical Perspective on Privacy Protection

Anne-Maree Farrell
The Politics of Blood: Ethics, Innovation and the Regulation of Risk

Stephen Smith
End-of-Life Decisions in Medical Care: Principles and Policies for Regulating the Dying Process

Michael Parker
Ethical Problems and Genetics Practice

William W. Lowrance
Privacy, Confidentiality, and Health Research

Amel Alghrani, Rebecca Bennett, and Suzanne Ost
Bioethics, Medicine and the Criminal Law Volume I: The Criminal Law and Bioethical Conflict: Walking the Tightrope

Kerry Lynn Macintosh
Human Cloning: Four Fallacies and Their Legal Consequences